Dirty Leeds

Don Revie & the Art of War

By
Dave Tomlinson

Foreword

The Heart – Being a Leeds fan

9 December 1967: Leeds United are playing Liverpool at Anfield with both teams in contention for the title.

A goal down, Leeds are struggling manfully to stay in the game as half-time approaches when suddenly Fate takes a hand. Big Jack Charlton slips the ball to goalkeeper Gary Sprake, standing out on the right edge of his penalty area. The Liverpool forwards trot back to their places as Sprake prepares to get Leeds moving. His first idea is to sling the ball out to Terry Cooper, over towards the opposite touchline. He has done it a thousand times before – it is a regular tactic for him in such situations and by now almost instinctive.

Out of the corner of his eye, Sprake catches sight of Ian Callaghan closing Cooper down and thinks better of it. Sprake checks for a moment but cannot halt his throw. The ball, instead of leaving his hand at the top of his swing, sticks to his glove a second too long and loops back over his left shoulder.

Referee Jim Finney, who had been looking downfield, asks Charlton what happened and what he should do. Jack replies, 'I think the silly so-and-so has thrown it in his own net; you'll have to give a goal.'

It could only happen to us ...

Supporting Leeds is not a science, a hobby, a trivial pursuit. It is a calling, an obsession, a thing born in the blood, which you cannot ignore. You do not choose Leeds, Leeds chooses you.

This book celebrates what it's like to be a Leeds fan, or any football fan, come to that, a masochistic member of a cult, usually left to wipe your eyes, but sometimes able to walk on air. And when you're on a high, there is nothing to compare with it – absolutely nothing.

They are rare, those moments. Otherwise, you end up acting like the Prawn Sandwich Brigade over at the Theatre of Dreams, with their insatiable demand for silverware and happy headlines.

They have been incredibly rare for Leeds, but oh so precious.

The Philosophy – The Art of War
'Great results can be achieved with small forces.'
Sun Tzu

The Art of War is a seminal treatise on strategy. Its insights into the use of psychology to outmanoeuvre opponents are as valid today as when it was written more than 2,000 years ago. It contains a myriad of examples which have become modern aphorisms. Some of the best have been used here to illuminate the philosophy and thinking of Don Revie as he sought to conquer the football world.

Some may think they've been shoehorned in for effect, as a cheesy gimmick – that's your prerogative. For the author, they add value and colour to this story of one of football's most enigmatic and successful characters.

'The art of war is of vital importance ... It is a matter of life and death, a road either to safety or to ruin.'

The Place – Dirty Old Town
'I met my love by the gas works wall, dreamed a dream by the old canal, I kissed my girl by the factory wall, dirty old town, dirty old town.'
Ewan MacColl, 1949

Post-war industrial England, a dirty hinterland in the North where the line of the smoggy horizon was broken by grimy old stacks and evil-looking factories, straight out of Orwell's back to the future doomview of *1984*.

It was a simpler time, less informed. If you said 'Prosecco', 'Paparazzi' and 'Literati' to even the worldly-wise gentlemen of the press, they might have guessed that you were discussing three members of some Italian club's forward line. The world of the working man was all fish'n'chips, warm ale and a packet of Woodbines. If you said 'Internet' then, people would think you were referring to where the ball would end after it met the muddy forehead of a bull-necked centre-forward, intent on despatching the keeper along with it by means of a full-blooded body check.

Opponents really were opponents then, hulking great full-backs who would come sliding in with a foot-up assault intended to send a nippy winger spinning into a hostile crowd.

'Try to make a fool of me again and I'll friggin' well hit you like that again, only harder …'

Look to the smoggy North East or the other side of Hadrian's Wall and you would spot the tricky ball-players, the men who pulled the strings, made others play. There wasn't a top-class club in the 1960s that didn't have a gifted Scot in its ranks.

This age was chronicled by David Storey, Keith Waterhouse, Willis Hall and Shelagh Delaney in kitchen-sink dramas like *This Sporting Life*, *Whistle Down the Wind*, *Billy Liar* and *A Taste of Honey*. The social realism genre popularised gritty depictions of domestic life for working-class families, living in cramped back-to-backs and whiling away their 'leisure' hours in spit and sawdust backstreet pubs. Their characters spoke with regional accents and they were committed to portraying England as it was experienced by millions.

Leeds was the archetype of this wasteland, a place deeply divided by money, class and race. The North-South Divide was very, very real, as were the West Indian and Asian ghettoes.

This is post-war Yorkshire, the setting for our tale. And out of this hopelessness came Don Revie, Harry Reynolds and their handcrafted football club, men from the margins who found themselves on the outside looking in and wondering why the riches on the other side of the pane of glass couldn't be theirs.

'We can have some of that, can't we, Don?'
'We can, Harry, and we will.'
'Leeds United are going to be one of the biggest clubs in the country, mark my words.'
'You're not wrong, Harry, you're not wrong.'

And Harry wasn't. They tilted at windmills, did Don and Harry.

Shuffling Off Stage

'The whole secret lies in confusing the enemy, so that he cannot fathom our real intent.'

June 1956: Life is sweet for Don Revie. He is at the zenith of his powers, with an FA Cup medal, four goals in five England games and a Footballer of the Year award to his credit. He looks a certainty for the 1958 World Cup.

He is happily married to Elsie, and the couple have a two-year-old son, christened Duncan after Johnny Duncan, Elsie's uncle and Revie's former manager at Leicester City.

They make a good-looking couple: Don, a shade under six feet tall and slim, often referred to in the sports pages as Mr Handsome; Elsie, an outgoing and smiley-faced Scot, less obviously attractive than her husband but more outgoing and always the centre of attention with her infectious laugh and permanently arched right eyebrow.

A contented family life was something Revie coveted. Scarred by the death of his mother from cancer when he was 12, he tried to mould his every club into a close family unit in which he could be the respected father figure.

Elsie knew football as few women did. Father Tommy was a pro with Raith Rovers before joining Leicester with her uncle Johnny while two of her brothers won Scottish caps. Always ambitious, Elsie urged Don to think big.

Revie was not short of ambition himself. He placed great stock in securing the financial independence needed to guarantee a comfortable life for his young family.

A child of the Great Depression, Revie was born in unemployment-cursed Middlesbrough in 1927, the son of an out-of-work joiner. His parents struggled to make ends meet – Don senior used to search for bits of wood to put on the fire while mother Margaret took in washing to earn extra pennies.

When Manchester City plucked Revie from Second Division strugglers Hull in a deal worth £28,000 in October 1951, he had the perfect opportunity to flourish.

Still coming to terms with life in the First Division, City were spending big to stay there after losing five of their first nine games – a couple of weeks before Revie arrived, City paid Sunderland £25,000 for Ivor Broadis, on the verge of a dream two-goal debut for England against Austria at Wembley.

Both Revie and Broadis coveted the deep scheming role, but it was the latter to whom manager Les McDowall entrusted the responsibility. Revie was forced to play up front, which he loathed. Dissatisfied with his lot, he requested a transfer. A few weeks later, he thought better of it and withdrew his request.

City ended 15th that season and followed up with two years in the bottom six.

The Revie-Broadis link was not a marriage made in heaven and McDowall accepted the inevitable and filed for divorce. Revie was the man that people expected to leave but it was Broadis who moved on in a big-money deal to Newcastle and a place in the World Cup finals.

The way was clear for Revie to assume his preferred position and he revelled in the responsibility. He performed well enough to be selected to play in a Football League XI against the League of Ireland at Maine Road in February 1954 and scored three times in a 9-1 victory.

11 weeks earlier, a superb Hungary side had inflicted a 6-3 humiliation on England at Wembley.

City colleagues Revie, Roy Paul, Roy Clarke and Johnny Williamson sat together to watch the game on television. Captivated by Hungary's innovation, Revie & Co resolved to copy the approach when they returned to training. McDowall listened with interest to their enthusiastic plans before dismissing them with a cursory 'Let's wait and see.' He was not convinced that the formation could work for City.

Undeterred, Williamson tried it out in the reserves, benefiting from the complementary thrusts forward of right-half Ken Barnes. The experiment reaped instant rewards – a 26-game unbeaten run took the stiffs to their championship title.

Williamson was certain that the tactics were made for Revie, but the man himself had mixed feelings. He was impressed by Williamson's achievement, but as uncertain as McDowall whether the tactics could succeed in the higher quality of the First Division. Nevertheless, Revie was an ardent advocate, extolling the virtues of the system to McDowall.

The manager was struck by Revie's enthusiasm and knew he had to try something. He felt obliged to seek the permission of the board for the experiment; it was a time in which know-it-all directors held all the power. They accepted the proposal but insisted that it should be tested out first.

McDowall told his players, 'We are going to play football this season. By football, I mean football. We are going to keep the ball down, no big kicking and no wild clearances from defence.' Revie glowed with pleasure while skipper Roy Paul glared at McDowall, knowing the comments referred to his no-frills style.

The manager led the players on a summer tour of Germany, where they could trial the tactics in anger. Revie was the cornerstone of a formation that proved extraordinarily effective. He had found his niche and McDowall was determined to go with it in the upcoming season.

The Revie Plan was a carbon copy of the Hungarian system, with Revie as deep-lying centre-forward. Working from midfield, he linked with his wing-half and inside-forwards in a triangular formation and roamed in the space on both flanks while the wingers looked to come inside.

Revie was delighted with the success, but he was unimpressed when McDowall announced that he had decided that pre-season training would start earlier than usual. Elsie was a schoolteacher and the pair could normally only get away for a holiday when the school year ended in July, by which time pre-season preparations restricted Don's availability. This year was different; Elsie had just given birth to the couple's first child, Duncan, and was enjoying an early start to her holiday. The couple were looking forward to an early break until that hope was shattered by McDowall's diktat.

Revie was furious. The matter gnawed away at his insides, but he kept the bitterness to himself.

3

The press got wind of City's plans and fostered wild expectations. The acid test, the first game at Preston, was a disaster with Tom Finney inspiring a five-goal drubbing. As it crawled its way through the Blackpool-bound traffic on the way back to Manchester, City's team coach was as silent as the grave. Several players happily accepted lifts from friends rather than fester in the gloomy atmosphere of the coach. Revie worried that it was going to be another wasted season, his lips tight as he pondered on what had gone wrong.

McDowall was every bit as disappointed as Revie but he was determined to give the formation a decent try. At the customary Monday morning meeting, he confirmed that he would be persisting with the experiment. 'We are going to play this system for a month. No matter what the public, press or anyone else says, one match is not a sufficient test.'

Revie put his finger on the problem; the formation's success depended heavily on mobile defenders and someone like Ken Barnes pushing forward. McDowall agreed and when he announced that he was changing the full-backs and recalling Barnes at right-half, Revie was delighted. He pushed the virtues of Barnes, 'an attacking wing-half who was not only clever in possession but who also had plenty of stamina and an ability to bring the ball up and use it intelligently'.

The tweaks brought immediate benefits – City beat Sheffield United 5-2.

The team blossomed, emerging as the most exciting side in the country. They carried all before them, reaching the Cup semi-final and riding high in the table. For once they had put Manchester rivals United in the shade.

McDowall decided to tweak things, laying out £25,000 for Hibernian's Bobby Johnstone, convinced the Scot could pull the strings more reliably than Revie. The decision smacked of superfluous tinkering. Revie had been outstanding and finally earned a call from Walter Winterbottom, scoring in England's 2-0 victory over Northern Ireland in Belfast in October.

Johnstone's arrival caused a rift – McDowall and Revie were constantly at odds, the former convinced that Revie was trying to undermine his authority. He put stock in a rumour that Revie and Paul were involved in an alleged case of bribery in 1952.

4

There was no evidence but McDowall needed none, he had not a shred of doubt that there was fire beneath the smoke.

For his part, Revie was convinced that McDowall didn't like him, preferring his blue-eyed boys. And, worst of all in Revie's eyes, he never fully appreciated his abilities.

He and McDowall had never got on and this was just the latest in a series of spats which grew into something darker. A man as principled as Revie could never forgive and forget – he couldn't hide his feelings and couldn't put on a show with McDowall – he couldn't abide him and could never get close to him.

When Johnny Hart fractured his leg in March 1955, it brought an uneasy truce. There was room for both Johnstone and Revie to figure when City beat Sunderland in the Cup semi-final, the game settled by a diving header from Roy Clarke.

City were also well-placed for the championship, though five other teams were in the running. A combination of injuries and loss of concentration derailed their challenge as they slumped to seventh after losing the final three games.

City faced Cup specialists Newcastle in the Wembley final – the Geordies had lifted the trophy in 1951 and 1952.

McDowall took the players away to Eastbourne for the week before the final to prepare. A disconsolate Clarke remained in Manchester to have an operation on his knee.

Elsie telephoned Don to complain about the seats allocated for the wives at Wembley. Revie and Paul threatened to withdraw from a television programme in London on the eve of the final. McDowall quickly reallocated new seats for the women but marked Revie's card with an even thicker pen.

City were undone on the day by injury to Jimmy Meadows after 17 minutes. With no substitutes allowed, the ten men were pulled hither and thither by a fervent Newcastle, who won 3-1.

Bob Stokoe, playing centre-half, sported a huge grin at the end after 'taking those f***in' big heads down a peg or two'.

It was a choker for Revie. He had dreamed of a Wembley masterclass to make up for the disaster that had befallen him six years earlier. Then, he missed Leicester's Cup final against Wolves with a career-threatening injury.

Revie's goal in the semi against Portsmouth secured their place in the 1949 final. When City then entertained West Ham on Easter Monday, Revie came away with a bloody nose from a scuffle. He thought no more of it and played in the next match against Blackburn.

On the way to the following game at Plymouth, Revie's nose began to bleed profusely; soon the blood was pouring down his face. Leicester boss Johnny Duncan thought it harmless enough and declined to send him to hospital until the coach got back to Leicester. When Revie finally sought medical treatment, the doctors diagnosed a burst blood vessel and said he had only just made it in time, another hour could have proven fatal.

Revie was ruled out of the final – Leicester lost 3-1. His mood darkened days later when he learned that, but for the injury, he would have been included in England's summer tour of Sweden, Norway and France.

Revie's Wembley debut had to wait until April 1955, when he scored in England's 7-2 hammering of Scotland. Dennis Wilshaw scored four times but the game was dominated by Revie's right-wing partner, 40-year-old Stanley Matthews.

Revie, ordered to keep Matthews fed, recalled, 'He gave the most amazing individual performance I have ever seen as he destroyed three and four players at a time. I shall never forget it.'

Despite the setbacks, it had been a wonderful season with Revie fulfilling his potential and able to console himself with his election as Footballer of the Year. Things appeared on the up but the feud with McDowall boiled to the surface in the summer after a show of defiance from Revie.

Still bitter about losing out on his holidays in 1954, he was determined to get away after City's gruelling campaign. Baby son Duncan would celebrate his first birthday on holiday in Blackpool in July.

Revie told the press that he had been given permission by trainer Laurie Barnett on the understanding that he reported for training two weeks earlier than the rest of the squad. A fortnight before departing, Revie reminded Barnett, who told him to talk to McDowall. The manager ordered Revie to commute from Blackpool each day.

Don told Elsie about the argument when he got home and was unusually defiant, almost snarling, 'Sod it, I'm taking it anyway.'

'Are you sure, Don? Is it worth all the trouble?'

'We deserve a break and I want to go away with you and Duncan. McDowall can't touch me after the season I've just had, you mark my words.'

Elsie sighed. She feared the worst but knew better than to argue with Don when he was in this mood, and a holiday did sound attractive.

Revie trained conscientiously while he was away and lost six pounds in the process.

McDowall and the directors were incensed, suspending Revie for a fortnight. City supporters slagged him off for his 'swollen head' and wrote letters supporting the board's stance.

Revie protested bitterly at the loss of two weeks' pay, £27, and made noises about a transfer but did not follow through.

He began the season well enough but was dumped in the reserves after the 2-0 defeat of Blackpool on 24 September, his place taken by Johnstone. Revie brooded on the injustice of it all. He was still regarded highly enough to be selected for England against Denmark in October and scored twice in a 5-1 victory but lost his place to Johnny Haynes after a defeat against Wales.

There was another council of war *chez Revie*. Don trembled with rage but eventually calmed down, his temper soothed by Elsie. She encouraged him to bide his time. 'It'll come right in the end, Don, what goes around comes around.'

Revie bit his lip and sat back to await a recall for City. He waited and waited and waited, not featuring at all from 12 November until 4 February.

His presence was marginal; Revie figured in only half the fixtures, though he excelled in the victory at Portsmouth that ended City's league season. McDowall remained implacably unconvinced of his worth. Revie only made it into the Cup final side because Johnstone and Leivers were injured and Billy Spurdle was laid low by an attack of boils.

The scenes in the Wembley dressing rooms echoed 1955. Roy Paul fussed over the younger players, trying to soothe anxieties while Revie, always superstitious, toyed around with two pieces of wood given to him by an old gypsy woman.

German keeper Bert Trautmann interrupted his reverie, asking, 'What are you doing, Don? What are those sticks?'

'They're nothing, Bert, just things I was given a few years ago. They bring luck.'

'Like rabbit's foot, ja? Did you have them with you last year?'

Revie blushed, 'Yes I did, but what happened wasn't down to them ...'

Trautmann chuckled at Revie's eccentricity. He had grown used to it since Revie arrived at Maine Road five years earlier.

As Paul led his team into the tunnel, he put the fear of God up everyone, including the startled Birmingham players when he suddenly raised his fist and boomed, 'If we don't f***ing win, you'll get some of this.'

Revie ignored the challenge, lost deep in his own thoughts, determined to show what he could do. His clutch of Wembley appearances over the previous 18 months helped ease his nerves. He took hold of the game from the off, creating an opening goal after three minutes.

It was the Revie Plan working to perfection. Revie picked up a short pass, swept the ball out to Clarke on the left and ran 50 yards for a return pass into the penalty area. He flicked the ball artfully inside for Joe Hayes to fire home.

City failed to build on the lead and Birmingham slowly clawed their way into the game, equalising after 30 minutes.

At half-time, Paul and McDowall urged the team to open up the play, use the full width of the pitch and make Birmingham chase. City's football after the break was a delight, with Revie giving a superlative display. After 70 minutes, they were 3-1 up after goals from Dyson and Johnstone. They eased off, allowing Birmingham a whiff of hope.

17 minutes from time, Birmingham's Peter Murphy beat Dave Ewing to a through ball and appeared odds-on to score. Trautmann raced from his line and dived headlong at Murphy's feet. There was a sickening collision, Murphy's knee hammering into Trautmann, knocking him out cold. Referee Alf Bond stopped the game to allow the German to receive treatment. Trainer Barnett rubbed away at Trautmann's neck and waved smelling salts under his nose. As he came to, the pain made him almost scream out.

'He was reeling around the goalmouth like a drunk,' said Paul, who considered putting Little in goal. Trautmann would have none of it and insisted he would play on. He made a number of saves but looked at death's door. He had broken his neck but no one was aware of this until he had an X-ray four days later. He had dislocated five vertebrae, the second of which was cracked in two while the third had locked against the second, preventing further damage. The slightest knock in the wrong spot could have seen the German lose his life.

City survived the Brummie barrage and lifted the Cup.

Trautmann stole the headlines the following day, though the match will always be remembered as Revie's peak hour, one in which everything came together. He would never enjoy the same playing success again.

Revie basked in the glow, his winner's medal offering material proof of his worth.

Bruised by the memory of the previous summer, the Revies contented themselves with three days in a Blackpool boarding house over one of the few sunny weekends in a dreary summer.

While playing with Duncan on the beach one morning, Elsie made one of her periodic pleas to Don to stop thinking about others and look after himself.

'You know Les will never forgive you, don't you? He only picked you because he had no choice and he'll drop you like a hot potato when he gets the chance.'

Don said nothing, continuing to stare out to sea. Elsie was right. He'd been upset when Trautmann took the headlines that should have been his. He was wracked by guilt at his jealousy and his mood wasn't helped by McDowall's attitude in the days after the final. Why the hell did McDowall have to be so …

'Don, are you listening to me?'

Revie was shaken out of his internal dialogue by Elsie's gentle admonishment.

'Yes, sorry, Elsie, I was miles away. You're right, of course, but Les will struggle to leave me out after Wembley.'

'He'll find a way,' was on Elsie's lips but she left it hanging there. She knew that nagging would not help. It would only set Don against the idea. She knew she would be proved right, but Don had to get these things himself.

Elsie had always wanted the best for her husband and nagged him to be more ambitious. God knows, the couple could do with more money.

Elsie's words on the beach came back to haunt Revie sooner than either of them expected.

City entered the 1956/57 campaign with Revie in his favoured No 9 shirt and given his head but the team misfired. They lost six games on the bounce in September and October, the only goals coming in a 7-3 hammering at Arsenal. McDowall recalled Johnstone at centre-forward and pulled Revie back to right-half. Revie was recalled to the England side in October but a disappointing 1-1 draw with Northern Ireland was his sixth and final appearance for his country.

His relationship with McDowall was as tense as ever and there was talk of a swap deal for Sheffield United's Colin Grainger, who had served under McDowall at Wrexham in 1950.

Elsie was understanding but firm about McDowall. 'You'll never get anywhere with that man, Don, you know you won't.'

Don sighed, his mind made up. His antipathy for McDowall was intense and his feet were itchy. He could not stop thinking about the extra money a transfer would earn him. When Barnes asked why he wanted to leave, Revie told him, 'There is one thing that will tell you whether you have been a good player and that is how much you have got in the bank.'

And it was the 'Bank of England Club', Sunderland, which was his next stop.

The Wearsiders were one of the game's earliest powers, winning the championship three times between 1892 and 1895, and again in 1902 and 1913. The 1930s brought another title and an FA Cup win.

Relegation from the First Division was a fate that Sunderland had never experienced but the club was no longer the force it had been. They earned the 'Bank of England' moniker for their attempt to buy their way to success. They broke the transfer record twice, with the signings of Len Shackleton (£20,500 in 1948) and Trevor Ford (£30,000 in 1950). Sunderland finished third in 1950, their highest placing since winning the championship in 1936 and continued to spend cash like it was going out of fashion. 1955 brought fourth place and the popular view was that one more push would be enough.

Cue the signing of Revie in November 1956 for £24,000, a deal which suited all parties.

During the obligatory checking out with Elsie, Revie received nothing but positive vibes.

'It makes sense, Don, a nice bonus for signing, a move to your own back yard, they want you and will look after you, which is something that man will never do.'

The signing-on fee was particularly welcome. Under the rules the most Revie would get via official channels was £10, though Sunderland were happy to blur the edges with other sweeteners.

Sunderland wasn't Middlesbrough, but it was close enough and the Roker club had a reputation for looking after its players. Revie was asked to 'slum it' in a top-class hotel, the Seaburn, a stone's throw from Roker Park, while the club searched for a suitable home.

It would be easy enough for Elsie to get a job; it was usually straightforward for good teachers to transfer location.

Sunderland saw to it that Don got a boost to his pay packet courtesy of a part-time job as a 'carpet salesman'. Whether the job was genuine or just a euphemism for a back hander is something that only Revie and Sunderland knew for certain.

The way that Sunderland cosseted their players struck Revie and was a lesson he took with him for ever; happy players make for a successful team, he thought.

The welcome for the Revies was warm, particularly from old friend Colin Grainger. 'In the evenings, he and I would sit in the bar talking nothing but football. Doreen and Elsie would often meet up to go shopping or to check out what the local estate agents were offering. Often, the four of us would meet for an evening meal.

'Revie was a complicated character and, in those days, something of a religious man. I went into his room once to find him kneeling down at the side of his bed saying his prayers. I am not even sure if he noticed I was there. I walked back out, somewhat embarrassed, and never mentioned the incident.'

Others were less appreciative of their new team-mate.

Len Shackleton, known as the Clown Prince of Soccer, resented the threat to his status as Roker's Big Time Charlie. One of the game's great entertainers, he was not prepared to let anyone steal his thunder.

Shack had a reputation for mickey taking – he once took the rise out of Arsenal, putting his foot on the ball in the penalty area and pretending to check his watch and comb his hair. He became a sports journalist after he retired, his autobiography including a chapter on the average director's knowledge of football – it was a single, entirely blank page.

34-year-old Shack was in the twilight of his career and Revie was bought to fill the void that would be left when he retired.

Sunderland were second-bottom after three victories from 15 games when Revie arrived, the run including a 6-0 defeat at Preston in November.

There was no quick fix. Revie's debut on 17 November at Cardiff brought defeat, the third in a row. It was 8 December before a victory, by which time Revie had lost his place after both his appearances ended in defeat.

He was recalled for the trip to Newcastle on 22 December but summarily dropped after a poor performance in a 6-2 thrashing. Losing so heavily to their hated local rivals was too much to bear.

As Sunderland laboured through a relegation dogfight, they were embroiled in an illegal payments scandal in January when an accusatory letter was sent to Football League headquarters in Lytham St Annes. It prompted the League and the Football Association to launch a joint inquiry.

At the time, the maximum weekly wage was £15 and signing-on fees were capped at £10. The six-man commission found that Sunderland's adherence to the rules was tenuous.

Grainger signed for the club a month after the allegations were made. 'The payments were why so many players wanted to go to Sunderland. We would get a decent signing-on fee … we would also get more money for winning than was allowed. The bonus should have been £4 but we got £10, quite a difference in those days. Footballers were paid more than the average wage, which was about £8, but still nothing like we should have been.'

League secretary Alan Hardaker: 'Neither the League nor FA found anything they could challenge … I made no more headway than the rest. The books looked perfectly in order. I more or less gave it up but decided to go through the books just one more time. I then noticed, for the first time, a lightly-pencilled question alongside a figure. It asked simply: "Where do I post this?" The sum was a big one, two or three thousand pounds, and was apparently money for straw.'

Hardaker rang brother Ernest, chairman of Hull Rugby League Club, and enquired, 'How much does it cost you to cover your ground with straw in a normal sort of winter? If I gave you £3,000, would you be able to manage for a season?'

'Blow me, for that we'd manage for 25 seasons!'

It was a payment for goods that were never received, meaning that the club would receive credit notes which could be cashed in to allow it to make covert payments to players. Hardaker trawled through the accounts and concluded that the straw 'must have been coated with gold dust'. He identified that, over five years, £5,450 had been misappropriated.

The club was fined £5,000, at that stage the largest sanction ever. Chairman Bill Ditchburn was permanently banned along with directors Stanley Ritson and LW Evans. Several players were sanctioned, including Trevor Ford, Ken Chisholm, Ray Daniel and Billy Elliott.

Manager Bill Murray was fined £200 and banned for life from any involvement in football. He departed at the end of the season a broken man after 30 years as player and manager at Roker Park.

Several players refused to answer questions, including Shackleton, who played the opening game of the following season before abruptly announcing his retirement on 'medical advice' after suffering an ankle injury. He had caused a dressing-room rift when he refused to co-operate.

The Players' Union, later renamed the Professional Footballers' Association (PFA), demanded a wide-ranging inquiry and launched a petition, asking all players who had ever received illegal payments to sign it. They banked on so many men confessing that the FA would be forced to drop their charges. It paid off – the Sunderland players got off with fines, which were later quashed.

The scandal stiffened the Union's resolve to end the stringent restrictions on earnings.

13

The maximum weekly wage in 1945 was £7 per week, which had risen to £17 by 1957. A player could hope for a benefit of £750 after five years' service, a £100 increase on the 1939 figure. The win bonus of £2 hadn't changed for 16 years. Whether the transfer fee was £1,000 or £10,000, the official signing-on fee had been capped at £10 since before the First World War.

Revie was confident that he had done nothing wrong but feared he might be implicated for receiving financial assistance from Sunderland.

The fear of God had been put into him. Several times he cried himself to sleep in Elsie's arms, wailing, 'What have I done? What have I done?'

Back on the field, a 5-2 defeat in February at Spurs left Sunderland a point clear of the relegation places. Revie was recalled the following week, after making just one appearance in 11 games. After netting his first goal in the 5-2 defeat of Sheffield Wednesday, Revie was appointed captain.

Now right-half, he played in all the remaining games. Sunderland's goalless draw at home to Preston on 16 March launched a seven-match unbeaten spell. A 2-0 victory against Leeds on 19 April was crucial. Leeds were captained by the magnificent John Charles; he was distracted by his impending transfer to Juventus and missed two easy chances.

The points lifted Sunderland to 18th, with 32 points from 39 games, five points clear of second-bottom Portsmouth. With a game in hand, Pompey could yet catch them.

The next day, against Man United at Old Trafford, keeper Johnny Bollands was injured after 55 minutes with the home side 1-0 to the good. Charlie Fleming took over in goal and watched three goals sail past him.

Elsewhere, Portsmouth beat Wolves and Man City overtook Sunderland by winning at Burnley. Losing 3-0 at home to Spurs, Cardiff was suddenly the club under threat, three points behind Sunderland with two games left. Charlton were stranded at the bottom, long since condemned to the drop.

Sunderland's goal average was far superior to their rivals, but the Roker men still needed a point to guarantee safety. Things looked dicey when they lost at Leeds two days later, but

Portsmouth won 2-0 at Cardiff to condemn the Welsh side to the drop and save Sunderland.

A reconstituted board appointed Alan Brown to replace Murray. A former player with Huddersfield, Burnley and Notts County, Brown had cut his managerial teeth over three years at Burnley, where he established a youth programme that would blossom in later years.

Sunderland, their reputation in shreds after the scandal, desperately needed a man of integrity, one who could restore public confidence.

Brown saw it as an opportunity to 'clean up' the club he had supported as a boy. At a time when bribing parents to persuade their youngster to sign for a particular club was *de rigueur*, Brown would not countenance it.

Playing-wise, he demanded a hard-running game – instead of running five yards and passing the ball 20, he expected the players to run 20 and pass the ball five.

'If Sunderland wanted the complete opposite of Bill Murray, the club could not have done better than Brown,' recalled Colin Grainger. 'A sergeant-major type with piercing eyes, he liked to promote himself as a paragon of morality.'

Revie did not warm to the abrasive Brown. The two men never saw eye to eye. Brown couldn't care less.

'The problem with Brown,' said Grainger, 'was that he seemed to have a suspicion of senior players. He did not even attempt to conceal his dislike of Don Revie. I felt that Brown resented Revie's reputation, experience and natural intelligence. Brown preferred to work with impressionable young players ... established professionals, by contrast, presented a threat to his authority.

'Perhaps his biggest mistake came in his first week when he asked four experienced players – Don Revie, Billy Elliott, Ray Daniel and Len Shackleton – to round up all the practice balls and bring them to the training pitch. Usually, the ground staff and youth-team players performed such tasks, but Brown had other ideas. He was asserting himself, sending out a signal about where the likes of Revie and Shackleton fitted into the new hierarchy at Sunderland.'

Again, Revie had found a mortal enemy, one with whom there was neither empathy nor respect – they were in very different worlds and the enmity between them only deepened with the passing months. Neither man could hide his distaste for the other – it was as plain as the nose on your face.

Brown's reign began with three defeats. Revie struggled and took until the seventh game to register his first goal in a defeat to Everton. Further goals followed against Bolton and Newcastle but the atmosphere was tense.

The team was a shambles. Supporters, accustomed to the entertainment dished up by Shack & Co, were disenchanted and soon openly castigating Brown. Sunderland were thrashed 7-0 at Blackpool, 6-0 at Burnley, 7-1 at Luton and 6-1 at Birmingham, but Brown never batted an eye.

The anger was laid bare during January's clash with Everton. It looked like nothing short of a miracle could save Sunderland and the fans chanted for the board to sack the manager.

Revie recalled, 'As we trooped off the pitch, I happened to look up into the stand and saw Alan Brown sitting there while the crowd was chanting for his blood. He never moved a muscle or displayed the slightest emotion. I remember being impressed by his self-control, and I'm certain I learned a great deal from him in that unhappy moment.'

In early March, with relegation looming, the team rallied. A draw with Sheffield Wednesday was followed by back-to-back wins over Spurs and West Brom before a point was secured at Chelsea. A Revie strike earned a draw at Manchester United.

It seemed Sunderland might escape for a second successive season but it all came down to the last day. A week earlier, they had beaten Nottingham Forest 3-1 to close the gap on Newcastle, Leicester and Portsmouth, who all dropped points.

Newcastle drew at Old Trafford during the week to virtually cement their survival given their superior goal average.

To stay up, Sunderland needed to win at Portsmouth and hope that Leicester lost to Birmingham. A 14-0 margin would have sent Pompey down but that was never going to happen.

Sunderland won 2-0 but Leicester scraped home by the only goal of the game at St Andrew's and that was that.

Sunderland had the same number of points as survivors Portsmouth and Newcastle, but a poorer goal average and were relegated for the first time ever.

For Revie, fast approaching his 31st birthday, an uncertain future in the Second Division beckoned. He was keen on leading a push for promotion but fell out of favour.

With Brown fixated on rebuilding with pliable youngsters, Revie was banished to the reserves as Sunderland lost on the opening day. Two defeats to Fulham persuaded Brown to recall him but a parting of the ways was inevitable.

It became clear to Revie that his time at Roker was up. He starred and scored in a 4-0 victory at Rotherham, the first away win, but it was obvious that Revie was not in Brown's plans.

There was no need for a conversation with Elsie. She knew exactly how discontented Revie was, working with a manager he despised in a division he detested. He was a forgotten man as far as England were concerned and had missed out on the World Cup he had set his sights on.

'Come on, Don,' Elsie said. 'It's time we were away.'

Revie was never one to stay where he was not wanted. He was soon packing his bags.

Harry Reynolds

'We cannot enter into alliances until we are acquainted with the designs of our neighbours.'

June 1956: Harry Reynolds is celebrating the club's promotion and the anniversary of his appointment as a director of Leeds United Football Club. Harry announces that he is taking the family for a slap-up meal. He and wife Agnes are joined at the swanky city-centre restaurant by their daughters, Margaret, with fiancé Peter, and Barbara, accompanied by husband Eric. A beaming grin lights up his face as Harry tells the Reynolds clan and everyone else in earshot, 'Mark my words, we're going to do great things for the city of Leeds. Mark my words.'

The only son of a working-class couple, Reynolds was born in March 1901 in a Holbeck back-to-back, a stone's throw from Elland Road. He was an enterprising soul with an eye for opportunity.

He enjoyed a happy childhood apart from the death of his only sister a few days before her tenth birthday. He enjoyed football, playing for Leeds Schoolboys, 'but never got anywhere'.

Reynolds' first job was in the office of Leeds Industrial Co-operative Society. He hated the work and quickly wangled a transfer to the grocery department as a flour lad. 'I got promotion to the shop weighing sugar and waiting on behind the counter on busy nights,' he said. 'I liked it, but I got an itch to move on and got a job as an assistant to a millwright.'

The pursuit of better wages saw him move again, this time to the railways. 'I started as a cleaner at 53s a week. Promotion was quick then because they were short of labour and I was passed out as a fireman after about three months. It was a good life and if you studied the job and used your brains and common sense it was money for old rope.'

Engine drivers never liked having Reynolds as their fireman because he would build enormous fires so that he could sit back and enjoy the journey in peace. Most firemen built small fires, stoking them regularly, so they could be put out quickly if the water level fell, to avoid any risk of an explosion.

The drivers would say, 'We've heard about you and your big fires – you'll come unstuck one of these days.'

Reynolds left the railway in 1924 and took a job with a tea shop, delivering to private homes.

'My customers had been asking for pikelets but the shop would only let me have two dozen. I could see there was more demand than that but I couldn't convince them. So I went and bought 20 dozen elsewhere and sold them. I made a good profit so I started up on my own.'

Reynolds also worked as a bookmaker, dealt in second-hand cars and machinery and entered the motor wrecking business. 'I could always see money and I started accumulating it. I was earning more than I was spending for the first time in my life, and I began saving. I had planned to retire before I was 40 ... but the Second World War came along and I decided to shelve the idea.

'We got contracts with various government departments breaking up tanks and Bren carriers, among other things. We were doing a good job but I didn't get a lot of money out of the war because of excess profits tax and the rest.'

When the war ended, Reynolds decided to retire again and got as far as selling out. It was only by chance that he returned to business and made his fortune.

A friend asked him to buy some steel sheeting to cover a barn and Reynolds came across some Anderson sheets, used for covering shelters during the war. He immediately realised the potential in an era when there was a worldwide shortage of steel.

Reynolds bought 140,000 tons of corrugated Anderson sheets, many of which were eaten away by rust. He straightened them out and obtained the sole export rights, catapulting him into international commerce.

He became the fifth largest customer of the Steel Company of Wales and they were rolling hundreds of thousands of tons of steel for him. He made his best deals with the Bethlehem Steel Company, the second largest in the United States, and crossed the Atlantic on the Queen liners 28 times after the war.

'One firm said Anderson sheets were not worth playing about with but I knew the chance was too good to miss,' he said. 'That's why I didn't retire. Some people used to say: "He's been a clever so-and-so." There was nothing clever about it. The world was starved of steel and I found the answer.'

Reynolds was into steel stockholding in a big way. 'The art of the thing was to buy your stock and then sell it again before getting involved with the cost of moving it.'

He incorporated H L Reynolds Limited in 1943 and acquired the Old Leeds Steelworks with its four blast furnaces in Balm Road, just south of Elland Road. Part of the attraction of the steelworks was its association with football in the city.

The men who laboured at Leeds Steelworks had formed a football club of the same name in 1889. Five years later the club was rechristened Hunslet FC, known locally as the Twinklers. Hunslet became a leading local club, winning the West Yorkshire Cup four times and reaching the Amateur Cup quarter-finals twice, including one celebrated victory over the mighty Old Etonians.

As Reynolds' wealth increased, the family moved to a bungalow in Hough Top, Bramley. Reynolds was the archetypal self-made millionaire. He had some refined interests, becoming an expert polo player with his own string of ponies and riding to hounds with the Bramham Moor Hunt, but he was always a down-to-earth, bluff Yorkshireman. He never forgot his roots. The comment in a Leeds United brochure that 'He never lost his common touch' made him glow with pride.

Reynolds had the time and money to indulge in his childhood love of horses. 'I went to a friend's riding school at Barrowby Hall. He told me about hunting and that whetted my appetite. I hunted with the Bramham Moor with riding school horses, at £2 or £3 a time. I was ambitious and their horses were no good to me. They were not up to it so I bought an old grey hunter just after the war.

'My progress was slow and gradual. My riding school friend was killed in a hunting accident and I bought his farm. I also bought a neighbouring farm and had 250 acres at one time.'

Reynolds took an active interest in the farm and began breeding pigs. He had about 10 head of pedigree breeding stock when he went to Peterborough and paid a world record price of £5,000 for four Landrace pigs.

By 1955, Reynolds had amassed considerable wealth and was starting to lay the ground for his retirement from H L Reynolds. He sold out to Knitmaster Holdings two years later, becoming a director, and pulled out completely in 1959.

Always a keen Leeds United supporter, he never had any ambitions to become a director, but knew chairman Sam Bolton very well because they were near neighbours and members of the Holbeck Pit Club in the old days. Bolton used to invite Reynolds into the boardroom after a game and even accompanied him to away matches, though he thought nothing of it.

'I remember him ringing me up one day in 1955 just as I was going home and he asked me to pop into his place. When he asked what my reaction would be to joining the board of directors, I could have dropped through the floor. Really, I couldn't say "Yes" quick enough but what I actually said was: "How much is it going to cost me?" When I first joined the board, it was strange. I found this public company rather different to my own board meetings.'

Bolton was another local industrialist, managing director at motor haulage contractor Thomas Spence Ltd.

Born and bred in Leeds, 60-year-old Bolton was the grandson of James Bolton, a veteran of the Charge of the Light Brigade. During the First World War, Sam served with the Coldstream Guards before joining the Royal Flying Corps.

Bolton was a football fanatic, playing for junior side Rothwell White Rose and watching Leeds City as a youngster before having trials with them. He became a director of Leeds United in 1945 and assumed the chair in 1948 when Ernest Pullan resigned after arguing with the directors over the appointment of Major Frank Buckley.

Bolton's board was in dire need of new blood. Hilton Crowther, the former chairman of United and Huddersfield Town, had been at the club since it was formed in 1919. He was as sound as ever, but he was 75 and since relocating to Blackpool was no longer as active at Elland Road.

Stanley 'Tiny' Blenkinsop, 63, had been on the board since 1934. Always immaculately turned out and blinking behind his distinctive spectacles, he was a mountain of a man, weighing some 20 stones and towering over most of his fellows. In its report of United's match against Rapide Vienna in May 1951, the *Yorkshire Evening Post* described Blenkinsop as 'the largest, widest and heaviest football director in the Old World'. Blenkinsop introduced radio match commentaries to hospitals in Leeds after a frustrating spell in a hospital bed. He used to provide commentaries himself alongside BBC light entertainment producer Barney Colehan and former Leeds City winger and broadcaster Ivan Sharpe.

Alderman Percy Woodward, 49, was short and squat. He owned a local packing case manufacturer and was well-known as a local Conservative councillor. Like Bolton, he was a regular on the Elland Road terraces from an early age and was vice-president of Leeds Wanderers before joining the United board in 1946 with Harold Marjason. Within a year he took over as vice-chairman from Blenkinsop.

Robert Wilkinson, 55, president of the United supporters' club, arrived shortly after Woodward and Marjason, and even 'newcomer' John Bromley had been on the board since 1949.

54-year-old Bromley was a solicitor and an active Freemason, serving as a director of the Leeds Masonic Hall Co Ltd.

The United board was brimming with larger-than-life characters, men from a bygone age, old and set in their ways. Fresh impetus was desperately required. The club had been marking time for years.

'Would you have much time to spare on something like that, Mr Reynolds?' asked Bolton.

'Well, I don't have to be at the factory that often these days, it pretty much runs itself. Anyway, in a couple of years' time I plan to retire. I've got time on me hands, all right.'

Bolton's eyes flashed. 'Would you be willing to put up some cash?'

Bolton didn't believe in beating about the bush. United badly needed new investment and the effervescent entrepreneur in front of him had energy and cash to burn.

The club was still toiling under the yoke of the bond holders who paid Crowther off in 1925. They agreed to delay 1944's scheduled buy back of all bonds for ten years, but when the war ended, the payment terms returned to normal. Some of the largest bond holders agreed to convert the debt into shares, but United still needed to find £1,400 a year to pay interest, plus a further £28,000 in cash to redeem the remaining bonds. The directors estimated that an average attendance of 27,000 was needed to remain in the black. Attendances rarely came within a country mile of that figure.

Former United manager Major Frank Buckley had worked wonders to clear the debenture and make the club profitable, but increases in the entertainment tax, running costs and transfer fees had seen the debt soar above £30,000.

Bolton badly needed new investment and when he heard that Reynolds had funds available, he offered him a seat on the board. Reynolds accepted and made an interest-free loan of £50,000.

One of his first tasks was to persuade manager Raich Carter to stay with Leeds. Employed on an annual contract, he was considering an offer from Derby County. Reynolds persuaded Carter to reject Derby's approach and sign a three-year deal with Leeds. It took some doing. Five years earlier, Carter had held out for a five-year deal when he was discussing the Elland Road manager's role and walked away when his request was rejected.

At first, Leeds was merely a pastime for Reynolds, but as the months went by, he began dreaming of what the club could become. He was an ambitious soul and began declaring publicly that Leeds United could become one of the powers of the game. He set his mind on giving substance to his words.

'Mark my words,' he said to Agnes, 'Leeds United are going to become one of the biggest clubs in the country. The game is changing and we're going to change with it.'

'Calm yourself down, Harry love,' she pleaded, fearful for his blood pressure.

'Mark my words,' he repeated, eyes shining. A new lease of life coursed through his body as he got his teeth into his new plaything.

Fire, Fire

'A kingdom that has once been destroyed can never come again into being; nor can the dead ever be brought back to life.'

28 April 1956: Jack Charlton is a fortnight off his 21st birthday. He has an excited grin all over his muddy face as he swigs champagne from a white china teacup in the Boothferry Park dressing room. He towers above the diminutive Jimmy Dunn as Raich Carter pours out a cupful for John Charles and a photographer snaps a memorable scene.

Leeds United Football Club has just secured its place in the First Division after nine years of second-tier football and Charlton has enjoyed his best season to date.

Charlton was a rock at centre-half and played the final 34 games straight after manager Carter recalled him, allowing the superb Charles to operate up front.

It was Carter who gave Charlton his Leeds debut in April 1953. When the 17-year-old asked what he was expected to do, Carter replied drily, 'See how fast their centre-forward can limp.'

Charlton wasn't the most gifted of players; he couldn't touch kid brother Bobby and many thought he only interested Leeds because of his family connections – uncles Jack, George and Jim Milburn had played for years for the club.

Charlton's first-team progress was stymied by National Service, an enforced two-year spell in the Army. The obligation persisted until 1960 with many clubs bemoaning the havoc that the break had on young players' careers and their own fortunes.

Charlton wasn't overly concerned, relishing his time away and even making a quick buck.

'Lads in the Army got four pounds a week retainer from their clubs,' Big Jack recalled. 'At Leeds, the rule was that you were paid £6 when you came home on leave to play … The real scam came in the expenses. People doing their National Service got chits to travel back to their families. But in the case of lads based at Windsor and living in London, these were pretty useless. I soon discovered that I could buy them for a few bob, use them to get to Leeds to play games, and then claim four or five pounds travel expenses from the club. The weekly wage in the Army was something like 25 shillings, but thanks to my football, I was making between £25 and £35 a month.'

Life changed for Charlton when he returned full-time to Elland Road in 1955.

'I came back to Leeds two years older and much more self-assured,' he said. 'I went away to the Army a boy of 18 and came back a man of 20 ... I was a bit too full of myself. I remember one run-in I had with John Charles when he came back for a corner and started telling me where to go, sort of saying, "You go over there and I'll go here." I said to him, "You f*** off! We've been handling this all game, we don't need you here." And he just looked at me. Anyway, when we got back into the dressing room he got hold of me by the shirt and said, "Don't ever talk to me like that again." I said I was sorry and told him we should just forget what had happened.'

'[Jack] was terribly confident about himself, even arrogant,' recalled team-mate Albert Nightingale, 'He used to give real stick to the players around him if anything went wrong. Big Jack did not care what he said to anyone, he was that cocky ... If you were having a bad game, he would lose his head and start swearing at you. He would badmouth players on the pitch and that would lead to a lot of rows. His head was too big for his shoulders. Because he was always shouting at them, people found it difficult to play with him. He was mean as well, never spent two ha'pennies.'

Charlton wasn't malicious and rarely bore a grudge, but he was abrasive and full of himself. He had an opinion on everything, whether he knew anything about it or not, and was always ready to argue no matter what the issue and who was talking about it.

Despite his tender years, it was inevitable that Charlton, the 'one-man awkward squad', was often at odds with the arrogant Carter.

'Raich was such a good player that he didn't understand how things that came easily to him might be difficult for others. The only training we used to do in those days was to run down the long side of the pitch, jog the short side, sprint the long side and so on ... Nobody taught you anything and nobody learned anything. It was ridiculous and I got bloody fed up with it.'

Charlton missed pre-season training in 1955, but he was fit as a butcher's dog after spending two months in barracks getting into shape. He did not take long to adjust to the rigours of the Second Division.

He was there to stay when Carter drafted him into the side and Leeds prospered in one of the most closely-fought promotion races for years. By 10 March, four points covered the top seven.

The attribute which set United apart was a special forward line, which Carter settled on almost by accident. He deployed Charles at inside-right rather than leading the line, with Harold Brook playing No 9. The acerbic Nightingale played inside-left and Carter had George Meek and Jackie Overfield on the flanks. It was a line-up that clicked as if made for each other; Charles top-scored with 29 of the 80 goals and Brook and Nightingale chipped in with 26 between them. Leeds were more dangerous than they had been for years.

Things came to a head on 21 April. Leeds, sitting third, welcomed second-placed Bristol Rovers for the match of the day. Elland Road was packed out with 49,000 fervent fans. Things looked ominous when David Ward headed Rovers into the lead after three minutes but United were not to be denied. They won a fourth game on the trot, with Charles and Overfield the scorers.

United's promotion hopes were finally in their own hands, although only one spot remained as Wednesday wrapped up the title with a 5-2 win at Bury.

Of the six teams below Leeds, only Bristol City were out of the running, but United were clear favourites and their match at Rotherham on 23 April, was crucial.

The gates closed on Millmoor's biggest attendance of the season with several hundreds more risking life and limb by clambering onto nearby roofs, slag heaps and chimneys to get a free view. Leeds' nerves were exposed in the first period with Charles and Brook both snatching at their opportunities. But when Rotherham found themselves down to ten fit men after Peter Johnson was injured, the odds moved in Leeds' favour. Nightingale won the game with two goals in the space of three second-half minutes. The victory left Leeds on the brink, in need of one point from their final fixture.

The team was in high spirits as Carter took them to Boothferry Park to face Hull, a club he had led to an unprecedented Third Division title in 1949. The Tigers had been doomed to relegation for weeks and seemed unlikely to present much of a barrier. After six minutes, Charles scored with a powerful left-foot drive, hinting that the result would be a formality. Hull had other ideas and were unexpectedly resilient. They were back in the game before the quarter-hour when Tommy Martin equalised. United's play was riddled with tension and the sides were still level at the interval.

'Just calm down, have some patience,' said Carter at the break, raising his hand to silence the dressing room. 'Our moment will come. Just be sure to take it when it does. And take your time, there's no rush.'

Carter had seen enough games in his time to know how these things work and he was confident Leeds would get their chance. He was not wrong.

After 62 minutes, George Meek danced into the Rotherham area, drawing a foul from a panic-stricken defender. Charles stepped up to bury the penalty, sending the keeper the wrong way with a smart feint. It was his 29th goal of a memorable campaign. Brook netted his 15th and 16th league goals during the final quarter of an hour to wrap up a flattering 4-1 victory. Leeds celebrated long and hard in the dressing room.

Carter strutted like a peacock around Elland Road for weeks afterwards, wordlessly telling everyone who cared to look, 'I told you so, look how good I am.' He was lord of all he surveyed.

There was a 31,000 Elland Road gate to witness Leeds face Everton in the opening game. Only Brook and Nightingale had First Division experience, but any doubts were banished as United ran out 5-1 victors with Brook grabbing a 21-minute hat-trick. The confidence that flourished in a triumphant spring saw the upstarts overwhelm supposedly superior opponents.

The day was not an unqualified triumph – Nightingale suffered a knee injury so severe that he would never play again.

His loss did nothing to curb United's enthusiasm for their new surroundings and a midweek win at Charlton left them top. This was completely unexpected, but it looked like a flash in the pan when they were victims of a 5-1 rout at Tottenham. There were knowing winks and nudges, and predictions that a rag bag side would be found out, but when Leeds trounced Charlton 4-0 in the Elland Road return, they were back up to fourth. Three wins in a week saw them rise to second spot on 15 September, a point behind Manchester United. Leeds were proving to be a durable force.

As the season moved through September, something happened which drastically changed the course of history for Leeds United.

Arnold Price, father of Audrey, the wife of Leeds full-back Jimmy Dunn, owned a fish and chip shop opposite the main gates of the Elland Road stadium. On Tuesday, 18 September, Price was torn from his fitful slumber around 2am as the sky lit up outside his bedroom window.

'What on earth's that, Arnold?' asked Mrs Price sleepily.

'Dunno, I'll have a look. You go back to sleep, love. No point both of us being up.'

'Bet some damned fool's been messing about with t'floodlights,' he thought as he rubbed his eyes and rose from his bed for a look out of the window. It would have been nothing new. The £7,000 lights were the most expensive in the country when they were erected in November 1953. Such a novelty had prompted many on the United staff to fiddle with them and Price's sleep was often disturbed.

But it was not the lights this time. As Price drew back his curtains, he saw the stadium gushing fire and smoke. 'Bugger me,' he muttered as he dashed barefoot and pyjama-clad to summon the fire brigade.

It was too late; the fire had had its evil way with a structure constructed almost entirely of wood. Five fire engines arrived within minutes but the West Stand was engulfed with flame. Though the blaze was under control in an hour, the damage had been done.

The roof had already collapsed into the seating area before the fire brigade arrived and the heat was so ferocious that an expanse of the pitch was left with scorch marks for weeks. The blaze consumed the entire edifice, including all the kit and equipment, the club records and the trophies. All that remained was a charred skeleton of twisted, smouldering metal.

There was no formal investigation, but arson was ruled out, an electrical fault in the roof deemed the cause. Damage was estimated at £100,000, and the club's insurance cover was woefully inadequate.

The stadium had never been great and had fallen into disrepair through lack of love and attention, as recalled by Jack Charlton. 'I had the wind knocked out of my sails when I saw the place for the first time. The terraces were made from ashes, not concrete, and there was more than a liberal sprinkling of weeds sprouting around the ground which had a look of untidiness … It did not quite come up to the standard I had envisaged.'

The utter devastation meant that the board HAD to do something. The stadium had gone almost untouched since Leeds United took possession in 1919 and the decaying image it presented impressed nobody. The fans had grown used to it, but to the newcomer it was an unlovely cattle shed. The atmosphere that did exist was despite the stand rather than because of it.

Harry Reynolds knew the tradition around the place and loved it, but for him and his grand vision of the future it was a liability, a dragging millstone around the club's neck.

Reynolds extolled the virtues of transformation, creating something to be proud of, something which would raise aspirations rather than grind them down. He painted a glowing picture of a new beginning and a symbolic cathedral of dreams to which devout supporters would flock in their tens of thousands. Even at this early stage of his stay in the United boardroom, his passion and energy made his a compelling voice.

As the players helped clear up the rubble and wreckage during the week, it was clear that it would be impossible to salvage the 2,800-seater stand and the directors launched a public appeal.

£60,000 was raised to boost the £55,000 insurance payout and at the start of the following season, a new West Stand was unveiled, built by local firm Robert R Roberts Limited. Fundraising efforts were co-ordinated by the newly established 100 Club, formed by United-supporting local businessman ready to dip into their pockets.

The 100 Club was a private members' club formed by Frances Gerard 'F G' Moorhouse, the managing director of Moorhouse's Jam and its factory in nearby Holbeck. The first meeting of the 100 Club was held on 17 June 1957 at the Queens Hotel in Leeds, and the first members paid 50 guineas each with the funds going to the football club.

Moorhouse was an impressive character with a flamboyant waxed moustache which gave him a Dapper Dan image. He was besotted with Leeds United, confessing, 'It's reached the point where on Thursday I start worrying about the team that the manager will pick, on Friday I worry about how they will perform, on Saturday I watch them perform, on Sunday I think about the game and read the newspaper reports, on Monday I think about what I am going to say at the board meeting, on Tuesday I worry about whether I said too much. Wednesday I have off!'

The 100 Club rapidly expanded as it raised funds and it had its own special room in the new West Stand near the boardroom. 200 lifetime season tickets were made available to members for 100 guineas each.

The new stand was a magnificent sight: 4,000 seats and a paddock area with standing room for 6,000 were located within a structure boasting an iconic blue façade. It bore the words 'Leeds United AFC' in large, golden letters above the city's coat of arms. The new stand was grandiose, putting the rest of the stadium to shame. At the south end was the infamous Scratching Shed, a shallow terrace with a barrel-shaped roof, built in the 1920s and now basic in the extreme.

Initially, builders estimated that the new stand would cost £100,000, but this was rapidly revised upwards to £130,000 and eventually ran to £180,000, blowing a £65,000 hole in the finances. Leeds City Council refused United's request for a loan but the board insisted there was no crisis.

The immediate concern was the next game, at home to Aston Villa. Carter was determined that the promising opening run should not be disturbed and insisted that the match went ahead as scheduled. The club ordered 40 new pairs of boots and the players had to soak and wear them in the days before, kicking the ball like hell to get them ready in time.

The stand ('a ring of metal girders looking for all the world like the dark skeleton of a whale' according to *The Times*) was cordoned off and the players and officials changed in the dressing rooms of the Whitehall Printeries sports ground in Lowfields Road before boarding a coach for the short trip to Elland Road. They had to pick their way through the burnt-out shell of the stand to reach the pitch.

A single Charles goal decided a tight contest, but Leeds then went five games without a win. Undeterred, they saw off Newcastle and Sheffield Wednesday at the beginning of November and continued to bob along in third.

52,401 were at Old Trafford on 17 November for the match of the day, Leeds in third against second-placed Man United. The Busby Babes were in their pomp, having stormed to the title in the spring and on track to retain the championship.

When Billy Whelan opened the scoring after 19 minutes, it seemed the Reds would walk it, but Frank McKenna equalised within seven minutes and the sides were level at the break. Jack Charlton's brother Bobby fired Manchester ahead in the 57th minute and Whelan's second goal seven minutes later seemed to have put the result to bed, but back came Carter's men. Within seconds they were awarded a penalty and an ice cool Charles made it 3-2 to set up a tense final 25 minutes. The result was in doubt to the end, but there were no further goals.

Eric Stanger lauded it as 'the best Leeds display since the war' but it heralded a slump with just two wins in the next 11 league games as the Peacocks slipped to seventh. The victories might have been rare but they were emphatic – 4-1 against Portsmouth, while a hat-trick from Brook and a Charles brace delivered a five-goal victory against Blackpool on Boxing Day.

Marking Charles at Bloomfield Road was future England captain Jimmy Armfield, who recalled. 'We took four hours to get there. No motorway, winding via Burnley and Keighley. It was midwinter and there must have been a foot of snow on the pitch when we arrived. We thought it was unplayable but Leeds were expecting a sell-out crowd, they needed the money and were determined that the game should go ahead. They had a right winger called George Meek who supplied the ammunition for Charles and the game had not been going long when Meek got away down the right and floated in the cross. I was under no illusions about what was about to happen. On cue, a steamroller by the name of Charles came hurtling into view, towering high above me as he leaped to plant a rocket-like header into the net. John headed two of them, easy as pie. I remember thinking "flipping heck!", he was so dominantly big. As they hit the net, I was still heading his chest.'

Leeds lost to a struggling Cardiff City in the third round of the Cup, the game Jack Charlton's farewell for more than two months. He was dropped by Carter after going off the rails, confessing later that he was going through a rough spell, staying out late, boozing, girls. He was still a rowdy bachelor.

Deputy Jack Marsden was out of his depth as United slumped 5-3 at Bolton. Performances grew patchy, but Leeds remained between 6th and 9th until the end of the season.

United's victories were rare, just four in the 19 fixtures since the trouncing of Blackpool on Boxing Day, but each was memorable: Leeds avenged their Cup exit by thrashing Cardiff 3-0, Portsmouth were routed 5-2, Charles hit a hat-trick against Sheffield Wednesday in a 3-2 win (taking his tally of trebles for Leeds to 11) and the closing day saw Sunderland beaten.

By the time United faced the Wearsiders, John Charles was in the departure lounge. The directors had bowed to the inevitable and agreed to sell.

The King is Dead

'He who advances without seeking fame, who retreats without escaping blame, he whose one aim is to protect his people and serve his lord, the man is a jewel of the realm.'

Early April 1957: Sam Bolton calls Raich Carter into his office to break some long-awaited news.

'Nah then, Raich, I'll not beat about the bush, we've decided to take offers for Charles.'

Carter says nothing immediately. He knows that the directors are ready to cash in on their prize asset. Finally, he breaks the silence. 'How much d'you think we'll get?'

Bolton, irritated at Carter's use of the word 'we', thinks, 'Who the hell does he think he is? That money's ours, not his.'

But he remains calm, saying, 'We'll be asking 70 grand.'

Carter's frown fades. 'And how much can I spend?'

Bolton isn't ready for an argument. 'We'll clear t'overdraft,' he says, 'and you'll have the rest.'

To Carter that means he would have 40 or 50 grand, quite enough to do the job, but to Bolton it means more like 20.

Assuming that they are on the same wavelength, Carter nods his acceptance and negotiations began.

Other clubs had pursued Charles for years, but the board had always been steadfast. Now, the cost of the new stand had seen the overdraft soar above £40,000 and the directors were convinced that drastic action was required.

Carter was not exactly dancing in the streets at losing his talisman but accepted the inevitable and consoled himself with the thought that he would have money to strengthen.

Italian giants Juventus had been tracking Charles for two years and Umberto Agnelli flew into Belfast in April to watch Charles lead Wales against Northern Ireland.

Agnelli had been alerted in January 1956 by club scout Gigi Peronace, who made contact with Charles after an outstanding performance against Arsenal the following November.

The Gunners had established a 3-0 lead but Charles got United back into the contest just after the hour when he headed home from a corner. Bobby Forrest added a second within three minutes and then Charles equalised with four minutes remaining. Peronace pulled Charles to one side at the end, introduced himself and outlined Juve's ambitions.

'I'm not interested, mister,' replied Charles. 'Leeds have never been willing to let me go, and that's good enough for me.'

'Is different now, John. They need money bad, and you're worth a fortune.'

'Oh, I don't think so, Mr Peronace.'

Charles was a home-loving bird, besotted with his wife, Leeds-born Peggy. The couple married in January 1953 and had the first of their four sons a year later, shortly before Charles, for the first time, asked for a transfer. When the Leeds directors decided against a sale, Charles took the decision with equanimity and reconciled himself to life with United.

Peronace refused to take no for an answer and was a frequent visitor to Charles' house in Morley, ingratiating himself with Peggy. He knew that if he could sell her on the delights of Italy, the player would be putty in his hands. 'You will love Italy and Italy will love you,' he said, as he courted Peggy.

When the couple were alone later, Peggy began her work. 'It sounds lovely, John. What do you think?'

'The club will never sell me,' insisted John. 'They've told me so, time and again. Let's not get our hopes up, love.'

'Will you just think about it?' she pleaded.

'Okay,' came the reply, but Charles put no stock by Peronace's wheedling. 'They'll never sell me, they've told me so,' he thought silently. 'I trust them.'

He was forced to have second thoughts when Carter broke the news to him in April 1957. Charles was confused by the change of message and uncertain what to do.

Juve's interest was mirrored by Real Madrid, Inter Milan and other clubs with the wherewithal to meet United's exorbitant asking price, but it soon became apparent that Juventus was the best option.

Sam Bolton announced that, while they would not sell Charles to another club in England, they would not stand in his way if one of the big clubs in Europe came in for him.

Bolton and Percy Woodward had lengthy discussions with Agnelli and Peronace in Room 233 of the Queens Hotel in City Square, talking late into the evening of 17 April.

Bolton told Charles, 'It's so sad that we're losing you, John.' Nevertheless, according to Charles, 'as soon as they got the cheque, they shot off to put it in the bank.'

Negotiations over the fee were straightforward but Charles' personal terms were a different kettle of fish. The player was represented by agent Teddy Sommerfield, experienced at negotiating with the BBC on behalf of people like Eamonn Andrews, and Kenneth Wolstenholme, there to advise on football matters.

The £65,000 fee smashed the British record and significantly boosted Leeds' bank balance. The previous highest fee involving a British club had been the £35,000 received by Charlton when Sampdoria signed Eddie Firmani in 1955. Leeds' own record had been £12,000, both paid to Cardiff for Don Mills in 1951 and received from Sheffield United for Len Browning two months later.

It was reported that Real Madrid were prepared to go to £70,000 with a £30,000 bonus for Charles. In addition to the money, Real held the added attraction of a place in the European Cup while Juve were struggling to stay afloat. The Madrid move was a non-starter, though, because Real already had its full quota of two foreign players.

'If the answer has anything to do with me,' said Peggy when asked whether she was happy with a move to Italy, 'it will most definitely be yes.'

John was every bit as positive. 'I shall get a new car and a flat with coal and lighting laid on. I should regret it all my life, as a married man with two children and a third due at any time, if I turned it down. I could never hope to earn that sort of money here, however long I played.'

The maximum wage in England limited his annual salary to £1,780. His basic in Italy would be £832, but he would also receive £28 for a home win and £40 away. For victory in the biggest games the figure would be between £100 and £200. That boosted his wages by around £1,500 in his first season in Turin, but it was the fully-expensed lifestyle and sunshine that were the clinchers. That and the £10,000 he received for signing, though a Leeds businessman had offered the same sum to stay at Leeds. Charles could have been forgiven for letting his mind wander, but one could not fault his commitment. He had games still to play for Leeds and put as much effort in as ever he had, though he was distinctly off colour at Sunderland on 19 April, fluffing two easy chances. He was on target twice in a depressing 6-2 defeat at Birmingham in the penultimate match and looked forward to leading out Leeds for one final time, at home to Sunderland.

Charles could not have dreamed of a more fitting end to his time at Elland Road.

Sunderland badly needed the points and were determined to stop Charles, but they couldn't. A *Yorkshire Post* reporter wrote, 'I shall never forget the way in which he overtook Daniel, the upstanding Sunderland centre-half, as they both raced towards the Sunderland goal and, as Daniel tried to keep the ball close to him, Charles calmly stole it and without a check in his stride, without deviation. It seemed as though one player merged into the other; red shirt was leading with the ball, suddenly a blue shirt was in front and there was no faltering.'

Charles' two goals came after Brook's spectacular 30-yard shot opened the scoring on 55 minutes.

But for some sound goalkeeping by Roy Wood, Sunderland would have scored more than the goal Grainger gave them between Charles' first and second. The visitors were 'too anxious to do the right thing quickly. Revie, except in finishing, was Sunderland's best player.'

It was a fitting end to a remarkable association. Charles had scored 154 goals in almost a decade, despite many years at centre-half, and shown himself to be a wondrous talent. His 38 goals helped Leeds finish eighth, and, but for a run of a single point from the five games prior to Sunderland, United could have enjoyed their highest ever finish. The lost nine points would have put them level with Blackpool in fourth.

The departure of such an immense talent left a grievous wound and Raich Carter could only scratch his head and wonder where (or rather whether) he would find a suitable successor. He had been planning for the future when he brought in Dunfermline inside-forward George O'Brien in March. Carter matched Leeds' record outlay when he splashed out £12,000 on Airdrie's Hugh Baird and then added South African right winger Gerry Francis, who became the first black player to appear in a Leeds team. He laid out £7,000 for Glenavon's Wilbur Cush and £5,000 for Noel Peyton of Shamrock Rovers.

Baird, already a Scottish cap, had scored 165 goals for Airdrie in six seasons. He looked a promising replacement, but the weight of expectation was a heavy burden.

Carter was disappointed to be given such sparse financial backing and feared the worst.

Things looked bleak when Leeds lost their first two games, at Blackpool and Aston Villa, without even a sniff of a goal. Baird got off the mark with a penalty and Overfield netted the other in a 2-1 win against Leicester on 31 August as the club christened its sparkling new stand. To help cover costs, ticket prices had been raised to 7s 6d for seating and 5s 6d for standing in what had always been regarded as the 'posh bit' of the stadium.

The new stand also played host to a representative match on 19 October, with a Football League selection facing a League of Ireland XI. Jack Charlton was named alongside the full-back pairing of Blackpool's Jimmy Armfield and Ronnie Moran of Liverpool in the Football League's defence. They won 3-1 thanks to a goal from Peter Broadbent of Wolves and a brace for Bolton's Ray Parry.

Baird added two more goals to his Leeds account and O'Brien and Brook the others in a 4-0 win against Villa. It was a false dawn. Leeds crashed 5-0 at champions Manchester United and managed a single goal during the two home defeats which followed. The team had four points from their opening seven matches and appeared toothless.

Leeds retained most of the players that had earned promotion, but much of their spirit went with Charles. All they could look forward to was a long hard winter struggling against relegation.

Baird was a regular scorer but was not in Charles' class and there was no one else who could take on the mantle of leader.

Carter nominated newcomer Wilbur Cush as captain, but he made his debut in the middle of a five-game losing run and by 23 November Leeds were three from bottom, a scant point clear of the relegation places.

Cush helped stem the tide and his maiden goal earned a point against Birmingham. A trip to Chelsea ended in another defeat, but Leeds then beat Newcastle and Blackpool. The victory over the Seasiders saw Leeds rise to 16th with a five-point cushion over the relegation zone.

They rallied, enjoying several important victories and earned a draw against Manchester United.

The FA Cup saw Leeds take their customary exit at the first time of asking but generated a gem of footballing trivia. In both 1956 and 1957, the third-round draw pitted United at home to Cardiff City and on both occasions the score was 2-1 to the visitors. 1958 saw the tie repeated and Leeds again lost 2-1. It was a disappointing way to mark their season.

At the time Jack Charlton was experiencing significant changes in his personal life, marrying girlfriend Pat Kemp in January and agonising over brother Bobby's brush with death in Munich a month later. The two events combined to bring a more mature outlook on life as the perpetual rebel cemented his status as the mainstay of the Leeds defence.

Three successive defeats in March plunged Leeds into the drop zone but wins over Arsenal and Burnley left them 16th as seven clubs were dragged into the battle. After a single-goal defeat at Manchester City on 29 March, the contest was perilously close with Leeds on 28 points, one point ahead of four clubs and two ahead of bottom side Sheffield Wednesday. Over the Easter weekend, the Whites strengthened their chances by taking five points out of six and the one they secured at Birmingham on 12 April confirmed safety with two games to spare.

A single defeat from the final nine fixtures was championship form but Carter had little cause for celebration. As Prime Minster Harold Macmillan assured the country they had never had it so good, the United manager's five-year contract came up for renewal. On the strength of one poor campaign, the directors decided against an extension. Carter was enraged, complaining that the failure to invest the Charles money scuppered his chances. The news that his contract would not be renewed was given by Sam Bolton on 9 May. The chairman said it was with regret that the decision had been reached and there were tears in his eyes to prove it.

The Silver Fox was never popular with players or board, generally regarded as an 'arrogant so-and-so'. Harry Reynolds, other directors and members of the 100 Club provided a ten-year loan of £58,000 to keep things going and weren't in the mood to continue tolerating the carping of someone they considered an 'odious little know-it-all'. 'Raich Carter was such a bloody big head,' commented Archie Gibson. 'Everything he talked about, it was always about himself.' Even the affable Charles detested him, claiming he 'loved himself … Carter was very opinionated.'

Carter, who said he wouldn't trust the directors enough to send them out to buy a packet of Woodbines, described the decision as 'a great shock … Under my management United went from tenth in the Second Division to eighth in the First Division and then last season to 17th after the directors sold the greatest player in the world and have given me far less than half his transfer fee to spend on replacing him. This last season could never be any more than a holding season.'

In recognition of his success, Carter was given a £500 pay off. When he suggested that the trainer and the groundsman should also receive a bonus, the parsimonious board agreed that the trainer should have £100 and the groundsman £50 but took both payments out of Carter's £500.

Carter's departure left United rudderless. A successor was needed who could bring experience and vigour, but there was little to attract such a character, with Elland Road more closely associated with financial restrictions than ambition. The club had been lucky with the appointment of Carter and predecessor Major Frank Buckley and now struggled to attract a man of any status. Bolton settled for a temporary appointment, promoting trainer-coach Bill Lambton to the role of acting manager, while indicating that he was merely 'chief-coach-and-trainer', declining to add 'chief cook and bottle washer'.

Lambton had been hired by Carter the previous November. He had no experience of running a football club and had not been a great success as coach, commanding little respect among the players. They sneered that he could forget petty rules about training starting at 9.45 rather than the usual 10, muttering darkly that the board should ready itself for some requests for transfers.

The directors began to push their noses into team affairs, insisting on 'working with' Lambton on selection and transfers and declined to pay him a salary befitting a successor to Carter and Buckley.

The World Cup finals in Sweden that summer set new standards. Brazil won the Jules Rimet Trophy for the first time with some breathtaking football, while the contributions of Northern Ireland and John Charles' Wales were outstanding.

His former employers at Elland Road could only look on enviously. While the rest of the footballing world was rushing expectantly towards the excitement of a new decade and a new era in football, humble old Leeds United were helplessly drifting. They were still a First Division outfit, but one with little hope.

The omens were not promising as United approached the new season. It was anticipated that they would continue to struggle without Charles: their 51 goals in 1957/58 was the lowest total in Division One and only three teams in the entire Football League were less productive.

Conversely, Leeds had a decent defence and only champions Wolves and runners-up Preston conceded fewer than the 63 shipped. This was due in no small part to the rearguard's collective experience.

The atmosphere around the club was toxic and the first 17 matches of 1958/59 yielded just three victories.

While Lambton enlisted no new blood during the summer, he could be forgiven for wondering what was happening as the normal defensive assurance evaporated. Leeds lost their opening game 4-0 at Bolton, setting an ominous tone.

Just as worrying as the defensive shortcomings was the lack of attacking punch. The previous March, Brook had followed Charles out of Elland Road, and Lambton was left with few options up front. United fielded a precocious 19-year-old right winger called Chris Crowe, but he was a rare exception and there were few others of any quality. Carter had let Major Buckley's cherished youth development programme slide into decline and Leeds were denied that particular avenue for recruits. It was to Lambton's eternal credit that he relaunched the programme, a decision for which his successors were eternally grateful. For now, he had to make do and mend.

Hugh Baird and George Meek missed the opener and in their absence there was neither presence nor bite. The two were soon back in action and on the scoresheet, but Leeds continued to struggle, winning just one of their opening nine games. The point surrendered in a 0-0 draw at home to bottom club Aston Villa on 18 October plunged Leeds into the bottom two.

The board had been unsuccessful in its quest for a permanent appointment but gave Lambton permission to reinforce and he forked out £5,000 for Ards winger Billy Humphries.

United twice came from behind to win in the final minute at Spurs. While never matching Tottenham's finesse, Leeds stuck to their straightforward game well enough to score three goals in a match for the first time all season. It could well have been four, so great was the forward improvement but Crowe smacked a penalty against the bar.

In United's rearguard, Charlton was inspired, constantly denying Bobby Smith. The *Yorkshire Evening Post*'s Phil Brown commented, 'If Charlton could regularly play even at only 80 per cent of this form, a lot of United's worries would disappear.'

On 27 October, Sam Bolton sought to allay concerns, telling former centre-half Tom Holley of the *Evening Post*, 'There is no dissension in the boardroom. There have been differences of opinion, certainly, that happens in any committee, but there has been no serious rift.'

There were disputes about the way that Lambton was running things. 'Nothing has been decided about a manager,' added Bolton. 'Mr Lambton will carry on until other arrangements are made, but anyone who says we have made up our minds is trying to jump the gun.'

Reports claimed that Jimmy Murphy, Matt Busby's well-regarded assistant at Manchester United, was the man Leeds wanted, though Richard Ulyatt of the *Yorkshire Post* championed the claims of former Birmingham manager Arthur Turner. The 100 Club was reported to be dissatisfied with performances and threatening intervention.

Lambton was gifted £8,250 to secure the services of Burnley's 24-year-old reserve centre-forward Alan Shackleton. Lambton recouped the outlay when Hughie Baird returned north of the border in October, joining Aberdeen in an £11,000 deal.

Shackleton scored in his first game for Leeds, on 1 November when they lost to Manchester United. 'Beaten, but far from being disgraced,' was Tom Holley's verdict on the first home defeat, but the truth was that Leeds were just not good enough.

After defeat to Chelsea, Bolton announced that a permanent manager would soon be in post. The *Evening Post*'s Phil Brown was not overly impressed, commenting that the directors needed to consider their own 'record of stewardship' and 'strengthening the board with new men'.

Brown was adamant that they had had long enough to build a decent side and had singularly failed to do so. He reported they would be offering a wage £2,000 greater than Lambton's and more in keeping with that paid to Buckley and Carter.

Brown added that there were plans for a new inside-forward, 'a really class man who can pull the line together'. The point was taken up by Tom Holley. 'United's big need sticks out a mile. They have no one who can control the game in midfield. It is an old, old Elland Road story, but a really good inside man could be United's salvation and give them the breathing space they so badly need.'

Leeds were chasing two big names and Brown thought the man for the job would cost twice the £12,000 they had paid for Baird.

Shackleton snatched a hat-trick in a much needed 4-2 victory at Blackburn as Brown reported little interest in the managerial vacancy. 'Otherwise there would be no need,' he wrote, 'for last night's patently "shot-in-the-arm" statement … that the club is determined to get the best available man, that the salary should attract some of the country's best men, that the manager will have absolute control of every football aspect, and that money will be forthcoming for any buying of players he will recommend.'

Soon the headlines were to be devoted to just such a transfer with Leeds initiating the club's relationship with the man who would transform them, Don Revie.

Welcome to Yorkshire

'When the general is weak and without authority; when his orders are not clear and distinct; when there are no fixed duties assigned to officers and men, and the ranks are formed in a slovenly haphazard manner, the result is utter disorganisation.'

26 April 1958: Billy Bremner, just turned 16, has broken into the Scottish schoolboys team. He is about to make his fourth appearance, the big one against England at Wembley with the second half to be broadcast live on BBC One this afternoon.

The Scottish schoolboys side is useful and includes future stars like Andy Penman, Ian Gibson and Bobby Hope, along with Bremner's great pal, Tommy Henderson. The England side includes Terry Venables, Ronnie Boyce and Peter Thompson.

The day did not go well – Scotland lost 3-1 and Henderson missed a penalty, but it could not take the shine off for young Billy. Even better, London giants Arsenal and Chelsea were suitably impressed and invited the pair down for trials. Neither boy was enamoured by the capital, though they agreed to think it over when they each received offers from the two clubs.

Sheffield Wednesday and Aston Villa joined the race for Bremner's signature and both Celtic and Rangers also expressed an interest.

'I really wanted to join Celtic,' recalls Bremner. 'My father had other ideas. He told me quite plainly that he was not going to have me get caught up with any religious controversy – and that automatically ruled out Celtic because of the sectarianism between them and Rangers. "You're going to England and that's that." I could never argue with my father … he would always have the last word.'

Harry Reynolds and Bill Lambton tuned in with thousands of others to watch Bremner and Henderson on TV and were impressed enough to throw their hats in the ring. The two men travelled north to try and sign the pair, but there was a weakness in their game plan. Bremner knew nothing about United and had to ask boyhood pal Henderson, 'Who the hell are they? Are they in the Fourth Division or something?' Henderson reassured Bremner, 'Dinna be stupid, they're in the First Division.'

Bremner and Henderson didn't warm to Lambton, he was stand offish and they thought he was ignoring them, choosing instead to speak over their heads to their parents and going on and on about discipline and 'knocking the lads into shape'. 'Who the hell does he think he is?' thought Bremner to himself.

However, Reynolds' down-to-earth air and straightforward manner were more to his liking.

'Okay, Bill, you've said enough. Let me talk to the lads ...' said Reynolds, raising his hand to silence Lambton.

'Ye've got that right, uncle,' thought Bremner to himself.

'Listen fellas, we don't mess about at Leeds,' continued Reynolds. 'None of the airs and graces you'll get at other clubs – we treat you like young men, not little boys. You couldn't join a club that cares more about the lads it signs. We're going places and we'd like you to come with us.'

Bremner had heard enough and he was soon bending Henderson's ear about a move to West Yorkshire.

They both signed for Leeds when the offers came, but began to have second thoughts as the reality of a move so far from home sank in. The pair were soon suffering homesickness and making this plain to all who would listen. Club secretary Cyril Williamson called them into his office to give them a piece of his mind about their disruptive behaviour. They listened attentively enough, but none of it sank in and it wasn't long before Henderson returned north; selection for the reserves against Preston persuaded Bremner to commit for another year.

Bremner remained unsettled but whenever he decided to up sticks and return home, something arose to dissuade him.

Bremner: 'I told the manager that I should have broken into the first team by now, I was consistently performing well for the reserves. I told him I was thinking about getting myself a move back to Scotland. He listened to me and understood my frustration. His parting advice was that it would be in my best interests not to seek a move away from Leeds but to stick it out, as bigger things awaited me while he was manager.'

Bill Lambton had negligible impact in his short, uncelebrated spell as manager, but he had the foresight (or fortune) to sign both Bremner and Don Revie, irrevocably changing the club's destiny.

Revie's priority when he quit Roker Park in 1958 was a return to the First Division but there was little interest in the market. Time had caught up with him; pace had never been a strong point and it had now gone completely but his mind was as quick as ever and he was still adept at pulling the strings. Hometown club Middlesbrough expressed an interest but it was Leeds United, struggling in the top flight after winning just four of their opening 18 games, who eventually stepped forward and paid Sunderland £14,000 on 28 November, setting a new club record.

It was quite a gamble. The club's financial results were poor, the profit for the year to July 1958 a meagre £521, after 1957's £59,967 (entirely due to the fee received for Charles), while the £180,000 reprovision of the West Stand and clearing the £17,500 overdraft had emptied the reserves.

Nevertheless, Leeds were suddenly back in the headlines and a genuine name had been found to compensate for the loss of Charles.

'I am very happy to be back in First Division football again, especially with a team in my native Yorkshire,' said Revie, indisputably the outstanding talent at Elland Road. Revie had two perspectives on this: he relished being the centre of attention but was downcast by the quality of his colleagues.

Revie and Elsie would go on living in Sunderland until the club found him a house in Leeds. 'The search will start right away,' said Harry Reynolds, now working as publicity director. Revie claimed that he was quite prepared to travel to Leeds for training until they got fixed up.

The *Evening Post*'s Phil Brown was enthusiastic, describing Revie as 'just the sort of signing that Elland Road … have wanted, a proven, well-known, skilful inside-forward, an English international of only a year ago, and young enough at 30 to be capped again … He is one of the best users of the ball the post-war soccer scene in the United Kingdom has known, and his spray of passes, long or short, has cut many a defence to ribbons.'

Revie's debut on 29 November brought victory against Newcastle, with the *Yorkshire Post*'s Richard Ulyatt writing of 'his deft through passes just in front of his team-mates of a type which no Leeds forward has made or received in the 25 years I have been watching them.' Alan Shackleton netted a hat-trick a week earlier to secure a much-needed 4-2 win at Blackburn, but before then there had been only three victories in 17 matches.

Three wins in the following four games boosted Leeds' spirits before they lapsed back into familiar mediocrity.

Revie was accorded the credit for the improvement. Eric Stanger wrote in his *Yorkshire Post* review of victory at West Ham that Revie was 'the man United have wanted for years ... that essential link between attack and defence which has so often been lacking. He was the co-ordinator, the Johnny-on-the-spot, bolstering up his half-backs when need arose and often transforming defence into attack with his shrewd strokes. Revie not only has that undefinable quality we call class but, on this occasion at least, the knack of making others play all the better for his presence.'

Six weeks after Revie's arrival, Wilbur Cush stood down as club captain, and the players unanimously selected Revie to succeed him. Delighted by the show of support, Revie said, 'I feel honoured and will give the job all I can on the field and off.'

The unbeaten run saw Bill Lambton's appointment made substantive following a lengthy board meeting on 9 December, with the decision reported as unanimous.

It was far from the truth; Reynolds was convinced that Lambton's bizarre methods could be effective and he was a strong advocate. The directors debated the matter long and hard in the new boardroom, located above the dressing room in the reconstructed West Stand.

Heeding the advice of Phil Brown in the *Yorkshire Evening Post*, the board had co-opted four directors in an attempt to appease members: former centre-half Jim Baker, who captained Leeds to the Second Division title in 1924, 100 Club chairman F G Moorhouse, Bob Roberts, whose firm had built the new West Stand, and Dr Norman Winder, a renowned local medic.

Brown pilloried the club's recent record as 'not at all encouraging ... Neither in the league or the Cup, nor financially

... have United made the progress the city and district want ... United have missed all the post-war spectator boom and all the income that went with it.'

Following the expansion of the board, Brown wrote a self-congratulatory note, 'I see the influence of the new members of the board at work', before welcoming 'the assurance that a new manager will have the money with which to buy players.'

Nevertheless, all four of the new men were excluded from the discussion about Lambton, allowing the big beasts the room in which to circle each other.

'Is anyone going to put their hat in the ring, chaps?' asked Reynolds, opening the discussion. 'We're not exactly spoilt for choice after the slagging that Carter gave us. And anyway, Lambton's methods seem to be working, we've won three games on the bounce with plenty of goals. Revie's making things happen.'

Tiny Blenkinsop shifted uncomfortably in his seat, his many chins wobbling as he peered like an owl at Reynolds through his round spectacles. 'You're right, Harry,' he said. 'Revie's making things happen, not Lambton. Everyone knows he's a complete joke. Charlton refers to him as a clown.'

'There's not a man in this club,' Reynolds retorted, 'that Jack hasn't called a clown at one point or another. That means nowt.'

Blenkinsop harrumphed loudly and linked his vast hands across his vast stomach. Reynolds had him there and he had no immediate response but he glared pointedly at Reynolds.

'He's nobbut an idiot, Harry,' tried Harold Marjason, his eyes bulging. 'Dunn, Kerfoot and Hair are going to walk. Think he's a bloody comedian, they do, knows nowt about tactics, nowt about football, nowt about owt. No bloody respect for him, they haven't.'

'They're just bloody nigglers, the lot of 'em,' snapped back Reynolds. 'They dunna like change, they dunna like hard work and Lambton makes them sweat. They dunna like the fact that he doesn't roll over and pay the maximum wage like Carter used to do. He's not a soft touch and they dunna like it.'

Sam Bolton was getting worried, he could see feelings were strong and the last thing he wanted was a divided board. 'Nah then, chaps, just calm down. Let's take a break and cool down. We'll think more clearly when we're not in temper.'

The directors retired to the adjacent lounge to mull things over as they savoured their glasses of Scotch and puffed at their cigars. An unrepentant Reynolds began to work the room. He knew he would get nowhere with Blenkinsop and Marjason, so he turned his attention to Woodward and Wilkinson; they hadn't spoken yet, but their views would be critical. Reynolds prodded and probed until he got some insight and it soon became apparent that they would go along with Reynolds if push came to shove.

Reynolds recounted the equation to himself. Two for, two against, Bolton would go with him, he was sure of it. And Bromley would go with Bolton. Reynolds rubbed his hands together in satisfaction.

Ten minutes later Bolton called his colleagues to order.

'I want no dissent, chaps, cabinet responsibility. We can have differences in here, but out there, we're as one. Now, let's see what's what.'

He asked each of his colleagues to declare their view. Reynolds and Woodward spoke first and were for Lambton, Wilkinson followed suit. Blenkinsop shuffled uncomfortably again. 'I'm uneasy, Sam, you know I am, but it looks like I'm outnumbered. Perhaps I've been around too long.'

'Not necessarily, Tiny,' mumbled Marjason. 'I'm with you. I won't break ranks, but I'm agin Lambton.'

'3 to 2,' thought Bolton to himself as he pointed to Bromley. 'What about you, John?'

'Things are going well, why rock the boat? I say give him the job.'

'Thank you, gentlemen. For what it's worth, I'll back Lambton too. Tiny, Harold, are you happy to go with the flow?'

'You know we will, Sam.' Tiny peered over his glasses, clearly uncomfortable with life.

Reynolds smiled quietly to himself as Bolton said. 'It's unanimous, then. Lambton's our man. I'll prepare a statement.'

Not a word of the debate was revealed to Lambton, who claimed that he had 'the complete support of the board of directors, who have promised to back me up in every way, as they have been doing ever since I came here'.

No contract was signed and Lambton insisted that he had not asked for one. 'If I cannot do the job, I have no right to hold it,' he said.

There was no new dawn and Leeds never found decent form, limping in a dismal 15th, with three wins in the final four games papering over the cracks. An indifferent fan base drifted away and there was only one crowd above 20,000 after January. It wasn't even necessary to open all the turnstiles every week because often there were less than 10,000 souls seeking entry. Crowds of at least 25,000 were required to ensure breakeven and the club continued to lurch into the red.

By mid-February, it was acknowledged that the Lambton appointment was a disaster. There was no respect for him and Grenville Hair and Jack Overfield both demanded transfers.

Matters weren't helped by a confrontation with Jack Charlton in the weeks before Christmas.

There was a club rule that only players and directors were allowed on the team coach. After a game at Chelsea in November, Charlton tried to cadge a lift for two relatives back to north London, only to be told that it was against the rules and there could be no exceptions.

A month later, following United's next game in the Smoke, against West Ham, Charlton heard that Lambton had permitted waiters from the team hotel to travel. The obstreperous defender angrily called out the manager: 'My relatives had to miss their train and spent hours getting home. Now there's four complete strangers sitting on our coach.'

'It's got nothing to do with you, I make the rules around here. You do as you're told.'

'I won't. You made a rule. You made me stick to it. Now you stick to it. If they're not getting off, I am.'

'Please yourself.'

Charlton furiously stormed off the coach. As he alighted, Tiny Blenkinsop boomed, 'Get them off the coach and get him on.'

In that moment, any vestige of authority crumbled.

Charlton said later, 'He wasn't a player, he wasn't a coach, he wasn't anything … One windy day, when we complained about the balls being too hard during a training session, Bill told us that anyone worth his salt ought to be able to kick balls in his bare feet and never feel it, so one of the lads said, "Well, go on then." Bill wasn't a pro, he'd probably never kicked a ball in anger in his life, and yet here he was running up to kick the ball in his bare feet, and of course you could see him wincing afterwards. This is the manager who's just been appointed, and he's making a fool of himself in front of his players. He finished up hobbling off the pitch, with all of us laughing at him.'

Bolton asked the players if they wanted Lambton to go and to a man they said yes. Lambton promised pathetically, 'If you let me stay, we'll have a new start,' but there was not one word of support.

A disastrous 6-2 defeat at Wolves on 14 February sealed his fate. With directors openly expressing their disquiet, the beleaguered manager bowed to the inevitable and resigned, muttering darkly that there had been 'interference ... in my training methods'.

The directors were quick to spread the story that it was the players who had got rid of Lambton in an eerie foreshadow of Brian Clough's fate 15 years later.

Lambton was not out of work for long. He earned a place in the record books after spending just three days in charge at Scunthorpe in April. It was later claimed that the appointment was only verbal and never formalised. He took over as caretaker manager at Grimsby immediately thereafter and lasted until the following February.

Leeds could not replace Lambton immediately and appointed head physio and former trainer Bob Roxburgh as caretaker. Somehow, he kept them clear of relegation. A closing run of three wins and a draw banished any lingering fears but the optimism of the Revie signing had long gone. Public interest had plummeted and the gates dwindled; it was as if no one could be bothered.

Leeds' 57 goals made them the division's lowest scorers and they could no longer counter with claims of a reliable defence. The shape had gone, with four or more goals conceded on six separate occasions, and another five when bowing out of the FA Cup at the first time of asking at struggling Luton.

The only defenders who came out of the campaign with any credit were Charlton and the ultra-consistent Hair, who made his 300th league appearance in the final game. The classy full-back had missed just 26 games since October 1951.

United's lack of appeal was exemplified by the preference of Arthur Turner to stay at non-league Headington (later Oxford) United. 'The Headington board can take its place with any in the country when it comes to allowing a manager to manage,' he said, with a barbed snipe at the Leeds directors and their reputation for interference.

Former Leeds favourite Tommy Burden also turned down the post when it was offered and there were unsuccessful attempts to lure Charlie Mitten, Archie Macaulay, Bob Brocklebank and Willie Thornton.

In the end Leeds settled on Yorkshire-born Jack Taylor, fresh from leading Queens Park Rangers to mid-table mediocrity in the Third Division. He was appointed in May on a three-year contract worth £2,500 per annum – brother Frank accompanied him as coach.

Taylor had brought little conspicuous success in seven years with Rangers but wishful thinking had it that with virtually no money, he would revive United. It was anybody's guess how he would achieve such a feat.

Charlton welcomed the arrival of the new regime, claiming that Frank Taylor 'was the first guy who ever took me out on a pitch and taught me how to kick a ball properly ... I could talk to the Taylors about the game, and suddenly I felt I had kindred spirits within the club. But the other players didn't respond well to the new approach. Their general attitude was that they came into the club to do their bit of training, played their matches, and then buggered off.'

In an attempt to improve training, the backroom team set up a circuit, with cones carefully laid out, along with other training kit. Some of the senior pros were in no mood for this and led by a contemptuous Charlton they hurled all the cones down the bank in one corner of the ground. 'I'll teach them to mess with me.'

Inexperienced as Billy Bremner was, he could still see that the club wasn't being run professionally. 'To go to see Mr Taylor: Christ, you had to go through one secretary, then another, and finally you would get to the third secretary and she would say he couldn't see you. The only time you ever saw the manager was if you travelled with the first team on a Saturday.'

The new broom earned considerable posthumous credit for persevering with the youth development policy that Lambton had revived. There was a steady incoming flow of young hopefuls from all around the country. One of those invited that summer was a lanky, raw-boned inside-forward from the North East, 15-year-old Norman Hunter.

He was spotted while playing for Birtley Juniors and offered a trial, playing inside-right for the junior side against Bradford Park Avenue. Leeds won 6-0 and Hunter did enough to earn an offer of a place on the ground staff.

Among Taylor's first duties was arranging the departure of two mainstays; Eric Kerfoot joined Third Division Chesterfield, while Jimmy Dunn moved to the Fourth with struggling Darlington. Both players had served the club loyally for years. A negative reaction might have been expected but there was merely passive acceptance, such was the lack of interest at Elland Road.

While the sale of George O'Brien to Southampton yielded £10,000, Taylor had little freedom to bring in new blood. He was allowed the whole of the O'Brien money to sign powerful Bradford City front man John McCole but only after Alan Shackleton had left to join Everton.

Revie was obliged to lead the line until McCole's arrival in September. Leeds were deep in trouble, losing 6-0 at Manchester United, and McCole's arrival coincided with three straight defeats which left the Whites with eight points from 11 matches and only Birmingham and Luton below them.

McCole impressed, getting off the mark in his second game and snatching six in his opening eight. He scored prolifically all year, one of the few to emerge with any honour from an abysmal season.

It was in defence that the problems lay, and no matter how many goals came from McCole, Leeds usually managed to concede one (or, more normally, several) more. The opening run was dismal – Fulham's 4-1 win at Elland Road on 5 December was the fourth defeat in a row and the 11th from 20 games. Leeds were second-bottom.

Taylor called all the players together from the first team down to the newcomers, including Norman Hunter. To Hunter's astonishment, no one took a blind bit of notice of Taylor's rallying cry. Several senior players ignored him completely, preferring to spend their time hurling Christmas streamers across the room. Hunter was shocked at the lack of respect.

Whether it was the Fulham reverse or Taylor's exhortations that had an impact it is impossible to know, but the team rallied. Revie scored the first goal in a hard fought 3-3 draw at Manchester City on 12 December. A week later, Leeds came away victorious from third-placed Burnley, a game played in atrocious conditions. The home side dominated and created most of the chances but just could not find the net. The longer the game went on, the more Leeds gained in confidence.

On Boxing Day, table-topping Spurs won 4-2 at Elland Road, but two days later Leeds pulled off a 4-1 victory in the return. The result lifted United out of the relegation places for a day at least and stirred frozen Yorkshire hearts. The game attracted over 36,000 fans, by far the biggest gate of the season.

This was a magnificent Tottenham side, on the verge of greatness and the Double in 1961. The star men were Danny Blanchflower, John White, Dave Mackay and Cliff Jones, one of the game's great midfields. Manager Bill Nicholson was building a superb outfit, though they were far from the finished article and Leeds tore them apart in the upset of the season.

It was all the more disappointing, then, to draw at home to bottom club Luton and lose to Second Division Aston Villa in the Cup. Decent form returned for a while and Leeds were at their best in defeating West Ham and Chelsea, prompting some to think that there could yet be salvation.

The Chelsea game was momentous, marking the debut of Bremner at outside-right with Revie inside him.

Revie took Bremner under his wing from the start, doing everything he could to settle him in, forging a bond that would keep them joined at the hip for 30 years.

Revie revealed the news to Bremner, taking the opportunity when he spied him in the car park. Taylor had mentioned his plans to Revie, who just could not wait to tell the youngster.

'Hello, Billy lad. Listen, I've got some good news for you.'

'Go on then, what d'ye know?'

'Well, you know that Chris Crowe's been called up to do his National Service?'

'Aye, I do, he was proper pissed off.'

'Well, the Gaffer's decided you're the one to fill the gap.'

'Eh? What d'ye mean?'

'You're in. Get your case ready, you're playing at Chelsea.'

Revie arranged for the pair to room together in the hotel where the squad stayed, seeing to it that Bremner was in bed by ten and rose at seven sharp to accompany him on a long walk. Revie gave Bremner an early touch of the ball to settle his nerves: 'I could see from the start that Billy had the ability to go right to the top. I wanted to see if he would use that ability. I didn't need to worry. He had no trouble with the big-time atmosphere, he was confident, even cheeky.'

Phil Brown reported in the *Yorkshire Evening Post*: 'His was no sensational debut with the miry pitch and rain all being against a lightweight youth shining. But all the main football qualities were there – enthusiasm, guts, intelligence, most accurate use of the ball and unselfishness.'

The game went well, Leeds won 3-1 thanks to a brace from McCole and one from Peyton.

Bremner recalled later, 'When I laid a pass on to Don Revie I immediately settled down into my game. Wilbur Cush constantly reminded me to ignore abusive and foul comments made by the Chelsea players and their crowd. He reminded me that the abuse should be taken as a back-handed compliment.'

Revie was determined to do for Bremner what others had done for him. He had always soaked up wisdom like a sponge and sought to pass on his knowledge. Bremner repaid the debt a thousand times over in the years to come.

Bremner did so well over the next few weeks that, when Blackburn made an offer of £25,000 for Crowe, Taylor was only too ready to deal. With United's finances remaining tight, he felt obliged to take the money but so telling had been Bremner's contribution that Taylor jumped at the chance. Crowe had great potential but always struggled to cope when the crowd was against him.

There was no happy outcome for Leeds. West Brom won 4-1 at Elland Road and there were then three straight defeats, including a 5-0 drubbing at Fulham.

Leeds struggled to a 3-3 draw at home to Birmingham on 9 March. Revie gave United a 2-0 lead inside 34 minutes. The Blues pulled one back just before the interval, but Bremner restored a two-goal cushion after 73 minutes. This was a brittle team, though, and Birmingham stormed back to equalise with two goals inside the next six minutes. There were only 8,557 spectators to witness an outcome which left United anchored in the bottom two. It was a massive opportunity lost.

Leeds were not yet ready to surrender and beat Manchester City, another struggling side. The crowd soared above 30,000 to witness the debut of Denis Law. Leeds won courtesy of two penalty kicks by McCole in the final stages which turned likely defeat into sudden victory.

United had sought to sign Law before he joined City, as recounted by Eric Stanger. 'Their debts were greater than ever. Yet a majority of the board had the courage to decide to chip into a pool and guarantee out of their own pockets an offer to Huddersfield Town of £40,000 for the up-and-coming Denis Law. I printed that story, too, only for it to be hotly denied by both clubs. It was true enough. My information came from one of the directors concerned, Harold Marjason.'

The two points saw Leeds leapfrog Birmingham, who had crashed 5-2 at home to Bolton, but United went four winless games before beating Bolton on 16 April. It was enough to take them off bottom, where they had been dumped by Luton's win at Blackburn the day before, but Leeds had fallen a couple of points behind Birmingham and looked in the greatest peril. There were five games left.

The Easter programme saw Leeds with two games in two days against Preston. United had the upper hand, drawing away and winning at home. They clawed back a valuable point on Birmingham, but the Midlanders had the superior goal average, thanks to Leeds' abysmal defensive record.

Things started to improve with the arrival of Manchester United's Freddie Goodwin in March. He brought a steadying influence but the damage had already been done.

56

Goodwin could not prevent Leeds losing by the only goal at Everton on 23 April. The same day, Birmingham won 4-2 at Sheffield Wednesday and Nottingham Forest thrashed Newcastle 3-0 to move three points clear of Leeds. The bottom of the table had an alarming look.

The following Tuesday promised to be decisive. Birmingham played hosts to a Burnley side still hopeful of winning the title, while Leeds had to travel to Blackburn, themselves not yet clear of relegation. With Blackburn and Birmingham meeting on the final day, Leeds' fate was in their own hands: win their final two games and they would survive.

United's preparation should have been meticulous, but not a bit of it. Bremner, wondering where they would eat, was disappointed when 'we stopped off at a café and had beans on toast. It was all a bit of a rush ... nothing had been arranged. And this was the most important game of the season. We lost 3-2. Even as a young fellow, I thought we haven't really prepared well for this game.'

As if to compound the agony, Birmingham lost 1-0 to Burnley, who went on to win the championship.

The die was almost cast, but United still had a mathematical chance of staying up. However, it required Birmingham to lose 4-0 at home to Blackburn, while Leeds would need to beat Forest by the same score. Stranger things have happened but rarely.

Leeds beat Forest 1-0 with a McCole penalty, but Birmingham confirmed their survival after winning by the same score. United's four-year stay in the top flight was over.

Theirs was a pitiful record, including 92 goals conceded. There was a stench of surrender about the squad and little to suggest they would bounce straight back. There was a major recovery job to do and Taylor had never hinted that he had the wherewithal to reverse the decline.

Harry Reynolds was distraught, Jack Charlton was hopping mad and the future was uncertain for Don Revie: five-year-old Duncan now had a four-month-old sister, Kim, and the family had settled well in Leeds. Elsie had got a teaching job locally, but Revie was coming to the end of his playing days and his thoughts were turning to management. That would almost certainly mean having to uproot them all and move on again. He viewed such a prospect with little relish.

Call Me Boss

'Ponder and deliberate before you make a move.'

June 1960: 16-year-old Norman Hunter and all the other apprentices on Leeds United's books have been summoned by manager Jack Taylor to be told whether or not they will be offered a professional contract.

The club has just been relegated and Taylor, scarred by the experience and let down by the players, has set his mind on a programme of fundamental rebuilding.

Bill Lambton had revived the youth development and scouting policy that fell into disrepair under Raich Carter and it is sprouting green shoots with almost 50 local youngsters taken on as amateurs. Given the scattergun approach, there is a huge divergence in capability and Taylor has to think carefully about who to retain.

He has bad news for Hunter, telling him, 'I'm sorry, I don't think you are big enough to make it as a professional.'

The youngster was devastated, but there was some hope. Taylor told Hunter that he would keep him on until the spring to see if he developed sufficiently to merit a contract. Hunter was pleased but fretted that it was just a stay of execution. He was still a growing lad, but at 5ft 7in he had much growing yet to do.

There was a clutch of players who did win contracts, including Ronnie Blackburn, who had starred in Hunter's trial game, Terry Cooper, Mike Addy, Paul Reaney, Terry Casey and Rod Johnson. Harry Reynolds, who was taking a keen interest in the club's development, regularly met the youngsters to talk to them about the club's plans. It was all part of the investment in the future. He posed in a team group with the youngsters at the end of the season.

The 'grow your own' policy needed time to bear fruit and Taylor did not enjoy the luxury of being able to wait.

Money was in short supply with the bank unwilling to extend further credit and Taylor was forced to raise funds by clearing the decks, shipping out Cush, Gibson, Meek and Overfield. He almost lost Jack Charlton as well, though not out of choice.

A deeply frustrated Charlton began agitating for a move and attracted several admirers, including Liverpool manager Bill Shankly, who was convinced that somewhere within the rough diamond there was a gem that he could polish.

Leeds were not receptive to the interest and quoted a price of more than £20,000. Shankly would have met the ask but could only get his board to commit to £18,000. It quickly became clear that the gap would not be bridged, much to the annoyance of both Shankly and Charlton.

Taylor's request for money to plug the gaps in his squad was greeted with little enthusiasm but after lengthy negotiations he wangled a small pot. The manager cast his net in the Scottish League, bringing in Eric Smith of Celtic, Queen's Park's Willie Bell, St Mirren centre-back John McGugan and Queen of the South winger Tommy Murray. He also signed Irish forward Peter Fitzgerald from Sparta Rotterdam. They were all unknown but Taylor went for a big name when he splashed £15,000 on Sunderland's former England cap Colin Grainger, known as 'The Singing Winger' for his vocal stints in night clubs. Grainger had played with Revie at Sunderland and his glittering past suggested the fee was merited but Grainger was hardly a success.

Tom Holley, the former Leeds defender but now a journalist, told Grainger, 'Y'know, Colin, Revie has put the word in for you at Leeds. He's influencing it for you. He wants you there with him.'

Grainger recalled, 'The first man to meet me at Elland Road was Jack Taylor … Warmer in person than he looked in photographs, Taylor seemed to lack ego and had no obvious agenda above and beyond wanting to take the club back into the top flight. And maybe that was part of his problem.

'The second man to meet me was Don Revie, who seemed as pleased to see me as I was to see him. Memories of happy afternoons at the Seaburn Hotel, Sunderland, in 1957, when Revie and I discussed the nuances of the game at length over coffee, entered my thoughts like a firework display and sent adrenaline coursing through my veins. And yet I noticed a difference about him. Here, in his post-Sunderland incarnation, he seemed more authoritative, more confident, happier, and not at all concerned that his playing career was drawing to a close. He was already planning his future. The Leeds United experience was clearly to his liking and he seemed to revel in his role as a respected elder statesman, even though he was only 33 and still, officially, the club captain.

'"You'll like it here, Colin," he said. I nodded, somewhat enthused, until I recalled that he said the same thing to me when I arrived for the first time at Sunderland three years earlier.

'As I cast my eyes around Elland Road, absorbing the sun and considering the possibilities of my new situation, I realised that Leeds the club, for all its attributes and traditions, did not quite match the size and status of Leeds the city … To reclaim our lost horizon, we needed new players and a fresh outlook to both reflect and embrace the onset of changing social attitudes. It was 1960 but, here, it might well have been 1950.'

In addition to the reshaping of the squad, Taylor also recruited two men who would have a major influence in the years to come – Syd Owen and Les Cocker.

Owen, a prominent centre-half, was elected Footballer of the Year in 1959 when he captained Luton Town to the FA Cup final. He was a full England cap, a member of the side hammered 7-1 in 1954 by Hungary. After the game, Owen said, 'It was like playing people from outer space.' After hanging up his boots, Owen was given the manager's chair at Luton but resigned in April 1960 over a 'fundamental disagreement on policy'.

'I was sacked as Luton's manager at the end of the season,' recalled Owen, 'and was thinking of taking a job outside football when Taylor contacted me. When he offered me the chance to join Leeds, he also asked whether I could recommend a good trainer. Well, as Les Cocker had been my trainer at Luton and we worked well together, I suggested him.'

Eddie Gray recalled, '[Syd's] appearance alone said a lot about him. He was a bit like an Army officer … immaculately groomed and put a great emphasis on discipline … Everything he did was done cleanly and precisely. He treated the game very seriously and, if any players gave the impression that they didn't, he would come down on them like a ton of bricks. One player who was clearly disconcerting to him was Peter Lorimer. Peter could seem somewhat casual and unfocused; half an hour before a match, while others might be thinking about what they had to do, he was liable to be trying to get a bet on a horserace. This did not fit Syd's perception of how a professional footballer should conduct himself.'

Cocker, a journeyman pro with Accrington Stanley and Stockport, was less celebrated. During his two years coaching Luton he earned a reputation as a hard taskmaster for his vigorous training routines.

The two had high standards and were appalled by what they found at Elland Road. Eric Smith was similarly unimpressed: 'The club was fifth-rate and the players were undisciplined ... Jack Taylor had let the thing go. I thought beforehand I was coming to a top club. I found out otherwise in the first three or four days. We would go on long training runs and at the end, some players, quite senior players, would walk in with ice lollies in their hands.' Charlton was one of the worst offenders, and the entire place reeked of indiscipline.

'We knew it would be tough going', recalled Owen, 'but not as tough as it turned out. Les and I managed to get the players in good physical shape before the season started, but there was only a limited amount we could do as far as technique was concerned. They were getting on a bit and were too set in their ways. We devoted a lot of time to the juniors. Taylor had some great prospects, like Paul Reaney, Paul Madeley and Norman Hunter, and the club's aim was to try and hold on to its Division Two status until these lads were ready for the first team. It was a race against time, and Taylor occasionally criticised Les and me for pushing the youngsters too hard in training. He felt this might do them physical damage, but I held the view that a lot of really hard work at the age of 17 and 18 would stand the lads in good stead in the long run.'

The sweeping changes had some supporters hoping that Taylor could get his rag bag assortment of players winning games. The newcomers freshened up the atmosphere initially, but they were quickly worn down by the general torpor.

Almost hinting at what was to come, Taylor introduced an all-white strip, trimmed with blue and gold, for the home game against Middlesbrough on 17 September. The match finished in a spectacular 4-4 draw, but both the club colours and normal service were quickly restored.

The excitement was a rare highlight in a dismal opening run that began with the team fortunate to depart Liverpool's Anfield with a 2-0 defeat.

Taylor rang the changes for the next game and the next and the next and continued to do so. He struggled to pin down his preferred XI, using 27 players, although injuries and poor form left him few alternatives but to fiddle while Rome smouldered.

The opening 11 games brought a woeful three victories and Leeds sat in the bottom eight after losing 5-2 at home to Ipswich on 1 October.

A year earlier, Leeds had been sloppy at the back, conceding 92 goals. There was little change in the second tier, their ranks breached 83 times.

On the positive side, McCole led the line admirably, picking up where he left off. He thrived in the newly established Football League Cup competition.

Revie scored United's first goal in the tournament in a 3-1 replay success at Blackpool, with McCole and Grainger finishing the job. McCole was on target again in the 4-0 win at Chesterfield and United hit four again in the next round, at Southampton, but lost a remarkable game.

The Saints stormed into a 4-0 lead with Derek Reeves scoring all four. Leeds showed uncharacteristic spirit by pulling level. With 25 seconds remaining, Reeves crowned a personal triumph with his fifth goal in a game which went on until 10.10pm due to two floodlight failures; it was the longest-ever match in England.

Matters continued in haphazard fashion and at the beginning of October, Taylor held a council of war with brother Frank, Owen and Cocker to hear their assessment of the squad.

Owen reflected on what he had found. 'You've got four decent players ... Smith, McCole, Hair, Bremner, good lad that, he's going to be great.'

Cocker nodded his agreement. 'Pick of the bunch, a pleasure to train.'

'A couple of reasonable lads,' continued Owen, 'Goodwin, Bell. They won't let you down, but they won't pull up any trees. A few lightweights, Fitzgerald, Grainger, Francis, Hawksby, they don't cut it. A load are frankly not worth the air they breathe, Ashall, Jones, Peyton, Cameron, McConnell, Murray, Caldwell, McGugan, Wright and all the keepers ... complete waste of space.'

Cocker continued to nod. The two men were of one mind about most of the players.

Owen finally turned to the two oddities. 'Revie, fine player, great mind, great bloke, but his legs are gone and I don't know how long he's got left in him. And then there's Charlton ...'

'Keeps calling me Cocker, he does,' interrupted the trainer. 'I've told him until I'm blue in the face but he doesn't give a f***. Won't take training seriously, thinks he knows it all.'

'Les is right, Charlton's a real pain in the a***, totally disruptive, won't listen and thinks he knows everything. He's offered me out a couple of times. He's got some talent and can do the business when he can be bothered, but that's not often. I'd get shot if it was down to me.'

'Or get him shot,' sneered Cocker.

Owen and the Taylors chuckled before the coach returned to his analysis. 'Charlton drives Revie to distraction. He's got a chip on his shoulder and Don told him straight that he was spoiling it for the others, Charlton's always charging up the field for corners, buggers off all over the place and completely f***s up the shape of the team. Revie took him to one side and told him, "If I was manager, I wouldn't play you – you're always messing about." Charlton laughed in his face, said "Well, you're not, so what the hell?" Revie was livid.

'The problem is he's taken a few coaching badges and he just won't be told. I would have thought the Army would have knocked him into shape, but if anything it made him worse.'

Owen shook his head with frustration as Taylor turned things over in his mind. A clear-out was badly needed and he'd probably got rid of the wrong players at the start of the season. There was no more money, the board had told him that. What could he do? He felt like weeping.

Leeds never looked in serious danger of a second successive relegation but the place stunk of despondency. The apathy spread to the fans; gates dwindled with the average below 14,000, lower than at any time since the very first steps of Leeds United in the 1920s. Often, there were fewer than 10,000 inside.

The shareholders forced a vote of confidence in the directors at an extraordinary general meeting in December. A resolution declaring confidence in the board was defeated on a show of hands but passed when shareholdings were taken into account, by 7,293 £1 shares to 1,210. There were raised voices, the air was blue and the unrest was tangible. Harry Reynolds was increasingly dominant behind the scenes, the only one with the energy to rise above the morass.

Three of the four co-opted board members, Jim Baker, F G Moorhouse and Dr Winder all resigned, as did John Bromley and Tiny Blenkinsop, both weary of all the stress and concerned for their health. The appointment of Lambton against Tiny's will had done it for him and he left a considerable void on the board, which was suddenly down to Bolton, Reynolds, Woodward, Marjason, Wilkinson and Roberts, although the last named was to resign due to his own health issues in December 1961.

Eric Stanger wrote later, 'There were rival factions on the board, soiled linen was washed at two shareholders' meetings. Leeds Disunited, in fact. All this lack of harmony and confidence behind the scenes was reflected on the field ... After one away game two players came off the field without so much as a stain on their shorts and, having previously been given permission to leave the main party, were away from the ground within minutes of the final whistle. They were anxious to get back to Leeds to back a greyhound in the first race and they had taken care to see they were not delayed by injury.'

Reynolds ingratiated himself with the 100 Club. He was often seen in close discussion with F G Moorhouse, still influential despite relinquishing his seat on United's board.

Moorhouse issued a statement: 'I would like to make it clear that the 100 Club was formed and exists solely for the purpose of giving powerful help and support to Leeds United and not for the purpose, in any way, of embarrassing them or adding to their difficulties. The 100 Club will not take a hand, either openly or behind the scenes, in what are entirely matters for the directors. Nobody is going to carry his dissatisfaction to the point of sparking the fuse.'

The revolt coincided with a brief revival in results – United went through December and January undefeated, winning five of their eight games and climbing to ninth.

Just as fortunes were on the up, those of Don Revie were in decline. His appearances were sporadic and he surrendered the captaincy, convinced that the fates did not smile on his leadership. Freddie Goodwin took on the responsibility but enjoyed no better luck. Revie played his final game of the season at home to Southampton on 14 January as his thoughts turned to a move into management.

The club still leaned heavily on his capacity to evaluate a player. One day Jack Taylor invited Harry Reynolds to travel with him to look at a player in Bolton. Reynolds told Taylor, 'It's no good sending a numbskull like me who knows nowt about the game. Don Revie's not playing so we'll take him with us.'

On the way to Lancashire, Reynolds talked at length about his ambitions. Much of what he said resonated with Revie's own views. A bond of mutual respect was forged between two kindred spirits and Revie was often to be found round at Reynolds' house as the two chewed over various things.

Still Revie's thoughts lay on a start elsewhere, anxious to secure a management appointment as his playing days wound down. In February, he applied for the job at Bournemouth while Tranmere were also interested and Adamstown from Australia hinted that they were prepared to offer a five-year contract as player-coach. It seemed Revie would soon be off.

The improvement in results proved to be a flash in the pan and February and March brought four straight defeats and 13 goals conceded. That was enough; Reynolds struggled to think of anyone who could turn the club around, but he was as certain as could be that Taylor was not the man for the job.

'F*** this for a game of soldiers,' he thought as he sought out Taylor to have it out with him. He left the manager in no doubt as to his concerns and made it clear that he would demand his dismissal. He told Taylor it was in his best interests to go of his own accord to avoid the ignominy of the sack.

The directors met in private to consider their options and Reynolds was quickly onto the offensive, urging them to sack the manager and make a new start.

The board were unanimous that Taylor must go but there were 14 months left on his three-year contract and they could not find the £2,500 it would take to pay him off. Roberts supported Reynolds but Marjason, Wilkinson and Woodward counselled pragmatism and Bolton was non-committal.

Reynolds called a board meeting for the Monday. The directors agreed with his recommendation and wanted to know who he had in mind for the job.

'Let's get t'other chap through the door first.'

Leeds beat Norwich on 11 March to end the losing run, but Taylor admitted defeat and resigned. The *Yorkshire Evening News* carried a fleeting report that Cyril Williamson would temporarily assume managerial responsibilities pending a permanent appointment. Bolton was more concerned with hosting arrangements for the Leicester-Sheffield United Cup semi-final at Elland Road. 'We have not yet had time to consider an official appointment,' claimed Bolton. 'We shall give the matter plenty of thought in the near future.'

But Reynolds was already giving the matter plenty of thought and it only took the germ of an idea to change the course of Leeds United's history.

Ronald Crowther, the editor of the *Evening News* and a long-time fan, made a crucial intervention. He had already written in condemnation of the directors, claiming that United would take the easy way out and carry on with Williamson in charge and Owen responsible for team affairs. When Revie asked Crowther to help him draft a letter of application for the Bournemouth post, Crowther instead urged Revie to apply for the Leeds job.

Revie had asked Reynolds to provide him with a reference. Reynolds was only too happy to do the necessary, clear about Revie's suitability for management, and he penned a glowing recommendation. The chairman of Chester had already approached Reynolds and asked him to let Revie go as player-coach. Taylor had been quite willing to agree his release but Revie turned his nose up at the prospect.

He was quite taken with the opportunity at Bournemouth and was convinced that the job was his.

Half-back Peter McConnell was sat in the communal bath at Elland Road chatting with full-back Jimmy Ashall.

Suddenly Revie appeared, and blurted out, 'How do you fancy going to Bournemouth?'

McConnell said, 'Bournemouth? What's going on there?'

'I've been offered the player-manager's job and I'd like you both – especially you, Peter – to come.'

A nonplussed McConnell could only say, 'I'll have to think about that one, Don.'

His wife was from Leeds and very close to her mother and the couple had just had a daughter. When he sounded her out about moving to the south coast, he could see instantly that that was never going to happen.

There was something else at play that ensured nobody was going to be moving.

Reynolds was having a Eureka moment. Revie's qualities stamped him out as someone who would succeed as a manager – why should piddling little Bournemouth, struggling to avoid relegation to the Fourth Division, benefit from those qualities and not his own club?

'I wrote to Bournemouth outlining Don's capabilities,' said Reynolds. 'But on the Saturday night I asked myself: "What the hell am I thinking about?" I ripped the letter up then and there.'

Reynolds called for an extraordinary board meeting. He got a positive response when he informally sounded out Bolton but the chairman wanted the whole board to be fully behind the move.

'Nah then, gents,' began Bolton as he called the meeting to order, 'Mr Reynolds has got it into his head that Don Revie could be the answer to our prayers. Best if I let him speak for himself.'

'Thank you, Mr Chairman,' Reynolds began. 'We all know that we're in a fix, no two ways about it. It was hard enough to get anyone when we were in the First Division. Now, even fewer men of any ability are going to be interested. Our financial position is well known, we've made no secret of it.'

There was mumbled agreement. The board had been badly embarrassed when they'd last advertised for a manager and they knew that beggars couldn't be choosers.

'There's much to be said for Don,' continued Reynolds. 'Got a good head on his shoulders, he has, he knows how the game should be played. I don't like the idea of someone stealing a man

like him from under our noses. If he succeeds somewhere else, we'll look blummin' idiots.'

Vice-chairman Woodward decided to intervene. 'There's a lot in what Mr Reynolds says. I've had many an interesting chat with Revie and he knows what he's about. I think he would do an excellent job. Plus, I think we can get him on the cheap.'

The other directors pricked up their ears at that. 'What d'you mean?' piped up the ageing Marjason.

'Well, Revie isn't ready to hang up his boots just yet. If we appoint him as player-manager, his money will be subject to the maximum wage and we'll only have to pay him £20 a week. It would be out of our hands, it's the rules. That amount will be buttons next to what we'd have to pay a real manager.'

Reynolds wasn't impressed. He argued that the decision would come back to bite them in future years. The others were sold on the idea and the appointment was unanimously agreed, although Reynolds abstained on the matter of terms.

'Well, if you're resolved on this course of action, chaps,' sighed Reynolds, 'I won't rock the boat, but please let me give him the news to make sure it lands right. He trusts me.'

They were all agreed on that and were relieved that it would be Reynolds who would have to deal with any reaction.

The next day, Revie arrived for lunch with Reynolds, who wasted no time in getting down to business.

'I guess you're wondering why I asked you to meet me, Don?'

'I assumed it was about the reference, Harry.'

'Well, in a way it is. I got to thinking when I was writing it, exactly how good a candidate you are. Just the sort of man, in fact, that this club needs. What would you say to the job?'

Revie sat back in astonishment. He hadn't expected this – he had been checking out house prices in Bournemouth. 'Are you in a position to make such an offer?'

'I'm certain I can convince the board. They've all been very impressed. What d'you say?'

'Well, I'd like to talk it over with Elsie, but I kept wondering which club might be the right one for me. This would suit me down to the ground. What are the terms?'

'A three-year contract, but it would be as player-manager. We still need you on the field for the time being, you get the best

*out of the players. Of course, that does mean the money would
be capped. We have no choice ...'*

*Reynolds' voice trailed off with a touch of discomfort as he
watched Revie's expression change, the delight vanishing from
his face as his shoulders sagged.*

*'That's a bit of a slap in the face, Mr Reynolds.' Revie's tone
had become sharply businesslike and his eyes narrowed.*

*'I know, Don, but you've no experience at present. If you do
as well as you and I think you can, we can go back to them in a
year or two and get what you're worth.'*

*Revie picked up on the 'we' and 'them' reference. 'Are you
saying that they weren't convinced?'*

*'I can only speak for myself and I am convinced. I know that
when I take over from Sam then we can put a lot of things right,
if you get me ...'*

*The two men exchanged knowing looks and Revie was the first
to break the silence. 'I'm trusting you, Harry ...'*

'And I'm trusting you, Don. I know you'll take us to the top.'

*Revie slowly extended his hand and the men shook warmly,
although Revie ended with a cautionary note. 'I'll need to talk it
over with Elsie ...'*

*'Of course, but dunna take too long. We need to get things
moving.'*

A managerial novice like Revie couldn't afford to pick and
choose, but he would remember the slight. He would ensure he
had his pound of flesh one day.

Revie kept his ire to himself when he discussed the matter that
evening with Elsie. He spoke in glowing terms of the favour he
thought Reynolds was doing him. Elsie wasn't convinced. She
had heard Don talk of the meanness of the directors.

Nevertheless, it meant that there was no need to relocate or
for Revie to put himself through a competitive interview down
south. 'Whatever you say, Don. You know I'm behind you.'

The deal done, the first job was to tell the players. Reynolds
called them together in the dressing room before training on the
Friday morning. 'Say hello to your new manager, lads.'

In walked Revie, posing for the obligatory photo shoot.

'I joined Derek Mayers, Peter McConnell, Gerry Francis, Grenville Hair, Jack Charlton and Jimmy Ashall in a contrived photograph,' recalled Grainger. 'I still have a copy of the image. Our smiles just about conceal our anxiety. Charlton is shaking the new manager's hand. In his lavish grey suit, Revie already looks five years older than he did the day before he took the job. His peppy expression tells the real story: the future begins here.'

Revie was determined to exert his authority and sought to distance himself from the players. 'It's not Don, or Mr Revie, it's Boss.' Only one player ever broke the rule. When John Charles returned to Leeds, he was sat one time with Revie as the team travelled to an away match. Charles asked Revie about something or other, 'What d'you think, Don?' His team-mates sat silently, expecting an outburst from the manager. There was no admonishment, but neither was there any response. He completely blanked him, continuing to hum quietly to himself as if Charles had never opened his mouth.

Of course, Charlton had to be different – behind his back he always referred to the manager as 'Revie', but never to his face.

Here Come the Mugs

'The skilful employer of men will employ the wise man, the brave man, the covetous man, and the stupid man. For the wise man delights in establishing his merit, the brave man likes to show his courage in action, the covetous man is quick at seizing advantages, and the stupid man has no fear of death.'

Friday, 17 March 1961: Don Revie has just been confirmed as the new manager of Leeds United. With the news sinking in, he meets Harry Reynolds for another chat.

'Harry, I have clear thoughts on how to run this club, how to treat the players and how they should treat others. We both know, if we're honest, that the club is a shambles. There are players I need to move on, they need a fresh challenge. Jack Taylor couldn't see that, and if he did, he never did anything about it. If he had still been in charge, we would have been relegated, no two ways about it. I need to make changes. Will you back me?'

'You have my full support, Don, let me know what you need. I need to know what's going on, I don't want any surprises, I know things will go wrong, but please keep me in the loop.'

Revie's first move into the brave new world was to step back a decade to when Major Frank Buckley experimented with John Charles up front. Revie announced that Jack Charlton would be asked to repeat the trick on a trip to struggling Portsmouth.

Charlton struggled to understand what was needed in the role but managed to score in a 3-1 defeat. Revie persevered, only pulling Charlton back when Fred Goodwin was unavailable. The manager also blooded a new talent on the left wing.

Albert 'Hurry Hurry' Johanneson, a 20-year-old black South African, arrived at Elland Road in January after the club was tipped off by Barney Gaffney, a schoolteacher. The popular story has it that Revie discovered the player and fast tracked him into the first team, but Johanneson told a different tale.

There had been some interest from Newcastle United, but Gaffney negotiated a three-month trial with Leeds, primarily because Johanneson's compatriot Gerry Francis was already at the club. No transfer fee was involved, and Leeds even insisted that Johanneson part-funded his transport from Johannesburg. Gaffney took a gamble and provided the upfront investment.

It was Jack Taylor whom the newcomer had to persuade, and it was no easy matter, as Syd Owen recalled.

'He was like a fish out of water, a scared rabbit caught in the headlights ... I told him he was going to meet Jack Taylor ... I shall never forget Albert stopping dead in his tracks, looking at me with a bewildered sort of expression, he said, "What is this person's name again, how am I to address him?" ... Albert was the perfect gentleman, he called Jack "sir" and had to be told not to do that as Jack preferred to be called "boss", which led to Albert adding "boss" at least three times in every sentence, which was equally as irritating.'

Taylor laid down the law and quite intimidated the newcomer.

'Right, Albert, if any of the directors speaks to you, you have to be very polite and proper. Never, ever tell them about what goes on in the dressing room.'

'I don't understand, Boss, why would they want to know about the players getting changed, Boss?'

Taylor chuckled to himself. 'No, Albert, what I mean is, don't tell them what we say, what the players think. It's important that we keep that quiet. I tell them anything they need to know.'

Albert sat there, saying nothing, still confused.

'Are you alright, son, you aren't saying a lot?'

'Where will I sleep, Sir? Will I be sleeping here in the stadium, Sir? Where will I eat, Boss? Will I be allowed out on my own, Sir? I don't have any boots, Sir, can I play in bare feet?'

Taylor laughed out loud at the naïvety of an innocent abroad. 'We will sort all that out for you, Albert, we have got another coloured lad here, Gerry Francis, so you are not on your own. Listen, I know that someone like you will find it difficult in England, but you have to act like the white people of the city. The best way to understand Leeds is to listen and learn, once these people know who you are they will take to you, until then, you have to prove yourself to them and to me and to the football club. I want no trouble from you. If I do have problems, you'll be on that aeroplane back to South Africa on the same day.'

Albert sat thinking for a while, then asked, 'Boss, do blacks and whites stand and sit together in the stadium?'

'Yes, they can and do, but we don't have that many black people here, Albert, I rarely see one in the city. You are unique not only in Leeds, but across the entire football profession here. It's not going to be easy for you to integrate, I can name maybe half a dozen black footballers who play professionally here. Many white people have a fear about your kind of people coming here. Someone has already asked me if you are a witch doctor. I have put that person straight, he won't speak so irresponsibly again. Your colour is going to be a real problem, Albert, just don't let the bigots get to you ... You will have to deal with rudeness and ignorance yourself. I cannot be there shielding you 24 hours a day. Don't ever retaliate with violence, just rise above it, let your football skill do the talking, show them that you are better than them. The other thing you have to remember is that you are representing Leeds United Football Club, so don't do anything that could ever put the reputation of the club into question. If you do, we will come down on you like a ton of bricks, okay?'

Johanneson's anxiety was reduced by the lengthy discussion, but his initial experience of Don Revie was not as comforting.

'He rarely spoke to me. He was very professional about his game and expected others to be the same. I didn't like him when I first arrived, he had an arrogant sort of way about him, an aloofness that made him different to the other players ... he had little time for trialists ... why bother making friends or getting to know someone if they were not going to be about for long?'

Les Cocker had to get Johanneson used to playing in boots, because back home he had always played barefoot. Johanneson appeared clumsy and slow as he got used to them, feeling as if he had lead diving boots on.

Billy Bremner quickly made friends with the newcomer, a kindred spirit who understood what it was to be a stranger in a strange land. 'Don't be scared to speak out, just ask one of us, someone will help you, we're all in this together, a team.'

Johanneson also received help from Grenville Hair, who advised him where to play and how to avoid some of the clatterings he received early on.

'Drop deeper towards me, Al, go wide left, you'll get more time there and the space to work in. You can avoid men if you give yourself room to work in.'

Hair caught Johanneson later in the dressing room, sat by himself, crying his eyes out at some of the racist comments he had been subject to as he got used to the city. Hair was oblivious to the cause, assuming that Johanneson thought he had let himself down in training.

'For what it's worth, I thought you were the best player in training today, Albert. I've not seen anyone cause Billy to miss a tackle and leave him behind like you did out there. We were all impressed by that, none more so than Billy himself.'

When Johanneson heard that Revie had taken over as manager, he was distraught, convinced that he did not like him. He was certain the new boss would not offer him a contract.

Johanneson was trembling as he entered Revie's office.

'How d'you think you have done in your three months here?'

'I have always given my best in training, Boss, and in games, Boss, and as a person representing Leeds in the city. I love the club and desperately want to stay.'

'I have had some contradictory reports about you. Some say you glide past players with ease and you can do almost anything with a football. Others say you don't like getting stuck in. I've been watching you in training, sometimes you amaze me, your skill and pace is breathtaking, your balance is majestic and the way you can leave players like Billy Bremner in your wake is bewildering. Everyone I speak to tells me you are a very nice man. I don't like you being a nice and polite man, I need you to toughen up, Albert, don't be afraid to get stuck in where it hurts, don't give up the ball easily, fight for it, shout for it when you don't have it. Can you do that for me?'

'I can, Boss, I can and I will.'

'Right then, Albert Louis Johannesen, I want you here as part of my Leeds United. You have got yourself a contract, it's of extreme importance for both you and me at this moment, because I'm making you my first signing for this football club. I want to see passion in your game … I want you to fight for the cause of Leeds United, I want you to give everything and if necessary, be prepared to die for the sake of this football club's success. I would do that, so I expect you to do it too. Don't let me down, Albert, if you do, you'll be on the first plane back to South Africa. I'm taking a huge gamble on you delivering ... Well done, lad, now stop snivelling and get yourself back up the hill.'

Johanneson had burst into tears of joy. 'Thank you, thank you for giving me the opportunity, Boss. I won't let you down.'

'Albert, make sure you get yourself a decent shirt and suit and a tie. You're a professional footballer now ... start acting like a man and not the shoeshine boy you think you are. People look up to you, Albert, act accordingly. No more hiding in the shadows, get out there and enjoy your time in Leeds.'

Revie pitched the South African straight into the first XI. He did enough in a closing run of five games to excite tremendous interest.

'I saw in Albert Johanneson a bright talent that I could develop,' said Revie. 'He was quick, exciting and different in every way ... He was a player I couldn't let go, he was already creating attention elsewhere with other clubs monitoring his situation and I saw it as a test of my own ambition and intentions. Albert didn't know it, but two First Division teams were watching his situation very closely ... Had he known of the interest then he may well have spoken to those clubs and been offered far better terms. I know he would have gone and we would have lost out. That speaks volumes for his ability, but also about my desire not to lose out on anything. I was a winner with a winning attitude, I wanted winners at my club. Albert was my first signing for Leeds United, I had doubts about him ... it was Les Cocker who finally persuaded me that Albert was of sufficient quality to represent the club. Les said that Albert would light up every football pitch in Europe with his blistering pace and ball control. In signing him I was helping my own reputation as a manager with real vision.'

Johanneson was Revie's first signing – his second was Norman Hunter, still on borrowed time after his discussion at the start of the season with Jack Taylor.

Since then, he had grown five inches and stood just short of 6ft. But he hadn't filled out and 'was just like a beanpole, still very thin and weak', according to the man himself.

'His tracksuit hung on him because he was so thin' Revie said later. 'He'd been playing at outside-left and inside-left, but in truth, had hardly blossomed … Even so, I was struck by his keenness to work hard and try to impress.'

Revie came up with his own solution to Hunter's lack of substance, 'a special potion consisting of a glass of sherry with a raw egg mixed in it'. It was vile but did the trick, or it might have been the diet of steak that the club pushed at him.

Revie also decreed that Hunter would be better deployed in defence than in midfield. He took him to one side after a game with the juniors.

'Hey, Norman, Jim Storrie was telling me the other day that you're a bastard to play against.'

Hunter recoiled in horror, thinking he was about to get a bollocking. 'I'm sorry, Boss, I … I …'

'No, don't get me wrong, lad, I mean in a really good way. Jim said that every time he plays against you in training, you always manage to get the ball off him – you get your foot in and do this, that and the other, and always come away with the ball.'

'I do my best, Boss, just trying to get the ball, it's my game.'

'It is that, Norman, it is that. Next game, you're in defence.'

'Okay by me, whatever you say. I'll play anywhere.'

That next game saw Hunter thrown in at the deep end, against Manchester United's British record signing Albert Quixall, who started in the reserves as Manchester gave him the opportunity to get used to their style. It wasn't the best day for Hunter – he scored an own goal in a 2-2 draw.

Revie persisted and Hunter quickly developed into a promising defender. He was always one of Revie's favourites, 'the best sweeper that's ever lived'. The manager adored him and would often play up to his reputation as a hard man. Revie used to joke, 'Norman left the pitch with a broken leg; try as we might, we couldn't find who it belonged to!'

But that was the future; back in the spring Charlton managed four goals to add to the one he scored at Portsmouth. Leeds squeezed out enough points to ensure survival, though the only win came in a 7-0 drubbing of already relegated Lincoln City. Those two points ended any lingering threat of relegation with a couple of games to spare.

'With our average home gate down to 16,000,' recalled Revie, 'Elland Road was like a ghost town. No one seemed to care whether we won or lost.'

Unimpressed supporters greeted their 'heroes' with snide cries of 'Here come the mugs' in this dreariest of seasons. It was an inauspicious start, but Revie did well to coax any return from a dispirited squad.

Changing of the Guard

'Never venture, never win!'

June 1961: Don Revie is planning his first full season in charge. He knows all about the playing side of the game but is a managerial babe in arms. There is much he needs to learn and one of his earliest steps is to cross the Pennines and seek the advice of the charismatic father of Manchester United.

'I went to see my old friend, Matt Busby. I badly needed advice ... He filled me in and I shall always remain in his debt.'

Revie parked his humble Ford Zephyr outside Old Trafford, in amongst all the Jags, Aston Martins, Mercedes and Rovers and filed quietly past the ticket office, through the main doors and up the ostentatious staircase to Busby's private office.

Busby stressed the importance of employing the same tactics and approach at all playing levels in the club, with youth players schooled in the same style as the first team. He left Revie in no doubt as to the wisdom of growing your own.

For all his support, Busby had no compunction about trying to lure Jack Charlton to Old Trafford. And for his part, Charlton welcomed the interest with open arms.

Charlton's disregard for tactics and team-mates prompted Revie to tear a strip off him but the defender shrugged off the criticism with disdain. He was not as *laissez faire* when it came to money, and he was enraged by one of Revie's decisions.

The lack of team spirit was a major concern for Revie, whose solution was to scrap pay differentials. He introduced a basic wage of £20 plus incentives: £5 for an appearance, £4 for a win plus a payment based on attendances; to qualify for the full 'crowd bonus' of £14 10s, Leeds would have to draw more than 31,000. Self-appointed union convenor Charlton insisted this was a con given the 13,000 they currently averaged. He would only sign the new contract when Revie promised to release him if the club received an acceptable offer.

Charlton rejected the captaincy and brother Bobby mentioned his disillusion to Busby, who tapped Jack up.

A combination of Revie's stubbornness and the meanness of the directors resulted in an asking price of £26,000. The valuation was way above Busby's and he ummed and ahed. Jack was not best pleased. He confronted Busby, demanding to know what was going on. Busby tried to placate him, claiming he just wanted to give a chance to 21-year-old Frank Haydock, and that the delay was temporary.

Charlton would have none of it. 'I can't believe this. I have caused ructions at Elland Road, I have refused to sign a contract, I have caused bloody havoc in the club, and now you want me to wait until you have had a look at someone else. You can stick your transfer up your a***.'

Charlton stormed back to Leeds and signed his new contract.

*   *   *

First-class tickets and first-class hotels were suddenly the order of the day. Revie had experienced the best at City and Sunderland. Harry Reynolds publicly declared, 'We're going to go first-class ... we're going to stay at good hotels.'

The players welcomed this change but dismissed another development as a gimmick. Revie ditched the club's traditional blue-and-gold in favour of spotless all-white. He gushed over the football of European Cup giants Real Madrid and he thought that aping their colours would see the players also copy their standards. Other than the odd cynical comment, there were few arguments, merely indifference.

'No one seemed bothered about promotion or even winning a match,' recalled Revie later. 'They played with cheap kit and travelled second-class. I never liked the strip so I changed it to all-white. I had said we would build a team as great as Real Madrid but they all thought I was mad ... I wasn't going to be satisfied until we had reached the same stature as the famous Spanish club and there was no future at Leeds for anybody who didn't think that way ... Just then I didn't think we had a cat in hell's chance, but they'd got to start believing in themselves. That was another reason for the improved travelling plan because you can't tell a team to aim for the sky and then put them in a dingy boarding house.'

For now, there was no badge at all on the shirt – the owl emblem was not added for three years.

Revie committed to giving the youngsters a grounding in life, saying later, 'We have a great responsibility to them when they come to us so young. We send monthly reports on their progress to their parents and also go to see them regularly. We give the youngsters sex talks, teach them how to dress well, which includes short hair, how to behave in hotels and how to look after their money. We encourage them to continue their education at day school or night school. My office door is always open ... If they want advice, I put them in touch with the people best qualified to help them.'

Revie's approach was having a positive impact on the players. Peter McConnell recalls, 'Don's the best manager I worked under by a country mile. He did all the little things. I played once at Portsmouth and got a really bad cut over my eye. We didn't get back until 2 or 3am and at 9 or 10 the following morning, he was at the house with a bunch of flowers and box of chocolates for the wife.

'I remember back then we had three or four teams at Elland Road. And the teams used to get pinned up on a Friday morning. Unless you were, say, John Charles you didn't know what team you were in. If you weren't in, there was no explanation. But Don never failed to call you into his office and say, "I'm not playing you this week because of ..." He'd talk rationally and you could accept that.'

This was new to many of the players who had become used to being spoken down to by Carter, Lambton and Taylor. Suddenly, they were being treated as adults and they responded as adults, starting to understand their obligations.

The changes evidenced the board's faith in Revie, or more accurately that of his sponsor, Harry Reynolds, who became more and more enthusiastic with each passing day. The rest were solid behind the Leeds revolution; Bolton admitted that he and four other directors had each made interest-free loans of £3,500 to keep things going, gambling on improved attendances. It was suicidally over-optimistic. Understandably, the board would only sanction enough money in the close season to purchase unknown Preston winger Derek Mayers. A bid from Arsenal for Billy Bremner could have eased matters, but Revie insisted that the Scot was not for sale.

The Leeds public were unconvinced. All they had seen so far was a tepid new-manager blip. The final home fixture against Scunthorpe brought in 6,975, the lowest attendance since 1934; the summer break distanced the memory enough to get the figure up to 12,916. Bremner scored the only goal against Charlton and his effort was also decisive three days later as Leeds won 3-1 at Brighton.

These were heart-warming victories, but old doubts resurfaced as Leeds were trounced 5-0 at Anfield.

It was a major setback. Brittle confidence crumbled as the team went into free fall, winning just twice in the next 15 games. A 0-0 draw at Elland Road against Leyton Orient in November left United second from bottom with 12 points from 17 matches.

John McCole scored all four goals in a League Cup trouncing of Brentford, demonstrating that he could still terrorise defences. It was a swan song – he was gone by the end of the month, returning to Fourth Division Bradford City. Whether it was McCole's choice, or an attempt to supplement dwindling funds is unclear, but Revie missed the Brentford win as he scouted for a replacement. The departure came as a shock, seeming to confirm that Leeds had accepted their role as a selling club.

Initially, Revie deployed Charlton up front again. He was a success, returning nine goals in the league and three in the cups, but he hated it, constantly bitching and moaning.

Strangely, there were no calls to 'sack the manager.' Revie was still enjoying a honeymoon period. Reynolds was a powerful advocate as the empathy between the two men grew through hours of conversation which built a shared vision. When Sam Bolton decided to step down, Reynolds suddenly had the legitimacy to turn words into action.

The club's line of credit with the bank was at its limit and to keep Leeds going Bolton drummed up investment. He cast around for interest in the local community and in came Albert Morris, Manny Cussins and Sidney Simon, three well-to-do Jewish businessmen. Bolton admitted them to the board as the reward for their cash. With Bob Roberts relinquishing his seat due to concerns about his health, the numbers round the board table were up to eight.

61-year-old Morris was thin, gaunt and bald with a huge, hawklike nose. He was president of the Leeds Jewish Board of Guardians and a founder member and former treasurer of the Leeds Jewish Housing Association.

Hull-born Cussins, 56, had a mane of slicked-back silver hair and sported huge glasses with a thick black frame. His face was always lit up by a toothy smile. Cussins built an empire from small beginnings, pushing a handcart around the city when he was 13 to collect furniture which he could refurbish and sell at a profit. When the Cussins Group was sold for £1m in 1954, he used the money to set up the John Peters Furnishing Group, a chain of shops which was rebranded as Waring and Gillow and expanded to over 100 retail outlets and a dozen factories.

58-year-old Simon, a director of a menswear manufacturing concern, was short and bespectacled, like Cussins, and, like Morris, his hair was almost gone. His attire of choice was a crested blazer.

Morris and Cussins, both members of the 100 Club, each advanced £10,000 in interest-free loans while Reynolds put up another £50,000.

There were fewer investors than Bolton wanted but he could do no more. His legacy to the club was a refreshed board and sufficient cash in the bank to tide it over. It was a job well done.

At 66, Bolton was weary of carrying Leeds United on his back after 15 years. He had other commitments at the FA and it all mounted up. Seeing Reynolds brimming over with energy convinced him that he could safely step aside.

Bolton announced his resignation at the Annual General Meeting on 8 December, saying, 'I have taken a lot of kicks ... I can't stand up to kicks like I used to.'

A delighted Reynolds assumed the chair with gusto, encouraging Revie to outline his plans at the same AGM. Reynolds had 'never heard such ideas better put. He will have all the backing the new board and I can give him ... Don Revie has more of the "sinews of war" – what we Yorkshiremen call brass – at his disposal than his predecessors had. How much more must remain our secret – the soccer market is as tricky a field of business to operate in as you will find. I have all possible confidence in Don Revie.'

Revie was delighted with the changes: the new men brought money and enthusiasm and Reynolds' elevation would give the manager *carte blanche*. Reynolds hung on Revie's every word and would deny him nothing. Revie had got on well enough with Bolton, but it had always been clear who was the boss and who paid the bills. Under Bolton, Revie had been an employee; under Reynolds, his power was absolute. He became the biggest man in the club, at liberty to do pretty much anything he wanted.

Reynolds and Revie resembled a proud father and doting son as they held court. The gameplan was simple – corner the market in the country's best youngsters and grow from within. *Yorkshire Post* sports editor Dick Ulyatt wrote that 'for years, the club built the wrong way round. They constructed a team from the top instead of from juniors ... The whole history of the Football League suggests that the teams who last longest as match-winners are home spun. I believe that Leeds United have reached the nadir of their fortunes and will shortly start on the way up.'

Revie's mantra was a constant in the matchday programme. He could never expect the same loyalty, he insisted, from outsiders as he could from players who graduated through the ranks. He extolled the virtues of the teenagers learning their trade in the Northern Intermediate League.

'We have a young team well worth watching ... but to get the best out of them, they must be brought along gradually. It is of course frustrating to a football supporter to be asked repeatedly to be patient, but I am afraid that is what is required.'

Reynolds would fondly recall a European youth tournament with a team that included unknowns like Gary Sprake, Jimmy Greenhoff, Paul Reaney, Norman Hunter and Terry Cooper.

'I had always favoured a youth policy,' he remembered. 'The youngsters had won the Northern Intermediate League. I went with the youth team to the Holland tournament and we played Birmingham in the final. We won. I just couldn't go into the dressing room afterwards. I opened the door and the tears were rolling down my cheeks. I had to go out and pull myself together

... That was my finest moment. The way they played that night I could see we were beginning to see daylight. 'It wasn't just a question of spotting these boys and signing them on. We had to keep them happy and look after their parents when they came to see them. I used to take them out for a meal. We wanted parents to know the boys were in good hands and that we were keeping them on the proper lines. I suppose we were sort of foster parents. We had a good press friend in Scotland and we arranged for him to meet McCalliog and Lorimer when they went home for a few days. He gave us a glowing report, about a full book page, and after that nearly every youngster in Scotland wanted to come to Leeds United. I also used to take the staff and their wives and girlfriends out for a meal.'

The Revie-Reynolds partnership worked perfectly when it came to convincing parents. Homespun philosophies, a warm personal touch and a family atmosphere clinched many a deal against the odds. Their success was astonishing given Leeds' lack of standing.

Eddie Gray had his choice of 35 English and Scottish clubs. The standard protocol at the time was for schoolboys to be given a two-year contract as apprentice professionals at 15 and their first full professional contract on their 17th birthday. There was a maximum of 15 apprentices at any one time and they could not be paid more than £7 a week for the first year and £8 for the second.

Leeds signed Gray as an amateur and arranged 'employment' with a local printer. Revie told Gray's father that Leeds had reached its full quota of apprentices and had no alternative. Gray earned three times what he would have received as an apprentice professional. It was a dubious approach and Revie stressed, 'On no account should you tell anyone what you are earning.'

Money was only part of the attraction, as Gray recalled. 'Another reason for my decision to join Leeds was Don Revie. He had tremendous physical presence and personality. He told my father, "I know you don't know much about Leeds United now, Mr Gray, but in the not-too-distant future, this club is going to be one of the best in Britain" ... When it came to making people feel special, he thought of everything. It was typical of him to celebrate the decisions of Jimmy Lumsden and myself to join Leeds. Don and Harry Reynolds came up to Glasgow and threw a party for us and our families.'

Revie fully appreciated that his high hopes might come to naught if he could not keep United in the division. Leeds were drifting badly and after a spell of two wins in 11 league games they were third-bottom. Revie named himself in the starting XI for only his third appearance since he was appointed manager but it was a sad misjudgement. A run of four games yielded two points as United slid into the bottom two.

Revie scouted the market for some seasoned performers to buy him time while the youngsters were maturing. As Syd Owen said, 'We had to get some mature, professional players to stabilise the position until the young ones came through.'

In came Scotland's World Cup keeper Tommy Younger and Revie's former Manchester City team-mate Billy McAdams.

Younger shed two stone and brought experience at the back but McAdams was a failure with just two goals in his first nine appearances, although his colleagues were no better. Derek Mayers and John Hawksby were fey passengers on the flanks and Albert Johanneson's four-month absence was sorely felt.

Bremner married girlfriend Vicky in November but her decision to remain in Scotland for the time being exacerbated his homesickness. Thankfully, it did not show in his performances and the Scot was the season's top scorer with 11.

November and December brought brief respite. After beating Middlesbrough and Walsall, Leeds saw off prospective champions Liverpool on 23 December with Bremner scoring the only goal. However, victories were rare thereafter and defeat at home to Plymouth on 24 February left Leeds bottom.

There was precious little between sides in the bottom half and Leeds' total of 22 points was only seven less than tenth-placed Luton.

Other sides had games in hand on Leeds, who were confronted by the very real threat of an unprecedented plunge into Division Three. So much for the Real Thing!

United's finances had always been precarious; relegation to the Third Division might have brought oblivion.

A significant loss of gate receipts exacerbated the money issues. The Lowfields Road stand was closed for the last ten weeks of the season after overnight gales damaged the roof. So strong was the wind that stanchions were ripped from their housings the length of the stand. Bob Roberts' building company was called into action to replace the roof for the new season.

It was said that staff used to open a gate at the back on matchday to allow the wind to pass through and prevent the roof being ripped clean off.

Revie knew that relegation would signal the end and that urgent action was needed. He was assured by Reynolds that the board would make money available for recruitment, suggesting he could raise more than £50,000. But March's transfer deadline was fast approaching and nimble footwork was needed to bring home the bacon. Revie set off in pursuit of six signings. Time was against him and selling clubs were hard to find, at least those who were prepared to release players within Revie's budget. In the end, he managed to bring in three newcomers.

The first arrival was Burnley reserve centre-forward Ian Lawson, for whom the Turf Moor club demanded an inflated price of £20,000. Goalscoring was United's major shortcoming and Revie reasoned that if the player came good the gamble would be well worth it.

Lawson made his debut on 3 March in the derby at Huddersfield, partnering Charlton up front. Revie named himself for his first game since November but Leeds lost 2-1, their eighth defeat in ten games. The only silver lining was that relegation rivals Brighton, Bristol Rovers and Charlton all lost and with 11 games left United remained just four points behind Newcastle who were 15th.

That was the end for Revie as a player. He heeded Younger's advice to concentrate on management. The pair sat together on the journey back to Leeds and Revie admitted, 'You were right, Tommy, I've played my last game for Leeds.'

Revie shelled out £10,000 to secure experienced left-back Cliff Mason from Sheffield United, an intelligent, cool head, relying on anticipation and smart interceptions to keep danger at bay.

It was the third arrival that was crucial.

The Times of 9 March reported the story in muted terms: 'R Collins, the Everton and former Scotland and Celtic inside-forward, was transferred to Leeds United last night. The fee (£25,000) was the highest paid by Leeds, and the highest received by Everton.' It was a terse record of a move which transformed the history of Leeds United Football Club.

The Difference

'The principle on which to manage an army is to set up one standard of courage which all must reach.'

The first week of March 1962: Bobby Collins wasn't in the best of moods as he pulled into the drive outside his house in Aintree a shade before seven o'clock in the evening.

Collins was a keen driver, he loved the freedom of the open road and the opportunity to clear his head after a difficult day. And it had been the most difficult of days.

That afternoon, Collins had a real set to with Harry Catterick, his manager at Everton. Collins had been a key member of the Toffees team that hammered Wolves 4-0 but Catterick was convinced Collins' best days were behind him. He had already earmarked Dennis Stevens, a recent signing from Bolton, to replace him and told Collins so.

When Catterick called Collins in to meet him earlier that day, the Scottish midfielder had thought that his display against Wolves had changed the manager's mind about him.

He was disappointed.

'Great game, Bobby, but it doesn't change anything. My mind's made up. Stevens will wear your No 8 shirt.'

'Are ye kidding me, ye ungrateful bastard?' exploded Collins. 'I've given the best years of my life to this club, I had a stormer against Wolves, played like a demon and ye're still not convinced. Just go to f***!'

He hurled his chair aside and stormed out. He went off driving for a couple of hours to clear his head but was still steaming as he arrives home.

When Collins entered the house, wife Betty told him that he'd got a visitor – Don Revie.

'What the hell's he want?' pondered the Scot.

The two had already discussed the possibility of Collins joining Leeds. When a journalist tipped Revie off about Collins' availability, Les Cocker watched him in Everton's Cup defeat at Burnley. A positive report set Revie off in hot pursuit.

Revie travelled to Goodison with Harry Reynolds and Manny Cussins to open negotiations and spent an hour with Collins after training. The initial discussions were not productive.

'I've still got a lot to offer the First Division and with all due respect it looks like Leeds could be relegated to the Third. Why would I want to join ye?'

'But we won't if you join us, Bobby. You could make all the difference in the world. We are planning big things.'

'Aye, well, that's what everyone says. I tell ye what. Let me think it over for a couple of days and I'll get back to ye.'

It smacked of a brush-off.

As the party headed home, Revie decided to have another go and drove to Collins' house, though he had to wait almost five hours to see him.

It was 2.30 the following morning before Revie & Co left for Leeds, but they had got their man.

Collins described Revie as a 'lovely fella … a good talker. He outlined his plans and he offered me the same money as I was on at Everton. Considering Leeds were in the Second Division, I thought that was something. It showed a lot of faith.'

The move was almost derailed by Liverpool boss Bill Shankly, who just failed to pinch Collins from under Revie's nose. He detected the same qualities which attracted Leeds: will-to-win, aggression, an expansive vision and a keen football brain. Collins would be an ideal leader for Revie's youngsters and a rallying point for an apathetic Leeds public – bottle and fight had long been absent from United sides, but you could never accuse the Scot of lacking either quality.

Eddie Gray: 'When I first came to Leeds and watched the team play, I was terrified. It was brutal stuff and definitely win-at-all-costs. Bobby was at the heart of all that. He was the main man and someone who taught the whole club how to win. Bobby would never admit when he was beaten or that the odds were against him. There was one night when Bobby had an accident and cut his arm badly.'

This was in March 1965 when the team stayed at a Harrogate hotel the night before a game with Burnley. Intent on winding Collins up, Jack Charlton knocked on the door to his room and threw a jug of water over him when the door was opened. Collins chased after Charlton to get revenge and accidentally put his arm through a plate glass door. Despite needing 16 stitches to repair the damage, he begged Revie to let him play. Cocker used so much bandage to protect the injury that Collins' arm was twice the size of the other one. He had an outstanding game, scoring twice in a 5-1 victory. At the end, covered in mud and dripping blood all over the floor, he grinned at Revie, 'I told you I wouldn't let you down.'

Collins changed everything. He brought something special to the club. Such moves come along once in a lifetime and for Leeds this was it.

The fee settled at £25,000, Collins became a Leeds player in one of the best bits of business that Revie ever did.

Many critics were astonished that Revie had staked the club's future on a 31-year-old who stood just 5ft 4in tall and whose best days appeared to be behind him but Collins was one of the most admired of post-war inside-forwards. After making his name with Celtic, he joined Everton in 1959 and cemented his status before the Merseysiders began to rebuild under Catterick. The chance to recover their initial outlay was too much to resist and Leeds' offer was swiftly accepted.

Collins wore Revie's No 8 shirt for the first time on 10 March at home to Swansea, among Leeds' closest relegation rivals. The crowd of 17,314 was United's third best of the season and Collins drove the side to a first win in seven games, scoring the opener himself in a 2-0 win. He brought much-needed urgency to the performance.

It was Leeds' third clean sheet in eight games, but that record disintegrated the following week in Southampton.

The evening before the game goalkeeper Tommy Younger was taken ill with a high temperature and sore throat. When his temperature reached 100 degrees the following morning, he was ruled out. Reserve Alan Humphreys was out with a damaged arm and third-choice Terry Carling lived too far away from the airport to catch the plane. Revie rang Cyril Williamson at 10am to arrange a specially chartered flight to Eastleigh Airport near Southampton's ground.

The only other goalkeeper on the books was Welsh apprentice Gary Sprake, still a fortnight short of his 17th birthday and enjoying his customary lie-in before a youth match. The Football League gave special dispensation for the game to be delayed until 3.15 but that was still cutting it fine. Sprake was whisked off in a 60-mile taxi ride to Manchester's Ringway Airport and thence on a 260-mile journey in a two-seater plane. The plane left the runway at 12.45 and five minutes later Sprake was violently sick before sleeping through most of the flight.

They reached Eastleigh with just over 20 minutes to go and Revie and Sprake, accompanied by a police escort, raced to The Dell. They arrived a quarter of an hour before kick off.

Sprake performed creditably but could not prevent Leeds losing 4-1. After 75 minutes, Southampton forward Derek Reeves barged into him, leaving stud marks in his chest and the keeper out cold for two minutes.

Someone else who had good reason to remember the day was Grenville Hair, playing his 400th league game for the club. He was the fourth player to achieve the feat, following in the footsteps of Ernie Hart, Jimmy Dunn and Willis Edwards.

Defeat left Leeds three points from safety, with only Brighton below them but the Collins influence began to bite in earnest.

He saw to it that the Revie gameplan was followed to the letter. Resolute at the back, fierce and combative further forward, they were now almost impossible to score against.

Collins demanded that Leeds became the most difficult of teams to beat. 'He wanted me to instil in the players a never-say-die attitude. The defence had to tighten up ... I sat in the middle of the park, leaving four in attack, with the wingers coming back to help when necessary. Don had been trying these tactics without success, but I made my point forcibly to the players that this would be our tactics come what may.'

Collins received sterling support from Charlton, now the dominant partner in a defensive pairing with Goodwin. Big Jack was a revelation as Leeds explored the dark art of shutting up shop – just four goals were conceded in a nine-match run-in, with Charlton demonstrating more discipline than for many a year.

Initially, the conformist Revie found himself at odds with the tearaway defender. The enmity between the two men seemed irrevocable. Charlton admired Revie and his thoughtful approach but couldn't bring himself to publicly acknowledge as much.

Relations had improved so much that Revie told Charlton, 'If you keep going like that, you'll play for England.' The words were prophetic, although Charlton was convinced that Revie had lost his marbles.

Billy Bremner also contributed much; his two goals saw off Luton at Elland Road on 24 March and he went from strength to strength, flourishing under the wing of Collins, his idol.

Bremner benefited from the same wisdom and insight previously offered by Revie but now laced with streetwise cunning, a telling combination of gifts which left an indelible mark on the 19-year-old.

After the Luton win came a hard-fought scoreless draw at Leyton Orient before a rare strike from Grenville Hair and an own goal brought victory at Middlesbrough. The threat of relegation stubbornly refused to recede and Leeds now faced a gruelling run-in – the Boro game was the first of seven to be played in 22 April days.

Bristol Rovers' 5-0 defeat at Middlesbrough and Swansea's enforced lay-off during a smallpox epidemic in South Wales meant that draws for Leeds at Preston and Walsall saw United edge momentarily away from the bottom of the table.

The point at Walsall came courtesy of a goal from Albert Johanneson, restored to the side after one game in seven months. He brought new edge up front. It was just in time.

Brighton were now all but relegated, but Leeds were in a desperate struggle with Middlesbrough, Bristol Rovers and Swansea to avoid filling the other place.

There were four games left, spanning the Easter holiday. The first came on Good Friday, against Bury. A day later, Derby were at Elland Road, which staged the Bury return on Easter Tuesday. A challenging trip to Newcastle concluded the campaign.

The battles with Bury provided the background for a controversy which was stoked up 15 years later by the *Daily Mirror*.

The paper claimed that Revie offered Bury player-manager Bob Stokoe money to throw the match at Elland Road. Stokoe, almost as new to the managerial game as Revie, had been in the

Newcastle side that defeated Revie's Manchester City in the 1955 Cup final.

Matters were never proven either way, but Stokoe was always a bitter Revie critic. 'He offered me £500 to take it easy. I said no ... He asked me if he could approach my players. I said under no circumstances ... and reported it to my chairman and vice-chairman.'

It's difficult to understand where Revie would have found £500 given United's precarious finances and even more puzzling why Bury did not report Leeds to the League or the FA. Nevertheless, Stokoe was emphatic about his story.

Whatever the truth, the Gigg Lane encounter was bitter, ending 1-1 after a second-half equaliser from Charlton. Bury went at Leeds as if their lives depended on the result, even though their own Second Division future had been safe for weeks.

The game with Derby was no less frenetic, with a goalless draw offering 'plenty of bodily impact'. Leeds could have done with the win but moved above Bristol Rovers on goal average and were three points clear of Swansea, who had two games in hand. The relegation quicksand still dragged.

The return against Bury, a goalless draw described by Stokoe as 'one of the finest games of my life', was a fifth successive draw. It left Leeds needing a point to guarantee survival – the previous day, Bristol Rovers had lost 2-1 at Charlton, but Swansea's Easter had brought a win, a draw and a defeat.

The final Saturday saw bottom club Brighton (31 points) and Bristol Rovers (33) travelling to Derby and Luton respectively, while Swansea (33) entertained Sunderland. Leeds (34) travelled to Newcastle with the best goal average, but equally aware that victories by Swansea and Bristol could yet doom them. Leeds had won two away games all season and the pressure was on.

There was little that Revie could do, other than to remind his charges to keep things tight and take no chances. He was apprehensive as kick off neared, but Collins really came into his own, taking control and driving out nerves with fierce nagging. He saw to it that they achieved the result at any cost, as recalled by Bremner. 'He never gave us a minute, because he was always telling us to do this, and do that, and do something else, and go tight there, and give it plenty of room in another place, and then get everybody running and running.'

United, playing into the teeth of a gale, gave their finest performance for years. Collins was on top form and pulled all the strings.

Johanneson was in peerless form and drove Newcastle's defenders to distraction. Not for nothing was he known as the Black Flash: bearing down at speed on a back-pedalling full-back, unable to fathom which way he would go, he was a wonder to behold.

Bremner came close to scoring early, but for all United's dominance it was 37 minutes before a goal, Johanneson lashing in off the bar. McAdams hit a post with a header but had better luck in the 65th minute when he headed home after goalkeeper Dave Hollins fumbled Johanneson's cross.

Ten minutes later safety was guaranteed when Bremner's centre was deflected into the net by Newcastle right-back Bobby Keith.

The Magpies had no stomach for the fight and Leeds were not troubled in the closing stages, able to take the trip home with both points and Second Division status safely in the bank.

With Bristol losing 2-0, the result was irrelevant. Still, the whistle saw Revie and Reynolds embrace in relief, their revolution granted time to flourish.

'How we escaped I shall never know. All I know is I hardly slept a wink at the time,' said Revie later. 'I knew if we slipped down, my short career as a manager would be over.'

'Well done, Don lad, you've done brilliant. What a team, what a team! Bobby Collins, what a man! And Albert – I've never seen anything like him.'

'They're good lads, but this is only the start. Leeds are going to do wonderful things, Harry.'

After a momentous and nail-biting season, Harry and Don's United had survived. The summer brought the chance to refresh tired limbs and stressed minds as Stage Two of the Revie Revolution rumbled into view.

Return of the King

'When your army has crossed the border, you should burn your boats and bridges, in order to make it clear to everybody that you have no hankering after home.'

July 1962: Grenville Hair whistles tunelessly as he makes his way to Fullerton Park for the first day of pre-season training.

Hair knows the first session will be hell after two months of doing nothing more strenuous than sunbathing. As a seasoned professional, he appreciates that it is a necessary evil and secretly rather enjoys shaking off the summer dust.

Leeds' longest-serving player by some way, Hair is making the journey for the 14th year. He joined Leeds on the same day in November 1948 as John Charles.

His career has interwoven closely with that of Charles – the two spent their National Service with the 12th Royal Lancers in Barnard Castle in County Durham and later Carlisle and starred when their team won the Northern Command Trophy in 1952.

Hair is in a positive frame of mind. This may be the year when he breaks the club's appearance record. After making his first-team debut in March 1951, he has been an automatic choice since October of that year. He has made 409 league appearances with 25 in the cups. Only Willis Edwards (417 and 27), former full-back partner Jimmy Dunn (422 and 21) and the legendary Ernie Hart (447 and 25) rank more highly. Hair hopes that with a good wind he will bypass all three in the new season.

He also anticipates the team tasting success and is intrigued by the speculation that has filled the newspapers all summer long – he is itching to find out whether there is anything of substance to the rumours.

The defiant trench warfare that Leeds United waged in the spring saved the club's status and Revie approached the summer with renewed confidence. The grateful directors continued to provide the resources required to fashion a competitive squad.

Revie sorted the wheat from the chaff, shipping out Billy McAdams, an abject failure in his short spell, along with peripheral players like John Kilford, Bobby Cameron and Derek Mayers. With just £22,000 raised, the debt remained a concern, but a newspaper headline had prompted Harry Reynolds to ask, 'What d'you think, Don?'

'Well, it would be a fantastic coup if we can get him, Harry. But would he come, and at what price?'

The two of them stared at the Evening Post headline of 13 March. 'Now what price John Charles for United?'

'He'll never come if we go down, you'll have to keep us up.'

'I'm trying, Harry, I'm doing my best.'

'Could we, should we?' they thought, dreaming their dream of football's top table and an agreement was reached. Reynolds would see what he could do.

Within days, Reynolds had convinced the board of the logic and economics of a deal.

'His goals will take us up and he will bring 'em in. We can bump up the prices – we'll be quids in.'

'D'you think, Harry? D'you think?'

'Aye, I do,' said Harry, his eyes shining.

The United directors set the wheels in motion.

Revie's long-term strategy still lay in attracting and nurturing the best of the country's teenagers, but the relegation battle saw patience cast aside and the cheque book flashed. The team's shortcoming had been lack of goals and, if Charles could remedy that failing, the directors reasoned, it would be money well spent.

And so began a protracted courtship.

On 5 May, Juventus were given the go ahead by the Italian football authorities to sell Charles. They were quickly inundated with offers from across Europe but Charles had already set his mind on a return to Britain. Wife Peggy pined for a return to the rain and gloom of Leeds and Charles knew he was adored in his spiritual home. He beamed with pleasure when he heard of United's overtures, seduced by rose-tinted memories of his salad days. Revie and the directors were equally besotted and resolved to raise the asking price, said to be around £50,000.

Charles said that Peggy was 'bubbling over with joy,' and so were his three sons. The oldest had already been sent back to live with his grandparents in Leeds. 'We don't know where we are going to live, but we are not very much bothered. All we want to do is to get back home. It is beautiful weather here, and I am certainly going to miss it, but there is one consolation – it will still be summer when we get home. What is the weather like in Leeds today? Is it overcast? I thought it might be. Never mind.'

It was still early days but Charles was set on his destination and Juventus were content to strike a deal with Leeds. Their directors cabled Elland Road on 7 June to say that Charles was returning to Britain. Over the course of the next fortnight, the United directors waited in vain for further developments.

At 2am on 3 July Reynolds was woken to be told that an urgent cable had been received. The Juventus board had met the previous evening and agreed to meet their United counterparts to Turin. By tea time, the *Yorkshire Evening Post* was carrying a report that Reynolds, Revie and Percy Woodward would fly from Yeadon Airport to Turin to talk turkey. Revie had been recalled from a golfing holiday with Elsie in Scotland and Albert Morris flew from his holiday in Monte Carlo to join his colleagues.

On Friday 6 July, Charles gave his employers an ultimatum. 'Let United have me or I quit,' he said, threatening that he would drop into non-league football when his contract expired at the end of the month if he didn't get his way. The following day he told the press that he had played his last game for Juventus.

Leeds' main rivals were Cardiff City, who had long coveted Charles, but his professed desire for a return to West Yorkshire made it advantage United.

It was still uncertain that Charles would be allowed to move. Juve would need a replacement and were in hot pursuit of World Cup ace Amarildo, for whom they were ready to fork out £185,000. The Italians were reluctant to sign any deal which could not be voided if they were unsuccessful in their chase for the Brazilian; Leeds were just as fixed on a deal without strings. There were complications in the Amarildo negotiations, and the move fell through with Juve president Umberto Agnelli resigning part way through talks.

On 23 July, Albert Morris, United's 'man on the Italian spot' while he holidayed in Monte Carlo, drove to Diano Marina on the Italian Riviera, where Charles was enjoying his own holiday.

'Hello there, John, we've never met, but we can get to know each other now,' said Morris, mopping his brow as he arrived.

'I certainly hope so, Mr Morris.'

The two travelled together to Turin. Morris had expected lengthy talks following the departure of Agnelli, but after 90 minutes he rang Reynolds to say that a deal had been struck. 'This is it!' declared Reynolds to Bill Mallinson of the *Yorkshire Evening Post*. 'Mr Morris told me that everything went off without a hitch and in a most amicable manner.'

The deal was finalised just after noon on 2 August following the completion of a medical. The fee of £53,000 shattered United's previous record.

The board made maximum capital from the signing. Scores of youngsters with autograph books flocked to the press conference they called, of which the *Yorkshire Post*'s Dick Ulyatt wrote, 'To background music of clicking press camera shutters, the whirring of television cameras and tape recorders and the bustle of newspaper men, John Charles yesterday signed his contract to play football for Leeds United for the next two years. Signed and re-signed that is, for the cameras had an insatiable appetite. He was writing for so long I thought he was starting the opening chapters of a new autobiography.'

Grenville Hair was in attendance to renew their long-standing acquaintance. The pair embraced warmly and reminisced about their times together. There were tears in Charles' eyes at the warmth of Hair's greeting – it was as if he had never been away.

Revie used Charles to persuade another player to up sticks for Elland Road. Free-scoring Airdrie inside-forward Jim Storrie turned down initial advances the previous season, but when Revie came calling a second time, the Scottish part-timer was convinced.

'I listened to what he had to say and was immediately impressed by his sincerity,' said Storrie, 'I remember his telling me, "The sky's the limit — we're going to be like Real Madrid." Well, I did feel that was a bit ludicrous; Leeds weren't even the best team in Yorkshire then. But he kept thumping it into our heads that we were great players and, after a while, we began to believe it ourselves! All managers like to think that their players are prepared to run through a brick wall for them, but this was true as far as Don was concerned.'

That was another £15,650 on top of the £53,000 for Charles as Revie's spending soared to within a whisker of £135,000 in less than six months. The debt now topped £200,000. While the initial cash came courtesy of the board, the purchase was a key component of Reynolds' new strategy.

He pushed for a rise in ticket prices, saying, 'We know that we need £83,000 a year from gate receipts to break even. Crowds averaged 13,500 last season and a price of 3 bob would give us 40 grand. John Charles will draw crowds of 20,000 and at the same ticket price we'd clear £63,000. However, we can push ticket prices up.'

'How much are you thinking, Harry?' asked Sam Bolton.

'I reckon the fans will stand seven-and-a-half bob. That would raise almost £160,000.'

'That's more than double.'

'It'll be right, chaps, have confidence. We are not obliged to foot the bill any more than the fans are. They clamoured for this, they wanted it and now they can pay for it.'

Heads shook in disbelief round the boardroom table, but Reynolds had his way. The *Yorkshire Evening Post* reported that Reynolds had even toyed with the idea of charging £1 for a while, and Leeds United were suddenly the most expensive side to support outside London.

The directors increased prices by 3s, proclaiming that they were 'giving the public a chance to show the firmness of the promises to support the club if the directors embarked on a policy of team-building and bringing personalities to Elland Road'. Season ticket holders were asked to pay 10 guineas for West Stand seats and 8 guineas for the Lowfields Road Stand. 'It is the first price increase in six years,' trumpeted a bullish Reynolds, who declared himself ready to meet anybody who objected to the increases and explain the logic behind them.

'I have already done that to dozens of people,' he said, 'After hearing our case, they all agreed we were doing the right thing. I am at Elland Road most working days from 10 to 12 in the morning, and from 2.30 to 4 in the afternoons. In those hours I will meet anybody who wants to have things explained.'

The first two home games would be all-ticket and prices were set at 5s for the Boys' Enclosure, 7s 6d for the 3s enclosure, 10s for the 3s 6d enclosure and 12s 6d for the paddock. Any seats that had not been taken up would be 20s for the Lowfields Road Stand and 25s for the West Stand.

Directors claimed that there had been scores of enquiries for season tickets. 'Name your own price for four,' one director said he was asked on two occasions. Nevertheless, stoic locals lived up to their flat-cap image with a 'Bah gum, that's a lot of money' response. Distinctly unimpressed, they reacted with vitriol, besieging the *Yorkshire Evening Post*.

Mr D Siddle wrote on behalf of 49 employees at a local printers, complaining that 'we supporters have finally been let down by this outrageous exploitation … the Leeds public have had to put up with a struggling team and second-class entertainment. Now, after all the promises, we have to pay these absurd prices.' He added that, unless there was a rethink, 'we shall not attend any first-team game.'

'Ten Angry Supporters' at another printing firm thanked the board for the return of the king before sighing, 'What a pity we can't afford to watch him!'

Reynolds was beside himself with rage. The board had given the fans 'what they have clamoured for' and demanded their support. He said in exasperation, 'I almost feel like saying to the board that if we cannot get support, and the public do not want football in Leeds, what is the use of trying?'

Revie's plan was simple: a pressing game to deny the opposition time and space, when Leeds get the ball, launch it to Charles, who would secure possession and bring the other forwards into play. It sounded effective, but there were flaws.

Firstly, the 30-somethings were ill-equipped for the hard-running game that Revie demanded.

Secondly, Charles had never been a target man in the usual sense. He often played off another forward and was more effective coming on to the ball than with his back to goal. He was a different player from the one who left in 1957, accustomed now to the more sedate style of the Italian game. The hustle and bustle of English football unsettled him.

Charles decried the focus on the long ball and 'hurrying and scurrying as if stamina was the main requirement for a footballer'. Italian football demanded subtlety and guile to avoid the cynical defensive tricks.

While Charles retained the physical presence to hold his own against brutish defenders, he preferred playing to scrapping and a love of pasta had left its mark. Tipping the scales at 15-and-a-half stone, he was an impressive physical specimen, but his edge had been blunted.

He had grown accustomed to less strenuous training and left Les Cocker speechless. 'The training at Leeds was very hard,' commented Storrie. 'It was a lot of stamina work and running and the big fella was having trouble with that. John would amble along and Les couldn't handle that. He would scream and shout at John and John would look at him as if he was daft. A lot of the young players like myself accepted it because we were young and enthusiastic but John was in the autumn of his career and he didn't want to go through all that crap. Charles did not possess sufficient speed and stamina for league football in this country. I will always remember a match at Huddersfield. They cleared the ball upfield following a Leeds attack, and our forwards made their way back into covering positions. After about ten seconds, the ball was booted into Huddersfield's area again – and John was still struggling up to the halfway line. He and Huddersfield's goalkeeper were the only players in that half of the field!'

On his first day in training, Cocker watched open-mouthed as Charles started running gently on the spot, going through his customary warm-up. The Welshman stood there with his arms out in front of him and started flopping his wrists while the other players were stretching and working.

A disbelieving Cocker asked Charles, 'What the hell d'you think you're doing, lad.'

Charles thought to himself, 'Who does this guy think he is? What has he ever achieved as a footballer?' He replied, 'Juventus won the Italian League and Cup on this stuff, boyo!'

Cocker stormed off in exasperation.

'We were a very physical, hard-working and hard-running side,' explained Storrie. 'We had to put the opposition's players under pressure all over the park. We harassed and chased ... I was a forward and my first job was to defend. That was the mentality. John was like a duck out of water playing that way ... He wanted to play one-touch football and flick the ball here and there. That wasn't Leeds' style. Long balls were played to the corner flag and John was expected to chase after them.'

At half-time in one game, Charles complained, 'I'm not running my pants off for long balls.'

Bremner retorted, 'You're making that f***ing obvious!'

Revie's team was a pack of hustling terriers, designed to collect points rather than play football. By contrast, Charles resembled a lazy Labrador. Cocker worked the squad hard and Charles, who missed pre-season training, found the going tough.

There were ominous signs in a friendly at Leicester. The *Yorkshire Evening Post* pulled no punches, deriding Charles as an 'ambling giant', his impact peripheral.

Other reporters were more positive.

'Not many clubs finish the last Saturday of one season sweating on relegation and start the next hoping for promotion,' wrote Phil Brown. 'But it is not as daft as it looks. The side finished the season with far better results and sometimes far better football than that with which it began ... Another ten points – and they threw away just about as many as that – would have seen them fifth.'

The opening day saw Leeds at Stoke, fancied promotion candidates who could boast their own superstar in 47-year-old Stanley Matthews.

Hair told Brown as they walked into the ground together, 'I have never had butterflies worse than this.' The full-back 'was feeling the high drama of the match. And behind John Charles' cheerful laughing there were signs of nerves, too. The big fella knew this was an occasion revolving around him and his team like nothing before in the history of the club.'

Stoke had the better of things but Leeds came away with the points after Storrie scored the only goal just before the break. When Eric Skeels miskicked from a throw-in near the corner flag, the ball fell to Storrie who drove past the helpless keeper.

The lure of Charles had the desired effect, attracting 27,000, but parsimony held sway when Leeds entertained Rotherham days later. A crowd of 14,119 was less than a thousand up on the previous average. Reynolds was apoplectic.

'Blummin' nigglers they are,' he stormed. 'These people want summat for nowt all the time.' He shook his head in despair.

Those who stayed away missed some rare excitement.

With Storrie pushed further forward, Leeds were light in midfield and they conceded after three minutes. Misreading each other's intentions, Hair and Younger allowed Alan Kirkman to tap home.

Rotherham were all over Leeds and enjoyed the better of things. The nippy Don Weston outstripped a leaden-footed Mason, Goodwin and Smith after 36 minutes to meet a free kick for 2-0. The same man made it three five minutes after the interval. A defender appeared to handle Butler's shot on the line but Weston netted the rebound with a spectacular overhead kick.

Finally seeming to realise they were in a match, United replied within a minute when Storrie headed in a free kick from Bremner which the crowd thought should have been a penalty.

They attacked frenziedly but it was 75 minutes before they pierced the defence again. Bremner was brought down in the area – penalty. Charles had always been the penalty taker but his confidence was shot after missing six spot kicks in a row in Italy. Johanneson stepped forward and converted with ease.

Five minutes later the fightback seemed complete as Charles blasted home the equaliser. His shot on the burst was cleared off the line but he recovered it, played a one-two with Storrie and drove home without breaking stride.

The crowd rose as one to acclaim a classic Charles score. The controversy of the ticket prices seemed an irrelevance as King John shook off the cobwebs and returned from the dead. But it was gallant Rotherham who snatched a last-gasp winner with five minutes left. Kirkman swept home a cross to finish things off; 4-3 and the Elland Road faithful were devastated, although they went away crowing at Charles' magic moment.

It was disjointed and disappointing, a normally tight rearguard exposed as hesitant and slack, the attack one-dimensional.

The acid test for the pricing policy came with Saturday's visit of Sunderland.

Despite Reynolds' early morning apology for his outbursts, the crowd was only marginally up at 17,753. After such heavy investment, an away win and a thrilling home match, it was too disappointing for words. It could have been worse; at 2.30 there were hardly 4,000 inside.

Sunderland were one of the division's big guns and featured the remarkable talents of Brian Clough, so it was a clear statement of protest. The visitors had the better of the opening exchanges but were thrown into disarray after 26 minutes when inside-left McPheat was stretchered off with a broken leg after a clash with Collins. Sunderland claimed the damage was intentional. The injury all but ended McPheat's career.

Leeds should have been ahead by then but squandered a penalty. Johanneson was again preferred to Charles, but his shot was weak and easily saved.

It was Sunderland's ten men who continued to dominate, but the numbers began to tell after the break as Leeds gathered momentum, scoring the only goal after 57 minutes. Bremner cleverly headed home from Johanneson's centre.

A chastened Reynolds scrapped the price increases, confessing that he had forced them through in the face of strong opposition from the other directors. 'I said a few things out of the heat of my disappointed enthusiasm that I should not have said,' he admitted. 'I am very sorry. I have been wrong, as wrong as could be ... I must take full blame for the whole business.'

Charles scored in a 2-1 defeat at Rotherham, a match remembered for a half-time clash in the dressing room.

'There'd been a corner against us in the first half,' recalled Jack Charlton, 'their centre-forward had sent in a floating header from the edge of the 18-yard box. Tommy [Younger] should have collected it easily, but, as the ball hit the ground, he dived over it and it bounced into the net. When Don came into the dressing room at half-time he was not best pleased. He pointed at me and said that I should have picked up the centre-forward on the edge of the 18-yard box. "Wait a minute," I said, "the bloody ball was headed from about 25 yards away. I'm not bloody responsible. If a guy gets in and heads a ball within ten yards, that's my responsibility. If I'd have gone out there and somebody else had headed the ball where I should have been positioned, then you would have bollocked me!" I had a teacup in my hand and I threw it against the wall. It missed Don by about a foot and smashed to pieces. Everyone else went quiet while I went ranting on.'

Charles looked around as if to ask, 'What have I come back to?'

Revie left the scene without a word. He vowed never again to criticise players until he had cooled down. A dressing room boiling over with emotion was not the place for harsh words.

Charles scored his third goal in a 1-1 draw at Huddersfield, although once again he was disappointing.

Dick Ulyatt, a stout Charles supporter ever since his debut as a youngster, offered an insight in the *Yorkshire Post*. Charles was finding life 'burdensome', knowing as well as anyone 'that he has a long way to go before he becomes the man who can lead his team to promotion'.

Charles had spoken in unguarded fashion to Alan Hoby of the *Sunday Express*, considering Hoby a friend. He was deeply shocked when the reporter included the chapter and verse of their discussion in the paper. It was a mark of his habitual naïvety.

In a special report to the directors, Revie insisted that Charles did not want to leave. It was a diplomatic truth. Charles had met Revie for an open conversation about how he felt. It would have been more accurate to say, 'He does not want to leave but …'

'It's not working, Don…'

Revie rolled his eyes in exasperation. 'You've got to learn to call me Boss, John, I can't be your mate. What's not working?'

'Righto, Don.' Revie sighed a deep sigh.

'None of it, err, Boss, none of it. I can't play this division. Maybe the First, but not the Second. I love this club, but it'll end up not loving me, if you get my meaning.'

'Okay, I understand. You'll need to give me some time and promise there'll be no more talking to the press.'

After five games, United were sitting in a disappointing 11th and questions were being asked about when Charles would start to deliver.

At least Reynolds could comfort himself with the knowledge that reducing prices had paid off handsomely. The midweek clash with Bury attracted 28,313, the biggest crowd at Elland Road since September 1959.

Matters went less well on the pitch; Charles strained his back in a heavy fall and ended the game a passenger on the left wing. Leeds were second-best despite Bremner opening the scoring after 26 minutes. They could not retain the advantage and the 2-1 defeat should have been heavier. Bob Stokoe revelled in putting another one over on Revie.

The manager knew, as his side slipped into the bottom half, that it was not good enough – things had to be done.

And they were; changes were made which transformed the history of Leeds United.

Storrie, Charles, Goodwin, Lawson and Bell were all injured and Revie was down to the bare bones for a game at Swansea. Disenchanted with the Bury performance, he also dropped Younger and Hair. It was particularly disappointing for the full-back, who had been struggling – he was just two games short of bypassing Willis Edwards' total of league appearances.

After astutely attracting some of the country's best young talent, Revie had been nursing them through the lower ranks. The reserve side which faced Liverpool earlier in the week had been one of the youngest ever, including teenagers Gary Sprake, Paul Reaney, Rodney Johnson, Paul Madeley, Barrie Wright, Mike Addy, Norman Hunter, Terry Cooper and Peter Lorimer.

Revie had hoped to let them learn their trade out of the limelight but he gambled with his team selection. He named Sprake, Reaney, Hunter and Johnson in the squad to travel and confirmed that the first two would play; Hunter thought he was only going along for the ride. His jaw dropped in astonishment as Revie called the four youngsters together in the gloom under the stand at Vetch Field for a covert meeting.

'You're all playing, lads. I've seen what you can do and I've every faith in you. Get out there and do what you're good at. You won't let me down. Norman, remember what I told you.'

Revie told his minders, Collins, Charlton and Smith, 'Look after the lads. They'll need your help. You know what it's like when you make your debut and the hard buggers get into you.'

'Trust us, Boss,' grinned Collins. 'They'll be right.'

Charlton used the opportunity to push something he had been considering for a while: 'I'm not going to play the way you've been playing with Fred. I don't want to play man-to-man marking, I want to play a zonal system where you pick up people in your area. I'll sort out the back four for you.' Revie nodded his acquiescence; beggars couldn't be choosers.

There were some nerves before the game, but Collins did his thing. 'If the Boss thinks ye're ready, boys, ye're ready. This lot are sheep shaggers, nothing more.'

They grew ten feet as the street fighter fussed round them, while Charlton repeated, 'Sheep shaggers, nowt more.'

Swansea might have been sheep shaggers, but United were second-best in the early exchanges with Jones and Webster testing Sprake. Both saves were comfortable, helping him to settle. This would not be another Southampton.

Things could have been very difficult if the 'goal' scored by Webster had been allowed but he was rightly adjudged offside.

Charlton and Smith began to show their experience, while the pace and energy of youth offered much that had been lacking. Johnson and Hunter were better equipped for Revie's gameplan than Charles and Goodwin, while Reaney brought verve and pace.

Swansea continued to dominate but failed to capitalise. Leeds opened the scoring after 11 minutes. Johanneson went on a characteristic run, passing inside to Bremner who played Johnson in with a lovely through ball. He had much work still to do but carved his way through two tackles before driving low from an acute angle past goalkeeper Noel Dwyer.

The goal gave Swansea pause for thought, allowing Bremner and Collins to assume control in midfield. Along with Peyton, they each came close to adding a second.

Swansea were still a threat and Sprake was often in action – indeed he was one of United's outstanding players. But Leeds made openings; Johnson's drive narrowly beat the bar while Smith fired just wide.

Swansea came out with guns blazing after the break, but Charlton soaked up all they could offer as Leeds waited to recover their momentum. They were soon two ahead, following close things for Johanneson and Bremner. Both men were integral when the goal came, and it was a real beauty, described by Phil Brown as 'the best United have scored this season'.

Johanneson forced his way up the wing and fed Collins. The Scot moved it on into the area for an onrushing Bremner to control, round left-back Griffiths and hammer past the keeper.

On the hour, Johnson was carried off after being flattened by the much heavier Dwyer. He returned after 12 minutes but was clearly suffering.

The ten men coped well in his absence and comfortably held Swansea who had to listen to a relentless slow handclap.

According to the *Yorkshire Post*, 'Bremner and Collins provided the best display of inside-forward work that United have had for years. United moved faster and played more accurately than at any time this season, or last, the youngsters bringing a zip the side has badly needed.'

Revie sat on the bench and rubbed his hands in glee. 'Bloody great, this. Harry will love it.' And he did. It was an impressive new beginning for Leeds United.

Charles was back for the next match, at Elland Road against a Chelsea side pressing for promotion. The injured Johnson made way, but Sprake, Reaney and Hunter retained their places. It was a gamble for Revie to rely on such unproven talent against one of the division's most powerful sides. Chelsea had dropped just three points.

Leeds started well, Collins' 'goal' ruled out for offside, but Smith was stretchered off with a broken leg after crashing into a tackle on Moore. The injury was bad and Smith played just once before moving to Morton in 1964.

The substitute rule was still but a dream and Leeds were left a man short. Bremner was withdrawn, stunting the attacking threat, but Chelsea over-elaborated; they would have been well advised to pull United wide and up the pace, but they allowed Leeds to get a foothold in a scrappy game. Two minutes before the break, Johanneson netted superbly. Charles and Peyton made the opening and the South African evaded three tackles with a shimmy and clipped the ball past Bonetti.

The Londoners fared no better after the break and Johanneson netted a second to make the game safe two minutes from time, seizing on Bremner's free kick.

The revival couldn't be sustained; the next six fixtures brought three draws and three defeats. Suddenly there was paper talk about Charles returning to Italy. Whether the interest came from feelers put out or unsolicited contacts it is impossible to know.

Torino tabled a bid, but Roma were favourites to secure Charles' signature. He played one tremendous game, away to Southampton at the end of September, when he was forced to replace Charlton after the defender was injured.

'Southampton had this striker called George Kirby and he had already sorted Jack Charlton out,' recalled Norman Hunter. 'He was giving all of us a bashing but John came back into defence and that was the end of Kirby. He was heading the ball away before Kirby had got off the ground. I was a very young man at the time and I remember John telling me, "Slow it down." He was telling me what to do and what not to do. It was a defensive display I'll never forget.'

But good as Charles was in defence, he had been bought for goals. The youngsters had shown what could be achieved without him, and Charles was agitating for a transfer. Despite denials, the board decided to cut its losses and call an end to a failed gamble.

Charles was out of touch during a drab goalless draw at Derby, constantly drifting deep. His frustrations were evident, but he would not be tortured much longer.

The directors met to consider Charles' transfer request on 22 October. Initially, they had rejected the request but were more equivocal now, though the absent Marjason and Reynolds were clear that Charles should stay.

The Welshman said he was 'surprised and disappointed' and when Gigi Peronace turned up in Leeds to press Roma's interest the following week the directors acquiesced to the inevitable. Reynolds said that 'owing to John and Mrs Charles not being able to settle in England and their desire to return to Italy, the

Leeds board are reluctantly compelled to grant his request for a transfer and are prepared to enter into negotiations with an Italian club. This is a great disappointment ... after the efforts to acquire and retain this player but in the circumstances no other course was left open to us.'

A party from Rome was due to arrive at Elland Road at 4pm on Friday, 2 November, but their flight from London to Manchester was delayed. At 7 they were met by a solitary and embarrassed Revie, the directors having departed home for their dinners.

Discussions finally began at 8.30 and Roma agreed to pay £60,000 in cash with the balance of £10,000 to be made up via a friendly between the two clubs. Charles denied newspaper talk of a £30,000 signing-on fee.

Charles had stayed just 91 days but handled the situation with customary humility, telling Eric Stanger, 'I am sorry it has turned out like this because I had looked forward to coming back to Leeds. It proved a mistake. Now I am glad I am going back, but money does not enter into it, I assure you. I am going because I feel my future as a player next lies in Italy.'

Charles flew to Italy to make his debut that same weekend against Bologna. The whole episode yielded a healthy £17,000 profit for Leeds.

Young Guns

'Regard your soldiers as your children, and they will follow you into the deepest valleys; look upon them as your own beloved sons, and they will stand by you even unto death.'

2 November 1962: Don Revie is considering life post-Charles. The £70,000 is hugely welcome but the promise of the club's youngsters means Revie and Harry Reynolds can be judicious in its use.

Against Southampton on 29 September, Peter Lorimer became Leeds' youngest player at 15 years 289 days old, while 19-year-old Mike Addy was playing his fourth first-team game, bringing the number of teenagers in the side to five.

The fact that Revie could snap up virtually any youngster he wanted was testimony to his sure touch with parents.

Lorimer was one of the hottest young properties around. He had scored 176 goals in a season for Stobswell School. Revie beat almost 30 clubs to his signature, driving through the night to sign him and receiving a speeding ticket for his trouble.

Not everything in the garden was lovely. Lorimer was given his debut because of the absence of Billy Bremner, refusing to come back from visiting Vicky. Still unsettled, he asked for a transfer. Revie said the request came 'out of the blue' as Bremner had trained only the day before and he and his wife were now living in a club house at Temple Newsam.

Bremner told Phil Brown that he 'thought it would be different when I was married but it is not so.'

The board reluctantly granted the request. Revie said he would consider either a cash offer or player exchange.

Reynolds felt obliged to address the unrest caused by the ticket price fiasco. He offered compensation to the 1,850 season ticket holders, announcing that they had a choice of a refund of two guineas, a similar reduction on the price of the following season's ticket or gifting the same amount to the club 'in our efforts to find new players'.

He had little option other than to open the cheque book when Revie asked for investment; the squad was decimated by injury and Younger announced his retirement following a recurrence of his old back problems.

'Mr Revie has our full confidence and the impending loss of Charles has deterred nobody at Elland Road,' Reynolds told Phil Brown. 'If Mr Revie wants new players and they are available, then the board will make every effort to get them.'

St Mirren winger Tommy Henderson was signed for £1,500 and Rotherham's Don Weston (£18,000) followed. Crewe's Brian Williamson arrived as cover for Sprake.

It was the same Henderson who had joined Leeds in 1959 with Bremner. He returned to Scotland for spells with Hearts and St Mirren and an appearance in the 1962 Scottish Cup final. He was to take Bremner's right-wing berth.

Weston was known for his power and pace and provided the sort of threat which Revie had hoped that Charles would deliver. He marked his debut on 15 December with all three goals in the defeat of third-placed Stoke City.

Leeds lost 2-1 at high-flying Sunderland after having two goals disallowed. They claimed stridently that Sunderland defender Charlie Hurley had pushed Charlton unfairly before he scored the winner. It was weeks before they could make amends – one of the worst winters on record put the season on hold for more than two months, leaving the players to kick their heels in frustration until 2 March.

Most of the country's grounds, and all those in the North, had been left unplayable by all-consuming ice. The loss of income from gate receipts was devastating. Reynolds, Cussins and Morris provided more loans and personal guarantees for an increased bank overdraft.

Leeds slumped to 13th during the lay-off. Les Cocker's tyrannical training regime brought the players to the peak of fitness during the break and they resumed action in far better condition than their opponents, announcing their return with an impressive 3-1 win against Derby.

United were the spring's form side, winning game after game. They had matches in hand on their rivals, and by the end of April sat on the verge of an unlikely promotion.

They put together a decent FA Cup run, ending a winless run dating back to 1952.

Leeds' third-round tie against Stoke was postponed 12 times – rather than the first weekend in January, the game was played on 6 March.

Superior fitness told and Leeds were two ahead in the first 20 minutes. Collins was in great form and opened the scoring, taking Hunter's pass to net from 20 yards. Eric Stanger: 'Collins strode the battlefield throughout like a pocket Napoleon, guiding his troops hither and thither with long passes to either wing or with shrewd lobs over the bogged-down Stoke defence.'

Eight minutes later Reaney added the second, coming up to collect a short corner and shoot through a packed area.

If Revie and his men thought they could coast home, they were wrong. Stoke got to grips with a pitch left heavy by the thaw, opting for a long-ball game. Sprake and his beleaguered defence stood up well – it was 70 minutes before Stoke narrowed the deficit.

There were a few jitters but acting skipper Hair, the only player who had experienced Cup victory with Leeds, netted to round off a 3-1 victory. Hair was now a regular once more, having switched to left-back. A week later he bypassed Jimmy Dunn's total of 422 league appearances when he played against Walsall. He could not now break Ernie Hart's record until the following season. It was just a matter of time, he thought.

Goals by Storrie and Johanneson secured victory at Middlesbrough in the fourth round but a tiring United XI were outclassed at Nottingham Forest to end a promising run.

Reynolds was not downhearted. 'It has only hardened our intention to make a hell for leather promotion bid for the rest of this season.'

He also confirmed that Bob Roberts, a director from 1958 to 1961, was back on the board. He had resigned because of ill health.

He had convivial words for Roberts but his return gave Revie issues in the years ahead. Most of the board went along with what Revie wanted, but Roberts was different, convinced that the board should hold sway.

Les Cocker's son Dave remembers it well. 'Bob Roberts owned Ringways and a building firm. He built the West Stand, the North Stand, the South Stand, the corners, everything. But the relationship with him was absolutely shocking ... Me, Dad and Don used to go in board meetings and they would be going, "We're not happy that you've booked a flight down to Southampton, you could have gone by road." Don's answer to everything was, "Well, Mr Roberts, if you don't agree with the flight, you drive and we'll fly. Next question" ... Bob had a say because Bob was owed money for the North Stand and the South Stand, he had them over a barrel.'

Reynolds' nonchalant prediction that the Cup exit would allow Leeds to concentrate on promotion looked naïve when United struggled at Norwich, trailing 3-0 before half-time. A rally brought them back to 3-2, and they had the chances to win but wasted them all.

Seven games in 22 days had left them jaded. They had games in hand, but were 12th, eight points off the promotion places. It was now, though, that Leeds discovered their form.

They hammered Grimsby 3-0. Bremner netted the first with a spectacular 20-yard drive and the game was dead shortly after the break when Collins added a second. He completed the rout in the closing seconds with the goal of the game.

When a fortunate win against Scunthorpe was followed by defeat at Plymouth, it appeared to end any promotion hopes, but Leeds responded, hammering Preston 4-1 and beating Charlton twice over Easter. Those games were among the first in which the negative, time-wasting tactics of later years were employed as Revie ordered his men to kill the game.

The crowd 'strongly objected to the way in which they taunted Charlton in the closing stages by rolling short passes to each other in midfield or putting the ball back to Sprake'. With promotion so tantalisingly close, Revie was unrepentant. The points were more important than style and he stressed the value of keeping possession with safe, short passes.

United inexplicably collapsed 3-0 at Portsmouth, before wins against Scunthorpe and Cardiff brought them back into contention. Storrie scored all three goals against Cardiff and was a revelation at centre-forward, though he did not welcome a move which he felt made him a poorer player.

The attack was more cohesive than it had been for years. The previous season, Leeds notched 50 league goals. They had already netted 47 in 18 home games. Johanneson, Bremner and Collins were regular contributors, although Weston's initial goal rush had dried up.

Revie was given a major confidence boost on the morning of the game at second-placed Chelsea on 30 April.

In October he had dismissed as 'ridiculous' a suggestion that he would succeed Walter Winterbottom as England manager while an unnamed lower division club had offered him a bigger salary as an incentive to join them.

The board offered a three-year extension, tying Revie down until 1967 and making him 'the best paid manager outside the top flight'. It was the material evidence of appreciation that Revie craved and appealed to his vanity.

He had just completed two years as manager and still had 12 months remaining on a three-year deal, but there had been a spate of clubs putting their manager on a long-term deal, including Manchester United, Aston Villa and Hull City

It was not the first time and it would not be the last when Revie used the press to wangle improved terms.

The announcement set things up nicely for the Chelsea game. Honours were shared in an enthralling 2-2 draw. Chelsea opened the scoring when Bridges forced the ball home, but Lawson's hopeful lob was fumbled into the net by Bonetti within three minutes and the same player volleyed Leeds into the lead seconds later. Chelsea refused to panic and equalised before half-time. The rest of the match was a battle of attrition.

That same evening Sunderland drew at Southampton and Newcastle beat leaders Stoke City 5-2 to keep things tight. When Stoke lost at home to Scunthorpe, the challenges of Sunderland and Leeds gathered momentum. The Black Cats hammered Southampton 4-0 while two Storrie efforts and one from Weston gave Leeds a flattering 3-0 win at home to Luton.

Collins, a 'presiding genius' according to Eric Stanger, was the architect of United's best football, creating two of the goals. He was a steadying influence on the younger players. 'A foot on

116

the ball by Collins to slow down play helped to calm taut nerves and give the others time to sort themselves out.'

Leeds were on the verge of a remarkable promotion, but the season collapsed as their luck deserted them. Sprake blundered twice in the first half at Middlesbrough to gift the Teessiders a 2-0 lead and even a fierce second-half fightback could bring nothing more than a consolation goal.

Revie dismissed the defeat as 'one of those things', describing it as 'one of the finest efforts this season'.

The effort of clearing the backlog told; defeats against Huddersfield and Southampton brought an anticlimactic conclusion to the best season in six years. When they closed with a rousing 5-0 defeat of Swansea to guarantee fifth spot, it recalled the heady days of September when Revie's teenagers announced their arrival against the same team. The manager used the final two games to blood 16-year-old wing-half Jimmy Greenhoff, who thus became the second-youngest player to appear in the first team, the eighth teenager to figure in an extraordinary season.

Revie confirmed his retirement as a player when he announced his retained list. The squad sparkled with youthful talent; of the 28 players retained, 12 were teenagers, 8 more were 25 or under. Lorimer, Harvey, Bates and Gray were still too young to sign professional forms.

In their customary end-of-season stocktake, Revie and Reynolds were phlegmatic about the failed experiment with Charles. Most of their conversation was focused on the future.

'You're doing a grand job, Don. I'm pleased as punch. Another year wiser, another year stronger ... these lads will get us there. I'm as sure as eggs is eggs.'

'Absolutely, Harry. I'm so proud of what we've done and so excited for the future. I can't wait to get on with it.'

Led by the phenomenal Collins, the new United looked as good as anything around. The revolution was under way.

Kicker Conspiracy

'If you do not take opportunity to advance and reward the deserving, your subordinates will not carry out your commands, and disaster will ensue.'

3 June 1963: Don Revie is laying his plans for a promotion push. There is only one cloud on his horizon, the continual uncertainty dogging Billy Bremner.

When his form stuttered at the start of the year, the fans gave Bremner the bird. Losing his place to Tommy Henderson provoked another transfer request.

Revie was wrongfooted – his grand vision had Bremner at its heart and he considered him his outstanding talent. The board refused to listen, reasoning that if Revie could cope without Charles, he could cope without the 20-year-old. They accepted Bremner's request and listed him.

Bremner complained that the £25,000 price tag was exorbitant and would put potential suitors off.

'Good!' thought Revie to himself, intent on doing whatever he could to stymie interest. He had already rejected a bid from Everton, who were prepared to pay the asking price.

Bremner did not realise it at the time but Hibernian were desperately keen to secure his services. 'They came in for me at £30,000 … The Gaffer had made up his mind I wasn't going. Don would want £35,000, then £40,000. Then I gradually settled down and started playing well, although I was on and off the transfer list.'

The offer had been a considerable temptation to the board, ever mindful of the crippling debts.

When Revie realised the directors were seriously considering the offer, he threatened to quit, warning, 'If he goes, I go. I want to build a team around him.' He stormed out of the boardroom and told Les Cocker to pack their bags.

Harry Reynolds sought to calm him down. 'Don, forget it, lad. Billy's going to stay … you can stay.'

Revie had lost count of the conversations that he and Bremner had about a transfer.

It was always the same every time the two bumped into each other. 'Let me go ... let me go ... let me go ...' Revie could do no more than sigh and make excuses.

Eventually Revie decided on drastic action and spoke to Bremner's wife Vicky.

'Leeds United are going places, we will be one of the best clubs in Europe and this will make such a difference to the place. And Billy is at the heart of my plans. He's a great player and a great man and one day he will lead this team to great things. He will become one of the greatest players in the game, but all that will be lost if he comes back to Scotland. It's not big enough for him. He needs to do it at the top and that means England. He will never have a better stage than Elland Road.'

Revie's persuasive abilities were legendary and Vicky soon became a Revie convert, enlisted into his campaign to persuade Bremner that his future lay at Elland Road. It needed the Leeds bandwagon to roll in earnest but eventually all Revie's efforts paid off and Bremner pledged his future to United.

At the time, Revie's intervention infuriated Bremner and he set his mind even more firmly on a move. He eventually agreed to come off the list at the end of September, seven months after making his request.

Revie also had to address Bremner's nagging about a move into midfield. His chance came one Monday morning. There was a knock at his door and Bremner walked into the windowless room.

'Hello, Billy lad, how are you doing?'

'I'm okay, Boss,' Bremner said as he took the offered seat. 'Have you thought about what I said?'

'I have that, Billy, I have that. And I'll do you a deal. We're off on tour of Italy in a couple of days. I'll try you out in midfield. How will that suit?'

'That's great, Boss.'

'Just one thing,' interrupted Revie. 'I'll only do this if you come off the list.'

Bremner had pestered Revie for months to use him at the heart of things in midfield. Revie had always resisted, arguing that Bremner was not ready for such a role. But when Eric Smith broke his leg against Chelsea in September 1962, there was a hole to fill. Willie Bell had played right-half for most of the season, but Revie had other plans for him.

'Not sure, Boss, let's just see how it goes for a bit.'

Revie sighed with disappointment, thinking the change would have been enough. Nevertheless, he was as good as his word and Bremner was at right-half against Roma on 5 June.

The tour had been arranged as part of the deal which took John Charles back to Italy and was how the final ten grand of the £70,000 fee would be generated.

Bremner took to the role like a duck to water, performing admirably in a 2-1 defeat. Charles wasn't quite so good; his contributions were fitful and he was clearly not in the best of spirits. His stay in Rome had been disastrous. Luis Carniglia, the coach who had wanted him, resigned after an argument with the directors just a few hours before the deal was done.

Charles was lobbying for a move back to Britain after making just ten appearances all season. His destination was Cardiff, who had long chased his signature, although the deal was held up by a dispute over money owing to Leeds.

When Roma failed to forward the £10,000 owed, United reported the matter to the Football League. They also confirmed that Juventus owed £6,000 after failing to arrange friendlies.

'The £10,000 is the sum we were guaranteed to play two matches out there,' said Harry Reynolds. 'We have made the tour but we have not got the money. Roma have not kept their part of the agreement which was that they should make payment within seven days of the second match. All we want is our £10,000.'

Bremner continued at right-half against a Cremonese Select XI and performed well in another defeat. He reverted to inside-right for the final game against Prato, but Revie had seen enough and began the season proper with the legendary Bremner-Charlton-Hunter half-back line.

A long-term solution to the resultant gap on the right emerged days into the new season but in the meantime, Revie used Don Weston in the No 7 shirt.

He had a difficult decision to make as he considered his defence. He had brought Grenville Hair back into the side for the second half of the previous season, but still had doubts as to whether he was right for the game Revie wanted to play.

Hair was an elegant, effective defender but offered little going forward. Paul Reaney had shown what a good, overlapping full-back could bring to the game and Revie knew that he needed as many attacking options as he could to compensate for the lack of a regular goalscorer up front. He had marked out half-back Willie Bell as the man who could do the job he wanted on the left, but that would mean denying Hair the opportunity to break Ernie Hart's club record. Hair had played 435 times in the league with another 29 in cups. Hart's record stood at 447 league games plus 25 in knockout football.

It broke his heart, but it had to be done. Revie called Hair in to break the bad news. The full-back didn't have an inkling. He had played left-back on tour and the other friendlies against Peterborough and Bradford City and thought his place was safe.

'You've been a wonderful servant to this club, Grenville ...'

Hair had wondered why Revie wanted to see him. To tell him about a testimonial maybe, or a presentation of some sort when he broke Hart's record. That would be a wonderful gesture, thought Hair, as his attention began to wander.

'... and I wanted to tell you face-to-face...'

Eh? Revie had got Hair's attention now, all right. This didn't sound like such good news.

'I've decided to make a change at the back. I'd like to try Willie Bell out.'

'But I'm full-back, Boss, how does Willie playing in the centre affect me?'

'No, I want to try Willie at left-back. Sorry, son, you're still in my plans. I know I can count on you when I need to ...'

Hair knew what was coming, the inevitable 'but'.

'... but Willie will be my first choice.'

Hair's heart sank as he slumped in his chair. 'Bloody hell,'
he thought to himself. 'After all I've done for this bloody club.'

Eventually, he reconciled himself to the decision and accepted a move to the periphery. He never did beat Hart's league record, falling four short, though he could console himself with the satisfaction of a higher number of Cup appearances putting him two ahead of Hart for all games.

Hair left the club at the end of the season to take over as player-manager at Wellington Town. It was a sad goodbye for one of United's most loyal servants.

Hair was later granted a testimonial. On 15 November 1965, United played a Grenville Hair XI which featured Gordon Banks, Nat Lofthouse, Jackie Milburn, Stan Anderson and Vic Mobley alongside Hair himself. Leeds won 4-2.

Most crucial of all the summer happenings was the rejection of external overtures for the services of Maurice Lindley and Syd Owen. Rejecting Hull and Tottenham respectively, they pledged their loyalty to Revie.

The manager was absolutely convinced that this would be Leeds' year and he would deliver success at last.

Bill Shankly once said, 'You can't play your way out of the Second Division; you've got to claw your way out.' In this most competitive of leagues, teams playing Fancy Dan football had no chance. Success was entirely dependent on hard work, application and consistency. Flash in the pan fannying about would see you kicked into oblivion. No one could have accused the United team of 1963 of being Fancy Dans; rarely has a more determined and dogged set of players been assembled.

Leeds' season began four days after the rest of the country. Opponents Northampton shared the County Ground with Northants County Cricket Club who had first refusal that weekend. United were left kicking their heels until the following Wednesday, when operations commenced with the visit of Rotherham.

They acquitted themselves admirably, winning by virtue of a 51st minute effort from Weston, in the right place at the right time when Johanneson's effort came back off the post.

Revie gave Bremner some food for thought by posting material notice of his ambition. With funds replenished by the repayment of the Italian debt, he completed the surprise capture of a man who was to transform the fortunes of Leeds United.

23-year-old John Giles was an outstanding footballer, the Republic of Ireland's youngest debutant at 18 years 361 days. He had fallen out of favour at Man United, along with Albert Quixall, after the pair featured in their FA Cup win. Matt Busby omitted both players from their opening game and Giles, a rebellious soul by nature, was convinced that his face simply did not fit and demanded a transfer.

Revie was a great admirer and wasted no time in contacting Busby. A deal was done within 48 hours of Giles being put up for sale. The fee was £33,000, a sum second only to that paid for Charles. It was an extraordinary coup for Revie.

During the negotiations, Reynolds told Giles, 'We intend to win promotion this season and become one of the leading clubs in the country.' The Irishman was 'positive Reynolds' conviction was based on more than just blind faith'.

Giles said months later, 'Leeds had had a good run the previous year. When you are in the game, you notice these things. There was a feeling about them.'

'We clicked almost immediately,' recalled Bremner. 'We knew instantly what the other would do and were able to work together without even talking about it ... I have never known a quieter or more modest player than Johnny Giles. He always did his best to walk away from trouble even though he could look after himself more than adequately if he had to. He just didn't want to lower himself to the level of players who were capable of little more than kicking and punching. It has often been said that Johnny Giles is the most accurate passer of the ball in the game and I would not dispute that.'

Giles was thrust straight into the team a couple of days later, replacing Lawson against Bury, with Weston switching to inside-right. He did well enough in a 3-0 victory, though Collins took most of the plaudits.

When Leeds lost at Man City after Jim Storrie fluffed a penalty, promotion hopes appeared to be on shaky ground but the return of Collins following injury prompted a run of 20 league games without defeat. They assumed leadership of the division on 12 October, despite having to manage for lengthy periods without Storrie and Charlton.

An ankle injury was the initial cause of Storrie's absence, but he later needed a knee operation after being stretchered off at Sunderland in December. It was an eventful season for the Scot; he pulled on the goalkeeper's jersey at Plymouth when Gary Sprake went off injured.

Every bit as serious was the loss of Charlton, now the senior defender, laid low for a while with a bout of tonsillitis and then a nasty knee injury.

The loss of Storrie blunted Leeds' cutting edge. Their attack was frenzied and prosaic in turns with Weston a chaotic force down the right, occasionally feeding the limited Lawson; the one touch of flair came from Johanneson who enjoyed a remarkable season on the left wing.

A mean-spirited approach spiced up with helpings of gamesmanship was the order of the day. A goal by Leeds meant that opponents might as well retire to the dressing room to remove their boots. On only eight occasions did opponents manage more than one goal against United, and there were 17 clean sheets. Bell was a success at left-back. It took him a while to adapt to playing wide and he was never as good as Reaney but he was wholehearted, a strong defender and better in the air.

There were far too many draws (15) along the way for Leeds to distance themselves from the pack, but the Whites proved to be the most durable of opponents. They also demonstrated how far they were prepared to push the rules. Many players fell foul of officials, with Bremner receiving a suspension, a punishment rarely meted out in those days.

He had already received a written warning from the FA as his list of bookings lengthened. Revie suggested he was more sinned against than sinning, complaining that 'this lad is singled out for punishment.' Bremner's temper and propensity for retaliation got him into trouble.

His bookings were mainly for dissent but his colleagues regularly took things too far. Many games degenerated into unsavoury battles.

The local papers were full of it, acknowledging United's provocative approach in their match reports.

Dick Ulyatt's report of the clash with Huddersfield was typical: 'There were 40 fouls ... almost evenly divided: it only seemed that Leeds United were the greater offenders. Morally, they were much more to blame. They started the roughness. The first three fouls in the first half and five of the first six in the second were committed by them ... For some time now over-zealous methods have been creeping into Leeds United's play to the detriment of both the quality of their football and their reputation.'

Leeds learned the worth of cynical gamesmanship and time-wasting at the feet of Juventus and Roma during the friendlies. As promotion became a distinct possibility, Revie's natural caution gave rise to a 'what we have, we hold' approach. In sharp contrast to the elegant artistry of his own playing days, Revie proved himself the master of spoiling tactics.

Geoffrey Green of *The Times* posed the question to Revie in 1970, 'How did he come to fashion a team like Leeds, so out of character with his own past?'

Revie answered, 'Our password here is "Honesty with each other" – and, to be honest, I have always felt that if I had been harder myself I would have been a better player. I doubt if even at my best I could have got into this Leeds side. What I lacked then I want now in others. You all constantly picked on their bad points, emphasising retaliation, provocation and the rest. Seldom if ever did anyone pay credit to their hard work and emerging ability as individuals or a group. Leeds were labelled as dirty and that was that.'

There is an often-told anecdote of the game with Derby in October. The players threw caution to the wind and found themselves two-down after 25 minutes.

When the players trooped into the dressing room at the interval, Revie slammed the door behind them. He was trembling with rage.

'What's all this f***ing namby pamby stuff? That's not how we've taught you to play; I want it the Leeds United way. You play the way I told you, no pissing about.'

Over the Tannoy, Reynolds insisted, 'Leeds will win promotion, the championship and the Cup. We will qualify for Europe. We will pour all profits back into building the club and making Elland Road into a magnificent stadium.'

Heeding Revie's directives, the players fought their way back. Goals from Charlton and Weston forced a draw which seemed more like a point gained than one lost.

Never again would Revie's directions be ignored; points were what mattered, not the manner of their gathering.

United's approach was designed to strangle the life out of games. They perfected a swift counter-attacking game, built on the long ball and the speed of Weston, Lawson and Johanneson.

They were unbeaten at home but struggled to finish off visitors to Elland Road. Swindon, Derby, Charlton, Preston and Northampton departed with a point in the first half of the season. Leeds were haphazard and uncertain when they had to make the going, running aground on the centre of a massed defence; on the break they were a different matter, incisive and sharp when exploiting their pace against a stretched rearguard. They excelled on their travels, winning at Northampton, Scunthorpe, Huddersfield, Southampton, Grimsby, Leyton Orient, Plymouth and Bury over the same period. It was their away form that set them apart. When Christmas brought a decisive double header with Sunderland, Leeds were three points clear of their Roker rivals at the top with a game in hand.

On the March

'Victorious warriors win first and then go to war.'

Christmas Eve 1963: Don Revie is deep in thought, not about the following day's celebrations, but exactly how big the next four days will be in Leeds United's history.

Leeds are top of the Second Division, three points clear of Sunderland with a game in hand and now play the Wearsiders twice over Christmas in what promises to be a season-defining double header.

Revie is furious at what he considers biased reporting of the two teams, who have been nip and tuck at the top all season. Sunderland are constantly written of in more positive fashion and it pushes all of Revie's self-righteous buttons.

Sunderland were widely acknowledged as the more exciting side but in fact had scored only one goal more. There was little doubt which defence was the more effective – Leeds had conceded 16 goals in 23 games to Sunderland's 27 in 24.

Leeds were branded the dirtiest team in the country; Revie's protests yielded little sympathy. The home draw with Preston in November was one of the most ill-tempered games in a confrontational season. The referee halted play on the hour mark to lecture the players.

An endless stream of niggling, disruptive fouls threatened to boil over and Eric Jennings' warning had little impact.

'The tenseness of the atmosphere kept the excitement blazing,' reported Eric Stanger, 'but it had a detrimental effect on football skill … it was mainly a grim defensive battle … Leeds, in the end, coasted home, tapping the ball about to each other in the continental manner in the last few minutes.'

The fractious nature of the game was nothing compared to the games against Sunderland.

The two matches stoked up the pressure on players who were already prone to temper and pushing referees to the limit.

United took better form into the match. As they enjoyed an eighth successive away win at Bury on 21 December, Sunderland crashed 5-1 at Northampton, leaving Leeds with a lead of three points and four over Preston. Sunderland had played a game more than the other two.

Revie ordered ground staff to spread 40 tons of straw across the pitch for the week before the game to protect against frost. Nevertheless, as Eric Stanger reported in the *Yorkshire Post*, 'Conditions were treacherous. Pools dotted both penalty areas and part of the midfield; peat blackened the goal areas and underneath the slimy top the ground was hard from the frost. Coherent, planned football ... was out of the question.'

Sunderland never played as if they believed they could win even when they opened the scoring after 55 minutes. The goal was against the run of play with Mulhall's shot creeping inside the far post with Sprake transfixed, unsighted and convinced the ball was going wide.

United poured forward in search of an equaliser but drove their thrusts through the overpopulated midfield when getting the ball wide to Johanneson would have been more productive.

Sunderland seemed to have weathered the worst until Weston chased his own through pass, panicking goalkeeper Jim Montgomery. Weston slipped the fumbled ball to Lawson who flicked home with Sunderland protesting in vain for offside.

The draw saw United's unbeaten streak extended to 20 games. It came to a sad end two days later at Roker Park.

With 60 seconds gone, Hunter committed the first foul. Hurley took the free kick from just inside the United half and lofted the ball to the middle of the area. Sprake came rushing out to gather but spilled the ball, allowing Herd to slam home.

Another foul by Leeds in the 25th minute led to a messy second for Sunderland, almost a carbon copy of the first. Ashurst lobbed a free kick from touch into the goal area. Sharkey had time and space to get in a back header which sent the ball rolling gently into the net off the far post.

The goals were mere distractions as the game degenerated into a running battle with the teams bitterly sledging each other.

Stanger's report for the *Yorkshire Post* noted that the match 'was so full of spite and malice that it did no credit to the 22 players, the referee or the huge crowd of 56,046. Where the tackling at Elland Road on Boxing Day was vigorous in the extreme, here it overstepped the bounds. 39 free kicks for fouls were given ... Two Sunderland players threw punches and got off scot-free: so did a Leeds player who deliberately kicked at an opponent. As for the crowd, it sickened me to hear them cheer when a stretcher was called for Storrie.'

The *Daily Express* claimed the game 'should have been given an X-certificate as it was not suitable viewing for children'.

The knee operation needed by Storrie kept him out of all but two of the remaining games.

'We were no angels, far from it,' Giles admitted, 'but I honestly believe we were more sinned against than sinning. We were young and inexperienced, and Sunderland knew full well that we could be vulnerable to physical and verbal provocation. They intimidated the Leeds players ... we lost our heads.'

United's recent history left them with most of the blame for the debacle, much to Revie's annoyance. He bitterly criticised the favouritism, claiming that it had become a 'positive gimmick with some newspapers and some people to call our side dirty. Our lads can't tackle or challenge at all now without somebody calling them foul.'

Pointing out that United had not had any player sent off and only Bremner booked all season, Revie protested stridently. He claimed that there were two occasions when Sunderland men went for United players with fists, yet the referee took no action, wondering darkly what would have happened if the boot had been on the other foot.

'I see no reason at all to lecture my players. I was proud of the way they stood all they did ... My lads are under orders to play hard, to tackle hard for the ball, and to fight for everything ... We have been given rugged opposition in nearly every game we have played, home or away, since we got to the top. Just because we have overcome it, it doesn't mean we are a dirty side but we are having to stand a lot of cheap sneering just the same. And I am afraid that referees are being affected by this sneering. We have had many a fair if hard tackle punished recently.'

The stirrings of a siege mentality could not hide the grim facts: United's three-point lead over Sunderland had been whittled down to one, though they had a game in hand. Preston, 4-0 winners over Cardiff, were level on points with Sunderland, with Charlton three points further away. The promotion battle was down to the four.

January brought temporary relief from the tension with an FA Cup third-round tie against Cardiff, whose ranks now included John Charles. Collins joined Storrie and Charlton on the injured list, and Fred Goodwin was the latest addition when he broke his leg in a collision with Charles. Cardiff had also been reduced to ten when McIntosh broke his leg.

The sustained menace of the Sunderland matches was absent as Leeds secured a comfortable win.

With Charlton and Goodwin unavailable, Revie was expected to dip his toe in the transfer market, but he chose instead to blood 19-year-old Paul Madeley at centre-half. The contest against Manchester City at Elland Road saw United field one of the youngest defensive units ever: Sprake (18), Reaney (19), Bell (26), Bremner (21), Madeley (19) and Hunter (20).

Leeds were back on form, despite missing a hatful of chances. Weston's goal saw United keep pace with Sunderland (4-1 winners over Bury) and Preston (2-1 over Southampton).

Leeds pushed Everton, one of the game's giants, hard in the Cup, only denied a victory at Elland Road by Roy Vernon's twice-taken penalty. They lost out in a Goodison replay to another Vernon effort with 12 minutes left.

Leeds tried to carry their Cup form into the league the following week against Cardiff but were held to the seventh draw out of 14 matches at Elland Road thanks to an inspired defensive performance from Charles.

Coupled with Sunderland's 6-0 trouncing of Swindon, the dropped point ended Leeds' nine-week occupation of top spot and emphasised their chronic lack of finishing power. They squandered a hatful of chances. Revie took immediate action.

Charles' short stay at Leeds in 1962 yielded a net profit of £17,000 which, when added to improved gate receipts, put the club into the black for the year to July 1963. Despite the purchase of Giles and debts of around £80,000, Revie persuaded Reynolds to open the wallet again.

'We're so close, you can smell promotion,' Reynolds told his colleagues. 'We have to strike while the iron's hot.'

'What d'you mean?' blinked Cussins.

'We have to give Don the money to finish the job. It's an investment for the future. We can't afford to miss out.'

'How much are you thinking of?' wondered Simon, preening his moustache.

'50 grand will do it. We need a man who can score goals.'

'50 THOUSAND? Are you mad, Harry?' queried Morris. 'We bought Charles to get the goals and look what happened there.'

'I know, Albert, but this is different. Don's got someone who is already doing it at this level. A proven talent in the division. No gamble this time.'

'On your head, be it,' growled Roberts, 'but it'll be worth it if we get up.'

Reynolds asked for a show of hands and their reluctant arms were raised in acquiescence.

'Thanks very much, fellas, you won't regret it.'

'We better not ...' grumbled Bolton.

Middlesbrough centre-forward Alan Peacock was Revie's quarry. An initial payment of £50,000 would rise by £5,000 if United secured promotion. It was a massive fee for Leeds if small beer for a player of Peacock's standing.

He had four England caps and played in the 1962 World Cup finals. Originally a foil to Brian Clough, Peacock inherited Clough's No 9 shirt when the latter moved to Sunderland. Peacock had scored 126 goals in 218 Second Division games, including 31 goals in 40 matches in 1962/63. He was renowned as one of the finest headers of the ball in the English game.

'It was a big thing for me leaving Ayresome Park,' said Peacock. 'I was meeting a lot of big names who were after me from different clubs, but it was Don Revie who won me over because he was a Middlesbrough lad and it wasn't far from home.'

A cartilage operation in November raised question marks over his fitness. Peacock had managed just five goals but Revie knew he needed a goalscorer to win promotion.

The new man came straight in at Norwich on 8 February. Leeds had to settle for another draw, but Peacock was an instant success, flicking home a beautifully judged header, and improving the forward line with his intelligent link work. It should have been a victory, for the Whites let a 2-0 lead slip in the final 25 minutes. Sunderland won once more, to edge further clear, but it was United's best performance for weeks.

Leeds beat Scunthorpe and then welcomed back the long absent Charlton for a home draw with Huddersfield. They had much to do to gain promotion with Sunderland two points clear and Preston just a couple of points away. The showdown with North End on 3 February was crucial.

Preston, on the way to the FA Cup final, roared into Leeds from the start. Collins tried manfully to turn the tide but Peacock was not firing on all cylinders, and Preston continually swept forward with long, incisive passing. They broke the deadlock after 20 minutes when Sprake parried Dawson's shot only for Ashworth to net from an acute angle.

Preston had the better of things with United's forwards wanting too much time to make and collect their passes. Storrie managed to force the ball home only for referee Jim Finney to rule it out for hands. Storrie and Collins protested so strongly that Collins was spoken to by Finney.

Close things from Giles and Charlton promised better at the start of the second half but Leeds were rocked after 57 minutes when Sprake was left flat-footed by Wilson's 25-yard drive.

Preston inevitably eased off and Giles struck the bar from 30 yards but Leeds never looked capable of turning the tables.

United's chances of promotion seemed slimmer by the day. They still retained second spot, but only on goal average, and were two points behind Sunderland after 32 games.

Revie rang the changes at home to Southampton. Storrie and Giles were relegated to the reserves and Greenhoff brought in. Lawson, after rejecting a move to Scunthorpe, was reinstated up front, along with Weston, fit after an ankle operation.

Lawson repaid Revie's faith with a goal in the first minute, but the United attack struggled. Lofted through balls from Collins were stymied by deep-lying Southampton defenders and when the Saints equalised after Sprake missed a cross, it looked like the usual story. However, Collins and Johanneson scored in the last 15 minutes to secure a victory that looked better on paper than it did on the pitch.

It was the first time Leeds had managed more than two in a game since beating the Saints 4-1 in October. With Preston inexplicably losing at Scunthorpe and Sunderland held to a goalless draw by Middlesbrough, valuable ground was gained.

Leeds now had to visit Middlesbrough themselves, and Revie recalled Giles to restore some midfield control.

The game marked a distinct return to form and United were at their best on a greasy pitch, regaining the leadership of the division with a display of fast, attacking football. They were constantly in their opponents' faces, closing them down. So intense was the press that Boro struggled to get out of their own half. Nevertheless, the sides were locked at 1-1 until four minutes from time, when Peacock emerged from a ruck of players to score. Giles gave the scoreline an emphatic look when he added a third from a difficult angle.

Preston were in Cup action and Sunderland lost at Newcastle, leaving Leeds a point clear, an advantage bolstered when Bremner returned from suspension with the second goal in the 3-1 defeat of Grimsby.

Giles was getting rave reviews and scored in a vital Good Friday victory at Newcastle. His first-half effort was fortunate, the wind taking a rushed centre into the net. The match was a triumph of concerted defence.

Four straight victories at such a crucial moment represented impeccable timing. Leeds were four points clear of third-placed Preston with six games left though the gap narrowed by a point with the other two Easter fixtures as North End reaped maximum points from their games. They moved temporarily into second place, for their match with Grimsby was a morning kick off. Sunderland dropped a point at Rotherham to leave them second, three points behind but with a game in hand.

Leeds dropped a point at Derby when Cullen scored from a speculative overhead kick with 90 seconds remaining, wiping out the advantage gained through Peacock's 81st minute effort, but victory in the return against Newcastle was crucial.

Newcastle finished with George Dalton in hospital and another limping. There was no malice involved, Dalton admitting he fractured his right tibia by kicking the sole of Giles' boot.

A 40,000 crowd saw Leeds secure their fifth victory in six games. Leeds took the lead after two minutes from Charlton's long free kick into the area. Shots from Giles and Collins were charged down before Weston forced the ball home.

The goal calmed Leeds' nerves and they began moving smoothly from midfield but the jitters returned when Newcastle equalised. Jim Iley launched a long-range free kick into the goalmouth and Sprake and his defence left matters to each other, the ball slowly crossing the line.

Leeds continued to press but were ragged and looked like missing out. As the match entered the final 15, Johanneson scored a fabulous individual goal to turn one point into two.

The South African was surrounded by three defenders as he brought down a long pass. Appearing certain to be shepherded away from goal, Johanneson sidestepped them all and nonchalantly slipped the ball past the keeper as he came off his line. It was his 15th goal of the campaign, the highest total by a Leeds winger since the war.

With four games left and far superior goal average, United needed five points to clinch promotion.

A routine Elland Road victory against Leyton Orient kept them on track. Preston lost 4-2 at Rotherham and were fading fast, but Sunderland beat Swansea and thrashed Orient 5-2 to maintain their chase. While a single point from the final three matches would all but guarantee promotion, Leeds required maximum points to claim the title.

As preparation, United welcomed Juventus to Elland Road for a midweek friendly. They emerged with a creditable draw, although the Italians rested some of their key men and took things easy. It was interesting to see Leeds cope so admirably against high-class continental opposition.

The game was very much an hors d'oeuvre, whetting the appetite for the main course – the weekend's trip to Swansea and a potential promotion party.

While a win was needed to make promotion mathematically certain, their goal average was so superior to Preston that a draw would be enough. Revie chose to blood 19-year-old Terry Cooper in place of Johanneson. Cooper started his career as a winger before Revie moved him to full-back; his inclusion hinted that Revie would settle for a point.

The manager was confident but anxious. Swansea were 18th, three points off relegation, but had come close to pulling off a shock before losing at Elland Road in November. They enjoyed a wonderful Cup run, beating First Division Sheffield United and Stoke on the way to a shock victory at champions designate Liverpool.

Leeds slipped quickly into top gear, intent on leaving nothing to chance – they raced into a 3-0 lead in little over half an hour. Cooper set the wheels in motion, supplying the cross for Peacock to slam home after 15 minutes. Peacock quickly repeated the dose after a Collins corner was flicked on by Giles.

There was no holding Leeds, although it was a quarter of an hour before another score. Cooper's corner reached Giles on the edge of the area. He caught the ball perfectly and, although his shot was partially blocked by defender Roy Evans, there was enough pace for his effort to find the net. The game was as good as over.

The improvement in United's goal average was too important to risk; Leeds settled for no-frills containment. Their conservative approach allowed Swansea back into the game but Sprake dealt with all their efforts.

United's promotion was confirmed and goalless draws for both Preston and Sunderland strengthened title chances. Reynolds cracked open the champagne after the game as he embraced Revie with tears in his eyes. Fittingly, success had come at the same venue where Revie had gambled so successfully on youth 19 months earlier.

'The Boss bought a few crates of champagne,' recalls John Giles, 'and we were all tipsy within half an hour of our train leaving Swansea! None of the Leeds players were entirely satisfied. We were sick of hearing what a great side Sunderland were; to hear some people talk, you would have thought we couldn't play at all. It became an obsession.'

Before the game against Plymouth, the players came out carrying a huge banner thanking the crowd for their support and took a lap of honour. They stumbled to a hapless 1-1 draw against a side battling to avoid relegation. Whether it was a delayed nervous reaction after a torrid season, or the result of too much celebrating, United looked nothing like champions.

Bell drove home from 30 yards after 18 minutes but Sprake gifted Argyle an equaliser on the hour with one of the mistakes that were becoming all too regular – he let Jennings' gentle shot slip through his grasp and into the net. United never looked likely to recover the lead.

Sunderland duly beat Charlton 2-1 to confirm their own promotion and set up a last-day duel for the title. The equation was simple: if Leeds, at Charlton, could match Sunderland's result at Grimsby, they would be champions. If Sunderland could outpoint Leeds, the championship would go to Roker.

Revie recalled Cooper for Johanneson, but otherwise Leeds were unchanged. Indeed, their line-up over the last five games was remarkably stable, with only Johanneson and Cooper not ever-present.

United quickly took control on a holding surface. They pierced Charlton's defence at will and kept their opponents firmly at arm's length. Their dominance never faltered.

Their incisive movement had Charlton at sixes and sevens. Peacock showed his value after 36 minutes, finishing off a splendid passing movement involving Collins and Weston.

It was the 69th minute before another score and once more it was Peacock, heading Cooper's cross home for his fourth goal in three matches and his seventh in eight.

If Peacock provided the cutting edge, it was the irrepressible Collins who took the honours, covering every blade of grass as he drove Leeds on. He saw to it that Charlton found no way back, even after they got a late penalty. Edwards drove his spot kick wide, but Athletic had long been resigned to defeat.

Sunderland's draw at Grimsby was irrelevant; Leeds had found form at the right time, capturing 18 of the final 20 points. Despite the odd stumble, they were worthy title winners, losing just three games, all away to sides in the top six, and conceded only 34 goals. Their 63 points was the highest in the Second Division since Spurs' 70 in 1920, and a club record.

The triumph came exactly 40 years after their only other silverware in that same competition, and two years after nearly plummeting into Division Three. This was heady stuff and Leeds United Football Club had their foot on the first step of a memorable climb.

Job done, Charlton hugged Revie while Reynolds looked on with a smile as wide as the River Aire, thinking of how the coffers would be swollen by the visits of the big fish.

'Our manager has untiringly worked to create a club spirit which has permeated through the whole of the staff,' beamed Reynolds. 'Leeds United have one of the best boards of directors in the country. They have given Mr Revie and myself encouragement and confidence on many occasions and they have supported us to the utmost without question.'

Revie acknowledged the support he had been given by the directors. 'But for it, the club could not have made such headway. We have a family spirit at Elland Road and everyone has been prepared to work that little bit harder and do that little bit extra. The players have given 100 per cent effort in every game, and no team, win, lose or draw, can do more than that. Their obedience to orders ... has been most gratifying and I know they have repeatedly lost the chance to make flattering headlines by making sure of victory or a point with unspectacular methods.'

The Leeds style might not have been attractive but it was ultra-effective and heralded the approach that would hold sway in England for the next decade. The Second Division had seen nothing like it before, and Division One was about to get a dose of the same unpleasant medicine.

'It's all right being Second Division champions,' said Reynolds, 'but really we've won nowt yet. Now let's get the championship.' It was said with some bravado, but his prediction proved to have unimagined substance to it.

White Riot

'In the midst of chaos, there is also opportunity.'

7 August 1964: Don Revie is sat in a hotel in Belfast. Phil Brown of the Evening Post is with him, there to cover Leeds United's pre-season friendly against Ards later that day.

Brown reads aloud some snippets from an FA report criticising the trend for poor discipline on the field. The report names Leeds as the club with the poorest disciplinary record.

No one at Elland Road has been given any pre-warning of the publication and Revie is caught off guard. He grows more and more furious with every word spoken by Brown.

Revie's hackles were up at what he deemed an unfair attack. He pointed out that the report referred to all of a club's teams, and told Brown, 'We did not have a single first-team player sent off last season and we had only one suspended, Billy Bremner. The majority of our offences were committed by junior second-team players and boys.'

United complained formally to the FA: 'We wish to register a strong protest regarding the statement ... We would point out that we have only had two players sent off at Leeds in the last 44 years ... We maintain that the dirty team tag which was blown up by the press could prejudice not only the general public but the officials controlling the game.'

Leeds' letter ended with a comment that the release of this 'private information' was ill-advised and showed lack of sensitivity. The club demanded 'an undertaking that there will be no recurrence' and hinted darkly that the report 'could lead to some very unsavoury incidents'.

The FA dismissed United's request out of hand, claiming the report was factual and that the article was 'fair comment'.

No one could seriously deny that Leeds pushed the boundaries of acceptable behaviour and Revie's tetchy rebuttal smacked of hypocrisy. The combination of Revie's rank paranoia, hostile press coverage and opponents who sought to get their retaliation in first made for a volatile mix.

Revie had not a hope of winning the public relations war. The Dirty Leeds tag was born and there was nothing he could do about it.

Revie's gamble on Bobby Collins had paid off but Collins was not averse to dubious tactics and his spiteful interventions earned the wrong sort of headlines. Revie might have been the visionary architect behind United's rise to footballing eminence, but had he not signed Collins, his grand design might have been smothered at birth.

The pocket-sized Napoleon was single-handedly responsible for the rebirth of a club cast adrift on a sea of mediocrity.

Collins was the heart and soul of the resurrection of Leeds, the rousing, restless spirit that translated Revie's plan into bloody action. He was one of the manager's favourites, 'a professional's professional'.

Revie raised an army to follow Collins, a bunch of nondescript youngsters whom the grizzled Scot could shape to his design – the war machine revolved around this one-man hit squad. It was Collins' presence which made the difference. United were soft touches no longer and the top clubs would learn to fear their high-tempo approach.

Revie chose not to strengthen his promotion-winning squad. His stance was branded naïve by critics who suggested that their physical approach would be found wanting but Revie insisted that his hungry young men had earned the opportunity and pointed to the recent achievements of Ipswich, Spurs and Liverpool in securing the league title following promotion.

When the board met in late June, Harry Reynolds' colleagues feared the worst, anxious that Revie might be asking them to splash big again. They were ready to tell him, 'You've had enough, son, keep us up and we'll see how it goes.' A pleasant surprise awaited them.

'How much does he want this time?' asked Woodward.

'Keep your money in your pockets, fellas, Don's very happy with the side,' Reynolds replied.

'Eh? What d'you mean?' enquired Simon.

'Don's very happy with the players he's got. He says we've spent enough.'

'Blimey, that's a turn up for the books,' exclaimed Roberts.

'He just wants to get on with the challenge and shake up the big boys ...'

'Good for him,' blinked Cussins.

'... but he wants five years.'

Revie's original three-year contract had come to an end and new terms had to be negotiated.

'Three years he's had, and three more years he shall have,' insisted Bolton.

'Don won't be happy with that.'

'I don't give a bugger whether he's happy with it or not. Three years he shall have.' Bolton, still a major shareholder, was resolute.

The accounts revealed a record loss of £84,930 driven by the net transfer outlay of £83,800, almost entirely spent on Giles and Peacock.

Income was up, with receipts for league games climbing from £89,725 to £115,890 – the contribution from the cups was up from £2,462 to £38,202, reflecting both higher crowds and increased prices. The gains were eaten up by huge increases in costs, the biggest hit the wage bill, soaring from £55,903 to £99,434, reflecting £40,000 in bonuses.

Reynolds was not worried, saying, 'The accounts represent the cost that has to be paid nowadays for having a really well-rounded and permanently first-class club.'

Morris asked rhetorically, 'Which way would you want it? Would you rather we be in the position we are today, having spent all this money to get there, or have £25,000 or £30,000 in the bank and be struggling in the Second Division?'

'After winning promotion,' recalled Jim Storrie, 'most managers would talk in terms of consolidation. He spoke in terms of finishing in the top four. He said, "We will come up against some world-class players, but we will be the best team in the league." So he had the optimists among the lads thinking we would win the league and even the pessimists thought we might finish halfway up.'

Reynolds was optimistic. 'It is my intention that we will get into anything that is going, including the European Cup and the Inter-Cities Fairs Cup.'

Revie had some pre-season issues to contend with. Alan Peacock was sidelined for months by a knee injury sustained in a friendly while Billy Bremner was arrested for being drunk in charge of a car, though he was eventually cleared following a 60-minute hearing in September, admitting to drinking 'about four pints'.

Revie was unconcerned about such things, his mind full of the wrongs that the FA had visited on his beloved club.

Peacock was absent when the campaign began at Aston Villa and Revie included only five players with First Division experience, including Bremner, whose exposure consisted of 11 appearances five years earlier.

Phil Brown suggested in the *Yorkshire Evening Post* that 'the spectators are hoping ... that a new attacking spirit will be abroad. I don't know about that, but although many a manager is working hard on how to score more goals, retention of league position is of paramount importance these days and defence is Priority One with so many sides. Leeds ... may well run into that attitude.'

When they took the field against Villa, the players' shirts bore a new club badge after three years without one – a perching owl on a white background circled by a dark blue border. The design was a surprise, given the superstitious Revie's morbid misgivings about the symbolism of birds. The owl came from the three on the city's crest, but fans argued that it was wrong for Leeds and would have been more suitable for Sheffield Wednesday. It went unchanged until 1971.

'When the whistle blew, we were like greyhounds let out of the traps,' recalled Bremner. 'We launched attack after attack in the first quarter of an hour and ran Villa ragged. You can imagine how we felt when they opened the scoring ... I don't often panic but I distinctly remember a dark cloud of self-doubt passing over. "We're not going to be good enough," I thought.'

Revie used the interval to sort things out. He told the players, 'For pity's sake, lads, stop running about like a set of madmen and get down to playing calm football.'

They played exactly as instructed. Johanneson equalised and Leeds now matched Villa pass for pass. Charlton put Leeds ahead and that is how it stayed until the end. The win was an important milestone in the development of Revie's Leeds.

Johanneson took to the occasion like a duck to water, tormenting Villa from the off. He took his goal coolly when keeper Sidebottom failed to hold Weston's vicious drive.

Revie was delighted with 'a very good result' but insisted the players remained grounded, 'taking each match as it comes, like we did last season'.

Villa were limited opponents but next came champions Liverpool at Elland Road. The Reds were led by Bill Shankly to the Second Division title in 1962 and spent a year consolidating before winning the championship in 1964.

Despite their opening victory, the popular view was that United would do well to avoid relegation, the limitations of their game badly exposed by classier opposition. Liverpool represented the acid test.

Reynolds anticipated the first capacity crowd since the 1920s and had reverted to the premium pricing policy, but the ground was only two-thirds full. Reynolds' hopes of 50,000 meant that the paddock stands were packed while huge areas of the terraces behind the goals were left vacant for expected latecomers who never materialised.

As per Eric Stanger, it was the pace of the two teams that divided them. Liverpool 'played rather too studiedly, often too short and too square', while 'Leeds used the longer ball for the most part and by constantly switching the direction of attack often pulled a slow-moving Liverpool defence out of position.'

Liverpool exuded the assurance of champions, confident that they would weather the early storm but Leeds nipped gamely at their heels. The Reds had already survived a difficult moment before United scored after 16 minutes. Byrne's back pass was misplaced under pressure and struck a post with goalkeeper Lawrence caught flat-footed. He was similarly helpless when Johanneson's shot from the edge of the 18-yard box hit Yeats on the shoulder and kicked up and under the bar to register a fortunate opener.

The lead lasted eight minutes – Sprake caught Hunt's header but collided with Reaney and the ball slipped into the net.

Five minutes before the interval, the Merseysiders' defence was slow to react when Weston nodded Storrie's centre past the keeper to give Leeds a 2-1 lead.

Revie made the most of his half-time team talk and ten minutes after the break Leeds made it 4-1, Bremner beating Lawrence with a powerful drive and then rolling a free kick to Giles who fired home from 30 yards.

The fans were in delirium, chanting, 'We want five.' A fifth was never likely but they had put Liverpool to the sword.

It wasn't plain sailing with the Reds pulling one back in the 70th minute when Gordon Milne forced home the rebound after Sprake pushed his initial penalty kick onto a post.

As Phil Brown remarked: 'Only time and a few more results to match, of course, will really tell, but last night's match could set even this fickle city alight.' How right he was!

Wolves made United fight hard for victory in the next match, twice leading before two goals from Storrie and another from Charlton secured a third straight win.

When United won just two of the next eight league games and slumped to tenth, people thought the rot had set in. There was a four-goal debacle at Blackpool with young Alan Ball terrorising Leeds. The memory of his performance remained long with Revie, who later spent months chasing his signature.

United's injury list was a contributory factor. In addition to Peacock, who faced a cartilage operation, Giles, Collins, Weston, Bell and Lawson missed games in the opening six weeks. Sprake, Johanneson, Bremner, Charlton, Storrie and Greenhoff soldiered on despite various sprains and strains.

Even worse, it seemed Revie was on his way out of the club.

Alan Brown had quit Sunderland for Sheffield Wednesday and news of the vacancy piqued Revie's interest. His own directors' offer of a three-year contract had gone down badly.

He talked the matter over one evening with wife Elsie.

'I'm interested, Elsie, it looks made for me. Leeds are doing well but Sunderland are bigger and they pay better. They're talking five grand, almost twice as much as I'm on.'

'Look what they did to that man, though, Don,' said Elsie, referring to Alan Brown who had been vilified by the Roker fans, disgruntled at his methods and style.

'Yes, but ...'

'Your mind's made up, Don, do what you want.'

Revie knew that the Roker job was his for the taking. It may have been down to some Machiavellian ruse on his part that the 16 September newspapers reported that he had placed his hat in the ring for the job. They were particularly well-informed.

Revie claimed his decision to leave was 'the most reluctant I have ever taken'.

The United directors met to consider the request for a five-year contract. Reynolds argued Revie's cause long and hard in a fractious meeting. Reynolds was forthright. 'I will resign if Mr Revie leaves.' He added for public consumption, 'Leeds will not release Don Revie from his existing three-year contract. Sunderland are wasting their time.'

The meeting finished in stalemate.

Revie had been due to travel with Reynolds and Don Weston to watch Rotherham play Portsmouth but took himself off instead to the Bradford derby. He had a lucky escape, for on the way back Reynolds' car collided with a motorcyclist, hit an electricity pole and ended up in a ditch.

Weston escaped with shock and played the next day against Blackpool, but Reynolds was less lucky, detained overnight in Barnsley Hospital with 64 stitches in face and head wounds. Milking the sympathy vote for all it was worth, Reynolds continued to press Revie's case. 'I have fought to get Don's contract amended to five years. Other directors on the board are behind me, but we are not strong enough to carry it through.'

The players were aware of the stories as they stripped for the game. Revie told them, 'Give me something to remember with this game, because it will be your last one for me.'

The fans bellowed their support for the manager; after a 3-0 victory, during which United hit the woodwork on seven occasions and Bremner missed two penalties, they gathered around the stand, begging him to stay.

The shocked players expressed strong support for the Boss.

Bobby Collins said, 'It has come as a great shock to us all. It is particularly tragic because United are doing so well back in the First Division. Mr Revie is a great manager, and if he does go to Sunderland he is bound to be missed.'

Revie and Cyril Williamson visited Reynolds. Revie asked Williamson to step outside while they had a chat. There was intense discussion, the chairman urging the manager to stay. 'I think they'll go for it, Don. Cussins and Morris are behind me all the way even if Roberts and Woodward have other ideas. Bolton and Simon will go with the majority.'

The board met again the next day with Woodward in the chair. They relented, granting Revie a five-year deal. Vice-chairman Woodward told the press, 'I personally am overjoyed that the question of Don's future has been amicably settled ... Don didn't really want to leave. We know that. It has been the unanimous decision that he remains with Leeds United and he is happy to remain with them. He has the five-year contract and the salary he asked for.'

The board upped Revie's wages to £4,500. Woodward's pre-emptive strike put Revie in a fix. He either had to go against the director and cause an argument or go along with the story. He bitterly resented the way that the board had seized back the initiative and left him looking like a money grabber.

Revie was furious at what he saw as double-dealing and said as much to Elsie.

'They're stitching me up. I've done wonders and they don't like it. Harry's great, but the rest can go whistle, for me.'

'You're going to look like you only care about money, Don. Be careful, you know you can't trust them.'

'I'll stress the importance of loyalty to the lads at the club, hitch my wagon to them and their families and have a dig. "They've been loyal to me, it's up to me to show the same loyalty." That sort of thing.'

Ever mindful of his public image, Revie went for the positive when he spoke to the press. 'I had landed the Sunderland job and was walking into the locker room at Leeds to collect my kit when I came face to face with a group of newly-signed apprentices. Believe it or not, they had tears in their eyes when I told them I was leaving ... It might seem trite to say that I looked upon my players as sons, but this is true. Most of them had been with the club since they left school, and I promised their mothers and fathers I would look after them.

'I was all prepared to go to Sunderland, but all the time in my heart I did not want to go ... Leeds United have a great future, although I think it will take another two years before we really see the full results ... When I was first appointed to this job three years ago, I said it would take five years and I still hold to that opinion.'

Storm in a teacup over, Revie and his charges returned to the job in hand. Within weeks, they were embroiled in controversy.

Their roughhouse tactics brought out the worst in opponents. After a defeat at Chelsea, Phil Brown wrote, '"Never mind the ball" seemed to be the order of the day as scything, irresponsible tackles ruffled tempers. The midget Collins once retaliated on Harris viciously and had his name taken when he might well have been despatched to the dressing room to ponder his action; McCreadie hooked up Giles painfully and, with half an hour gone, left Leeds permanently reduced to ten men as the wounded winger was carried away from the scene on a stretcher.'

That tussle was as nothing to an ill-tempered affair at Everton on 7 November. Four straight wins took Leeds fourth and they were in no mood to leave Liverpool empty-handed. Collins' former club had a proud tradition and were determined not to roll over for such uncouth upstarts. It was a case of unstoppable force meets immovable object: something had to give, and it was very nearly the good name of football.

Everton's players were patently aware of United's reputation. Indeed, only those lost in the Arctic could have been in the dark. The atmosphere at a partisan Goodison Park was passionate. For many of his former team-mates, memories of Collins' readiness to take liberties were still fresh, and they awaited Leeds with trepidation.

Within seconds, Fred Pickering was fouled by Bremner and almost immediately Charlton suffered a similar fate. The battle lines were drawn, this was going to be a tasty affair.

After four minutes, Giles tangled with Sandy Brown. When Brown rose and swung a fist he was instantly dismissed, complaining of stud marks to his chest.

'We collided in challenging for the ball and our legs became accidentally entangled,' recalled Giles. 'Brown wriggled free, leapt angrily to his feet, and aimed a punch to my head ... Brown's behaviour that day ties in with my point about the prejudice against Leeds. I did not foul him, nor did I attempt to provoke him in any way. But, due to our reputation, he wasn't prepared to give me the benefit of the doubt.'

There was no going back and players on both sides threw themselves into the tackle with reckless abandon. An enraged home crowd bellowed their ire.

After 15 minutes, Leeds took the lead following a free kick out on the right wing. Collins swung the ball high into the Everton goal area. Bell came running in at speed to find space and met the ball perfectly, his header flashing into the net.

The stadium was in chaos. Any Leeds player foolish enough to come within throwing distance ran the risk of being struck by missiles – for Gary Sprake there was no hiding place, his goal was pelted by a hail of coins.

Things came to a head after 36 minutes. Bell and Derek Temple were following the flight of the ball and seemingly unaware of each other. They collided at full speed, laying each other out. That was the signal for the crowd to get completely out of hand. Missiles rained down on Bell and Temple and the trainers attending them. Les Cocker and referee Ken Stokes were struck by flying objects.

Stokes ordered both teams to the dressing rooms to give them and the crazed crowd time to cool off.

It was some minutes before Bell came round sufficiently for Cocker and Giles to carry him off, while Temple required a stretcher.

For a time, nobody knew whether the game had been abandoned. Eventually, the loudspeakers announced that play would restart in five minutes, though Stokes warned that the match would be called off if more missiles were thrown.

The referee laid down the law, marching into the dressing rooms to tell both teams that if they didn't stop kicking each other, he would report both clubs to the FA.

The game resumed after a ten-minute interval on a pitch festooned in cushions and rubbish. The break did little to soothe the mood. Some of the tackling, particularly by Norman Hunter and Vernon, was brutal in the extreme. Hunter was booked, and the referee lectured Bremner, Collins, Vernon and Stevens for dangerous play. Several players were fortunate to avoid joining Brown in the dressing room.

Collins became dominant, relishing the kind of hostile environment in which he thrived. His generalship and shrewd distribution ensured Leeds had all the possession. They made the most of their man advantage, Collins exhorting his colleagues to stretch the play.

United resisted Everton's closing assault, squeezing out the victory in the face of fierce antagonism from the 40,000 Scousers in the crowd.

Furious supporters had to be dispersed by mounted police. The Leeds players stared from their coach windows as it was pelted with missiles.

There was some predictably hysterical press coverage.

'Goodison Park has already gained an unsavoury tribal reputation for vandalism,' thundered *The Times*. 'Leeds United, too, more recently have earned black marks for ill-temper on the field ... One remembered the old days when play certainly was equally rough, if not physically rougher. Yet now the modern sophisticates can be more sinister, more subtle in their methods. The high rewards at stake, the financial incentives, have brought new, more savage pressures ... Stern, practical steps must be taken now to cure the malaise.'

Revie fell back on his favourite ruse of deflection. 'I must defend my club and my players after all the bad things that had been said about them. It started last season when we were in the Second Division and tagged as a hard, dirty side by the press. I am disgusted by these attacks on us and I ask that we be judged fairly and squarely on each match and not on this unfair tag ...

we were wrongly labelled by the press and then by the Football Association. The result has been that opposing teams have gone on to the field keyed up, expecting a hard match. I think the number of opposing players sent off in our matches proves it.'

The episode raised the hackles of football's establishment. The patriarchal president of the Football League, Barnsley's Joe Richards, hinted at firm action to follow.

Richards was determined to show the strong leadership that he thought the public would demand, saying, 'The time has come to investigate the whole question of these ugly scenes and rows. They are bringing a bad image to football ... Something must be done and we must find out the causes. We shall certainly look at it from the bonus point of view and find out whether that is causing the trouble. Competition is healthy and we must have promotion and relegation, but things seem to be getting too keen. It may be that players are getting too much money for points. It is all very disappointing ... this trouble is happening too regularly.'

Despite his declarations, the only punishment meted out by the FA was against Everton. Brown was suspended for two weeks and Everton were fined £250 for the behaviour of their supporters.

The episode cemented the reputation of Revie's United in the minds of many for years to come – a bunch of thuggish yobs who would stop at nothing to win a football match. To a polarised public there was no grey, only black and white; for them, Leeds United and everybody associated with the name wore the black cowboy hats.

Leeds were slated for their readiness to remove the gloves. Their aptitude for securing points was much more important than being loved. Revie would look back in later years and regret the attitude, but at the time his judgement was swayed by the success of the physical and mental aggression.

A blistering performance by Collins and goals by Charlton, Belfitt and Storrie brought victory against Arsenal and a four-goal hammering of Birmingham secured a seventh consecutive win. Leeds were third, a point behind Chelsea and two behind leaders Manchester United.

Defeat at West Ham rudely interrupted the winning streak, but then came four single-goal victories, the second of which saw Man United bested on their own pitch at the start of December.

The game began with the ground shrouded in mist which gave way to even thicker fog, but neither could mask the tactical supremacy achieved by Leeds. It was shrewdly planned by Revie and brilliantly executed by his troops. The nominal wingers, Giles and Cooper, provided security on the flanks with Bremner and Collins patrolling the centre. The expected twin strike force of Johnson and Storrie spent much of their time chasing down the Manchester defence and midfield. It set a strangling web in which the home side were often enmeshed.

Manchester contributed to their troubles through Crerand's insistence on carrying yards forward before making his pass. It gave Leeds extra seconds and their cover was smothering – they always had a man spare.

The longer the game went, the more Matt Busby's men struggled for coherence. They would have been well-advised to hold the ball in defence to draw Leeds onto them and thus create more room for themselves. Whether Leeds would have fallen for the trick will never be known, for the Reds could find no way of coping with Revie's game plan.

Leeds' play was not purely defensive – on the break Johnson and Storrie were regular thorns in the flesh and there was always Collins, harrying his opponents.

In the first ten minutes of the second half Leeds won the match, springing from deep defence to take Manchester by surprise with a series of assaults before they broke the deadlock. Giles and Bremner probed down the right and Bremner played Cooper through. Goalkeeper Dunne pushed Cooper's effort away but the ball fell to Collins, who buried it.

After that, the fog descended and so did Manchester's chances with Sprake catching everything which came his way.

Ten minutes from time, referee Jim Finney was forced to call off the players to see if visibility would improve. Thousands of Leeds supporters left for home under the impression that the game had been abandoned.

The veil lifted sufficiently for the referee to resume after a delay of eight minutes and Leeds secured a famous victory.

Leeds rose to second, with only Manchester's superior goal average keeping them at bay. That they were so successful without Peacock, still two months from fitness, was a miracle.

On 2 January, Leeds had the chance to go clear at the top as they hosted Sunderland, with Man United-Fulham postponed.

The game drifted towards a goalless draw as United let their frustration show. The goal the game needed came after 72 minutes, Charlton heading home from a Collins free kick. Within nine minutes Hunter had made it 2-0. Leeds looked home and dry, but Hood pulled one back a minute later, shooting out of a ruck at close range.

Writing in his weekly column in the *Yorkshire Evening Post*, Revie let his joy spill over, the victory making him 'just about the proudest manager in soccer'.

London-based critics deplored United's style but accepted that they would be a team to watch in the FA Cup.

The third-round draw was kind, at home to Fourth Division Southport. Leeds had the better of the first half, though they only had a goal from Greenhoff to mark their dominance. Southport battled manfully but Johanneson wrapped up the victory after 81 minutes and Johnson knocked home Cooper's centre at the death to give the score a flattering look.

Collins and Bremner (twice) struck the woodwork, and a couple of goals were chalked off for offside, but Leeds had made heavy weather of things, trying to be too clever and precise on a pitch made quagmire by heavy overnight rain.

They faced Everton next at Elland Road but a 1-1 draw left people predicting defeat in the replay. 50,051 were in attendance, the highest crowd thus far, and Leeds collected £13,000 in gate money. The Goodison replay three days later attracted 65,940 with receipts of almost £15,000.

Charlton conceded the penalty at Goodison which allowed Pickering to cancel out Storrie's opener but made amends with a goal. It was his seventh of a campaign in which his regular lolloping forays into the penalty area were a feature. He was in the form of his life in defence but it was his contributions at the other end that got him noticed. Only Storrie, with 16 in all competitions, and Johanneson (8) scored more goals.

Leeds struggled in the fifth round against hard-working Shrewsbury, despite going ahead through a Giles penalty. They confirmed their place in the last eight when Johanneson netted the second goal with ten minutes remaining.

Joining Leeds were their two biggest rivals for the championship, Chelsea and Manchester United. The three clubs had pulled away from the rest of the pack and had seven points in hand on fourth-placed Tottenham.

Leeds' unbeaten league run was stretched to 11 by a fiercely fought victory at Arsenal and Peacock returned to action on 27 February at Spurs. The game finished a tame goalless draw but it wasn't long before Peacock was back among the goals, hitting two in the Cup against Crystal Palace.

It was the first time that United had been drawn away from home, and they had to wait until the Wednesday for action, as Selhurst Park was unplayable due to frost at the weekend.

Palace manager Dick Graham was determined to spring a shock and blithely instructed his men to kick Leeds out of the competition. He also attempted to confuse by mixing up shirt numbers but Leeds players simply picked up whoever was nearest to them, nullifying the gimmick. Palace committed 17 fouls in the first half but United refused to rise to the provocation and their opponents ran out of steam.

Peacock broke the deadlock just before the hour and ten minutes later, he added a second after a great ball from Cooper, who set up Storrie for the third goal after 73 minutes.

Leeds struggled to a draw with Fulham at Craven Cottage and then fell a goal behind at home to Burnley. With Reaney hobbling on the wing, a sluggish United were feeling the effects of three matches in six days but the Lancastrians could not build on their advantage and United took control, firing back to win 5-1. It was their best performance of the season, and certainly their most convincing result, although they remained in second position to Chelsea on goal average.

The eyes of Revie and Reynolds sparkled with anticipation.

The First Failure

'One may know how to conquer without being able to do it.'

19 March 1965: Paul Reaney, injured at Burnley, is coming to terms with missing his third league game since making his Leeds debut two-and-a-half years earlier. He has been the model of consistency, but his fellow debutant, Norman Hunter, has gone even better, playing in every single game since.

The pair were rocks in the defence that drove Don Revie's Leeds from 12th in the Second Division to their current lofty standing of the second-best team in the country. In the 111 games that Hunter had played, Leeds had kept 40 clean sheets.

Hunter rarely made it into the papers but by comparison Reaney could have been the invisible man. But Don Revie certainly knew how good he was; Alf Ramsey, too, who gave Reaney his first Under-23 cap against France in April 1964 and then took him on the summer tour.

The entire United defence was making waves. Hunter was in the Football League XI which beat the Irish League 4-0 in October and then played three times for the Under-23s. Reaney was selected alongside him in that third game, a 0-0 draw with Scotland in February. Hunter and Jack Charlton were at the heart of defence when a Football League XI drew with the Scottish League at Hampden on 17 March. But for his injury, Reaney might well have made it three Leeds men in defence.

19-year-old Gary Sprake was the daddy of the bunch, with five Under-23 caps and five full caps for Wales to his name. Willie Bell had played at amateur level for Scotland and would win two full caps within a year, while Charlton would become the most celebrated for his work with England.

'Speedy' Reaney was born in Fulham to a mixed-race couple but had lived in Leeds since his family moved north when he was 14 days old.

He was a manager's dream, one of the fittest players at the club. He had pace to burn, tackled ferociously and pioneered the overlapping full-back play that became the norm by the end of the 60s. But ask the man in the street and all you would get, even from the knowledgeable, would be, 'Paul Reaney ... plays for Leeds, doesn't he? Don't know much about him.'

Reaney, still feeling the ankle he turned on Monday against Burnley, and Charlton, who had gone down with flu, were out of the game the next day against Everton. Paul Madeley and Terry Cooper were summoned from the reserves to replace them. For Madeley it was a ninth start and for Cooper his 14th.

The two slotted in smoothly as Leeds secured a convincing 4-1 victory lit up by two goals from Albert Johanneson. It extended their unbeaten run to 20 games and took them top for the first time in seven weeks as Chelsea enjoyed a day off. The Londoners were in the midst of a two-legged League Cup final with Leicester and had an FA Cup semi-final clash with Liverpool to look forward to.

The other team in the title running were Manchester United, who lost to Sheffield Wednesday. Their impressive recovery since the Munich disaster made them the people's choice.

Leeds were not yet the iron-clad defensive giants of future legend and both Chelsea and Manchester had better defensive records. The fact that the three teams had virtually identical goals scored tallies also gives lie to the myth. The bias of the London-centric popular titles was already in play.

Don Warters, who covered the club for the *Yorkshire Evening Post* for 29 years, wrote, 'Leeds against the world. In London, they weren't the favourite team ... The Revie team used that as a spur, the fact that they were disliked and didn't get much support from the Football League whenever they tried to postpone a match for Europe. They had an "us against them" attitude. I'm sure Revie used that to his advantage.'

The top three had all made it to the last four of the Cup and harboured hopes of the elusive Double, with Chelsea even dreaming of an unprecedented treble. 27 March was semi-final day, with Leeds facing Manchester United at Hillsborough, and Chelsea pitched against Liverpool at Villa Park.

The Londoners lost 2-0 to Bill Shankly's revitalised team, in high spirits having just secured a European Cup semi-final spot.

The FA Cup records of the two Uniteds could scarcely have contrasted more. Leeds had only once gone as far as the last eight, losing to mighty Arsenal in 1950. Their normal fate was an early exit, and the ten seasons between 1953 and 1962 yielded not a single victory.

By contrast, the Red Devils had won the Cup on three occasions and were twice runners-up during the 50s. Add in five championships and six second places, and the divide was clear. In terms of major silverware, the Peacocks could cite only two Second Division titles.

Nevertheless, Manchester had little reason to look forward to the clash. There was a bitter and unlovely tension developing between the two teams.

Reaney and Charlton were both back for the game and the former was given the job of man-marking danger man George Best as he had so effectively done when Leeds won at Old Trafford in December. Best ('the slim Irishman now reckoned just about the best winger in Europe') didn't get a sniff with Reaney never more than a foot away and touch-tight whenever he had the ball. 'If George had gone to the toilet, I'd be there,' Reaney said in later years. The tactic reduced Reaney's attacking threat, but it was a small price to pay to negate Manchester's totem. Eric Stanger wrote in later years, 'Best found himself playing rabbit to Reaney's stoat. It is remarkable how Reaney masters the talented Irishman game after game. This time, he finally had Best in such a tizzy that on one occasion he twice stumbled and almost fell over the ball looking out of his eye corner for Reaney.'

From the first seconds it was clear that this was to be a war of attrition and anger, as reported in *The Times*. 'This was a rough and tumble: tough, with the rumble of trouble from the start when Bremner sawed down Charlton in full flight … He retaliated immediately in anger, wagged his finger in admonition and from that first act the battle quickly slipped into a black mood that only matched the dark stage itself, a heavy churned-up pitch made sticky by heavy overnight rain. Manchester, having heard of the dog's bad name, clearly were themselves determined not to be bitten.'

Bremner provoked the early enmity with aggressive assaults on Law and Charlton, but he was the one who was wronged the most during the opening 20 minutes. Felled on a number of occasions and once climbing off the floor with a bloodied nose, he then came close to putting through his own goal as he volleyed Connelly's centre from two yards out.

When Leeds went on the offensive, Peacock almost steered home Collins' free kick but it soon became clear that there would be no rhythm or flow to the play. No one was allowed the time or space to show control or skill. When anyone attempted to do so, they were quickly reprimanded.

In an ugly first half Leeds restricted themselves to launching long-range free kicks high into the Manchester goal area for Peacock, Charlton and Bell to dispute but goalkeeper Pat Dunne dealt confidently with everything. When Leeds tried a more cultured approach, using Giles and Johanneson down the flanks, both were brutally dealt with, Stiles being the main enforcer. It was no surprise that the first half ended goalless.

Things degenerated after the interval, with Stiles and Crerand leaving Johanneson a limping passenger, and Bremner doing the same to Best. With Peacock blotted out by Foulkes, and Law and Bobby Charlton more concerned with demonstrating their tackling than attacking flair, the game slumped into a messy, undisciplined struggle for survival.

Stiles and Law were booked for bad fouls on Johanneson and Bell, and the only surprise was that more players were not cautioned or even dismissed.

The refereeing of Dick Windle was tolerant to the point of weakness. One clash after an hour transcended everything that had gone before. Windle bottled it, declining to take the action that could have restored order. Law chased after Charlton, intent on making a point. He caught up with the centre-half and barged into him, infuriating Charlton and fists started flying. The players took it as the signal to let their simmering rage overflow, and players from both sides piled in. Crerand and Bremner clashed violently and Stiles and Hunter had to be separated.

It was several minutes before calm was restored, with Law's shredded shirt hanging loosely from his shoulder. Windle took no action, choosing only to tick Law off and award a free kick to Leeds. His patience was inexplicable.

The match rumbled to a goalless draw, with a final scoreline of 24 fouls by Manchester to ten by Leeds.

There was concern that the replay would be spoilt by the settling of scores. Windle officiated again, but clamped down on any misdemeanours from the off. The change brought noticeable improvement in discipline. There were too many fouls, 20 against the Reds and five against Leeds, but most were for petty offences, rather than aggressive play.

The improved conditions helped. Hillsborough had been a bog of a pitch, mitigating against expansive play. Nottingham's City Ground offered a fast, dry surface that the players were thankful for, taking the opportunity to rise above thuggery.

Leeds were again content to rely on defence. Phil Brown noted that a dominant Collins was 'invaluable, pulling United out of trouble at one end of the field, and touching off their attacking at the other,' while Eric Stanger branded the Scot a 'cool, masterful general'.

Leeds saw to it that Crerand never got the chance to exploit his wonderful armoury of passing skills, detailing Cooper to mark him. Leeds strangled his supply, leaving the more prosaic Stiles and Foulkes starting forward moves. The goalkeeper was left to kick upfield where Jack Charlton would win it in the air.

After early Manchester dominance, Giles took control and Leeds several times went close. Most of their openings came from high balls into the Manchester area for Peacock to contest.

Busby's men were on the front foot after the break and this time their dominance was total. For the first 20 minutes there was only one side in it.

Gradually, the storm abated as Leeds forced their way back in. They gave the Red Devils food for thought when Charlton headed inches wide, the catalyst for a match-winning rally.

Revie was never one to let an opportunity pass him by and noted the change. He could see Busby's men fade and issued orders to capitalise. He withdrew Giles to a deeper, more central role, moved Storrie wide and thrust Bremner up front. Bell and Reaney pushed forward on the overlap at every opportunity, foregoing their marshalling of Connelly and Best.

157

The tide had perceptibly turned. At first, Leeds merely held their own and assumed equality of possession, but as the game moved into its fateful last quarter, they dominated, attacking with passion and pace.

The seconds ticked by and the lottery of extra-time beckoned. As the match moved into its final two minutes, Stiles floored Bremner with a late tackle in the centre circle, happy to trade a long-range free kick for the certainty of nullifying a quick break. Giles floated the ball unerringly into the heart of a crowded goal area.

Bremner darted past three or four defenders and moved in under the steepling kick. With his back to goal, he dived to flick the ball with his head past the keeper and into the top corner.

Ecstatic Leeds players mobbed Bremner as he reached the corner of the pitch. Leeds had done it! They had broken the deadlock with a goal owing much to sharp thinking, but most of all to their never-say-die spirit.

Leeds were in no mood to surrender to Manchester's last-ditch assault and repelled the Red Devils' feverish attacks.

At the end the crowd swarmed onto the pitch, Manchester fans angry at what they saw as one-eyed refereeing. Windle was struck by a Manchester supporter and fell to the ground, requiring attention from ambulance men and protection from the police as the culprit was arrested.

Leeds had kept their Double hopes alive, hopes that grew stronger as they returned to league action with victories against West Ham, Stoke and West Brom, taking their unbeaten run in all competitions to 25 games.

Peacock's return had boosted United's threat with seven goals in ten appearances. As the decisive Easter holiday beckoned, things looked good.

Only Chelsea were in action on Good Friday, hammering Liverpool 4-0 to exact revenge for their Cup defeat. They had just lifted the League Cup and still fancied their chances.

Most eyes were on the following day's match at Elland Road as Leeds faced Manchester United for the third time in 22 days. A win for Revie's men would take them five points clear. They had every reason to anticipate victory with two wins and a draw in their head-to-heads and had yet to concede a goal.

Revie tried desperately to play down the importance of the occasion, but he knew that this was crunch time – it was the most important game that Leeds United had ever played.

They were unchanged from the 2-1 win at West Brom, with Greenhoff continuing to deputise for the suspended Bremner.

The Scot was often in disciplinary hot water for retaliation and backchat. Don Revie sought advice from wife Elsie, who always seemed to know exactly what to do where behaviour was concerned. Her experience as a teacher had equipped her to deal expertly with childish behaviour.

'The other teams pick on Billy, Don, because they know it works. They know which buttons to press, get in his face. He falls for it every time. He's the one that the referee sees and he gets the blame. These other bullies get away with it every time. Your lads need to close ranks, share out the job, point out to the ref what's going on.'

'I never thought about it like that, Elsie, I just want him to calm down.'

'Scots can't calm down, we have a short fuse.' Her eyes shined.

Don called the players together the next day.

'Okay, boys, we need to do something. Billy's being targeted. We need to look after each other, make sure that no one gets isolated or picked off. If they target Billy, he must walk away while the rest of you draw the matter to the referee's attention. Take nothing lying down.'

'Anything you say, Boss,' chorused Reaney and Hunter while Collins growled, 'Leave 'em to me ...'

'Hang on, Bobby, I mean talk to the ref, not do their lads.'

'Whatever you say, Boss, leave 'em to me.'

Revie sighed and rolled his eyes.

Bremner feared the worst as he awaited news of his punishment, dreading that he would be kept out of the Cup final. Four cautions, he thought, would get him a three-week suspension and put paid to any Wembley hopes. Collins said it would be one week and a fine, which turned out to be bang on.

Bremner missed two games, the league showdown with Manchester United his most crucial absence.

The Reds enjoyed much of the early play, taking a deserved lead after 14 minutes.

A combination of strong wind and a rock hard playing surface played their part when Jack Charlton's headed clearance fell to Law, who fed Connelly. As Hunter ran out to engage him, the winger spun on the ball and fired goalwards. He didn't catch it true but it went through Hunter's legs and an unsighted Sprake didn't stand a chance.

It was a bitter blow. Manchester were much the better side, defending sternly and showing their greater experience. Leeds were done. A massive opportunity to cement their charge had passed them by, and worse was to follow.

On Easter Monday, it was announced that Collins had been elected Footballer of the Year, receiving almost 50 per cent of the votes of the Football Writers' Association, but he would have exchanged the award and his recall to the full Scotland team for a win later that day at Sheffield Wednesday.

With Peacock and Collins unavailable, United slumped again. Leeds were never at the races in a 3-0 defeat. Bremner partnered Storrie up front, with Greenhoff on the right and Madeley in midfield. Completely out of sorts, Leeds looked jaded by too much football and too much tension. Wednesday were two-up in 26 minutes and running riot.

Leeds were a point behind Manchester but appeared on the verge of collapse, slipping back to third, even though Chelsea lost at Anfield. The pressure of having to win every game was telling and Leeds were in desperate need of a tonic.

Just as it seemed they had shot their bolt, Leeds bounced back to form, beating Wednesday 2-0 in the return and then emerging 3-0 winners from a visit to Sheffield United.

Chelsea's challenge evaporated in a bout of indiscipline – a rout at Burnley after a late-night boozing session which brought a falling out with manager Tommy Docherty. Eight players were sent home in disgrace, giving the tabloids a field day. Terry Venables was stripped of the captaincy and all eight players were omitted from the side thrashed 6-2 by Burnley.

Just as the Londoners crumbled, Manchester grew stronger. As Leeds were beating Sheffield United, the Old Trafford club hammered Liverpool 3-0 to register their sixth win on the trot. They had dropped two points in 11 games, enjoying a goal record of 32 for and seven against.

Leeds were somehow still top but had only one game left, away to relegated Birmingham. Busby's team were a point adrift, but had two games to go and a superior goal average.

Revie accepted that the title was slipping away. There was still the Cup final to look forward to and he was torn between saving his best for Wembley and really going for it at Brum. In the end, he rested Storrie and Bell but otherwise sent out a full-strength side.

There were no ifs, buts or maybes – United's only option was to go all-out for victory. Even then they would have to rely on Busby's side dropping points, either at home that same evening to Arsenal, or a couple of nights later at lowly Aston Villa. The chances of Villa doing Leeds a favour were remote – they had crashed 7-0 at Old Trafford.

It was a tenuous possibility (after the Saturday results, bookies quoted Manchester United as 5-1 on with Leeds 7-2 against), but stranger things have come to pass in football.

Birmingham had enjoyed a disastrous campaign, registering only seven wins and were already doomed to finish bottom. It looked a straightforward task for Leeds, but within seconds it was apparent that their pipedream was not going to be realised.

United started tentatively and fell behind after four minutes. Blues winger Dennis Thwaites scored after being put clear by Terry Hennessey. Two minutes later Manchester United took the lead against Arsenal through a wonder goal from George Best.

Another minute gone, and Birmingham winger Alex Jackson went off with a dislocated shoulder after a clash with Cooper, who was vigorously booed every time he touched the ball.

The ten men fought like tigers to hold their advantage but Leeds could well have been ahead before the interval. Peacock missed two good chances and Weston hooked wide with the Birmingham defence waiting for an offside decision that never came. But the Blues had the momentum and took a 3-0 lead six minutes after the interval.

Nine minutes later Law increased Manchester United's lead to two goals just as Arsenal were threatening a rally. With the scores as they stood, Leeds' cause was lost. Revie signalled to 'take it steady', urging his men to save their best for Wembley. Bremner saw him on the touchline waving his arms about but misunderstood, assuming Revie wanted them to get back into the game. From somewhere the Yorkshire fighting spirit returned to breathe fire into their play.

In what was now a customary move, Bremner became an auxiliary centre-forward. After 65 minutes, City left-back Green brought him down and Giles coolly converted the penalty.

Minutes later, George Eastham netted at Old Trafford to haul Arsenal back into the other contest.

Those incidents provided the explosive catalyst for the high drama of the final 20 minutes. An intensive Leeds bombardment of the Birmingham area ended with Reaney contributing a rare goal. 3-2, and the momentum shifted to Leeds as the crowd in Manchester started to chew their nails. There was a hint that this could yet be an incredible evening for West Yorkshire.

Charlton, now a full-time attacker, thumped home an equaliser two minutes from the end, throwing Birmingham into a panic. With everyone permanently camped in the City area, Hunter smashed the ball against a post in injury-time.

But there was to be no salvation – the game ended in a breathless 3-3 draw. In the closing minutes at Old Trafford, Law tapped in a third to confirm Manchester as 3-1 victors. There was still an improbably remote mathematical possibility that their positions could be reversed (Aston Villa would need to have scored 19 against the Reds in the final match to have given Leeds the title), but the game was up – Busby's club was crowned champions for the sixth time.

Villa beat Manchester United 2-1, leaving Leeds as runners-up by dint of goal average. Their 61 points was the highest total ever achieved by a team failing to win the title, and enough to have won the championship on all but three occasions since the war. Leeds had come desperately close to glory.

The plaudits and congratulations were no consolation to a disappointed squad. They had come within a whisker of footballing immortality, but the first case of 'so near and yet so 'far' left a bitter taste. If anyone had offered Leeds the runners-up spot twelve months previously, they would have snapped their hands off, but now it felt like a hollow achievement.

The Yorkshiremen retained one final chance of silverware, the FA Cup final on 1 May against Liverpool.

Johanneson, Storrie and Bell were all back from injury and selected by Leeds, who were rated narrow favourites. There were far more red favours at Wembley than white, however, and the Leeds players came out of the tunnel in trepidation.

Bill Shankly turned to Collins. 'How are ye, son?'

'To tell the truth, I feel f***in' awful,' muttered Collins, reflecting the mood of his camp.

He was almost resigned to failure, telling himself, 'There's no chance of winning at Wembley unless the lads have played there and know what to expect. Don's got this one wrong.'

Collins' team-mates had been carried away by the hullabaloo surrounding the final. Their week had been spent in Sheffield, Birmingham and London, three different beds in five days.

Revie loved being away with the squad, secluded in the Selsdon Park Hotel in Croydon. He could forget the burden of running the club and instead build team spirit with games of indoor bowls and dominoes. The players would have preferred being at home instead of getting bored and overly focused on Revie's game plan, but the captain said nothing for fear of upsetting the apple cart.

The tension spilled over at times, peaking during a five-a-side game on the Friday. A driven clearance by Hunter caught Collins full in the face. It was accidental but the Scot saw the red mist as well as the blood from his nose and took his revenge, leaping into Hunter with both feet raised. There was a tussle and Collins ended up on top, punching Hunter. Charlton hauled him off. 'Come on, Bobby, calm down, we've got a Cup final tomorrow.'

'F*** off, ye tw*t,' growled Collins as he stomped off.

When Collins and Ron Yeats came forward for the toss at Wembley, there were fully 12 inches between the giant and the midget. Collins called correctly, opting to change ends and allow the Reds to kick off in overcast conditions.

The pattern was clear: Liverpool, battle-hardened from three years of top-flight action and 12 months of European competition, were assured, playing within themselves and preferring the certainty of easy ball retention to the gamble of a panicky forward pass. Their forwards were in constant shuttle, offering width and the comfort of a short square pass. St John and Hunt combined in slick one-twos to leave Charlton and Hunter nonplussed.

By comparison, United were as rigid and static as the stance of Peacock, their defence entrenched on the edge of their penalty area; Bremner, Giles and Collins clustered tightly in midfield with only the long ball as an outlet; Johanneson, strangely out of sorts, and Storrie, rendered immobile and ineffective by early injury, made only fitful contributions.

Leeds looked one-dimensional and emasculated. The stage had been set for Johanneson to take the cause of the black footballer in Britain to fresh heights. He could have cemented his reputation as the most exciting winger in the game, but the occasion swallowed him. The one Leeds player who could excite crowds, he was a shadow of himself.

Sprake was the only man to shine, saving countless efforts to keep United in the contest far longer than they deserved.

The match was colourless. Few teams were better equipped to ensure that outcome. Leeds and Liverpool had perfected the method football demanded by the physical rigours of the Second Division. They set a grim trend in the English game.

The opening minutes were typical of the day, untidy, with the most active men being the trainers. With three minutes on the clock, Hunter strained his ankle in a tackle as he nailed his man out on the left. Seconds later Collins stamped into a challenge on Gerry Byrne. Play was held up for almost two minutes as Hunter and Byrne received treatment. At the time, Hunter's looked the more serious problem, but Byrne suffered the greater damage, recalling later, 'I went in for a tackle with Bobby Collins. He put his foot over the ball and turned his shoulder into me. I'd never broken a collarbone before, so I wasn't aware of what damage had been done straight away. It didn't cross my mind to leave the field and I played on with my arm dangling motionless by my side.'

Byrne hid his discomfort so well that none knew until much later that he had broken his collarbone. Indeed, he played admirably, making the time and space to avoid further damage.

Charlton, Bremner and Storrie all required Les Cocker's attention within ten minutes of the start. Storrie's damaged left ankle rendered him a hobbling passenger on the right wing.

Only once in the first 20 minutes did Leeds threaten. When Bremner released Johanneson, he made some progress and the overlapping Bell won a corner, but Peacock's header was aimless. Bremner's telling pass was a rarity from United's midfield. Most of their contributions were long and aimless, pumped down the middle for the head of Peacock, and easily snuffed out by Yeats. Had his colleagues learned from Bremner's example or Johanneson been more effective with the little possession he enjoyed, Leeds might have fared better.

Rain began falling heavily after 25 minutes, making conditions difficult. There were no goals in a drab first half.

Liverpool dominated after the break and several times went close, forcing Sprake into perpetual action. On occasions the United defence were camped in their own area, Liverpool's slick pass and move game pinning them back for long periods.

Bremner pushed forward in the latter stages, providing fire but no clear-cut openings as Liverpool became tentative. They were content to hold possession as they shifted crablike across the field but fashioned enough chances to have won easily. Surely, Leeds would concede sooner or later?

But they didn't, somehow reaching 90 minutes without a breach; never threatening a goal themselves, they proved a durable nut to crack.

It was the first time since 1947 that extra-time had been necessary, and there was a suspicion that there might be the first replay since 1912, so resolute was Leeds' rearguard.

United kicked off the extra 30 minutes with Bremner leading the attack but their concentration had been disrupted. Stevenson slipped through several tackles as he danced towards the edge of the Leeds area. He slid an incisive through ball to the overlapping Byrne and a clipped cross from the byline was met by a stooping Hunt. 1-0.

Liverpool should have safely seen out time but Leeds then contrived to create their only opening. Hunter launched the ball into the penalty area for Charlton to nod down; the advancing Bremner met the dropping ball perfectly and fired into the open net. Against all expectations, Leeds were back in it.

Liverpool launched several assaults as the second period began. Sprake saved Strong's shot and Hunter volleyed clear when St John got away. Leeds couldn't hold out – after six minutes Liverpool regained the lead.

Smith fed down the right to Callaghan, socks rolled down to his ankles. He rounded Bell, skipped to the byline and centred for the plunging St John to net in fine style.

The exhausted United players had no more to give. Liverpool ran down the minutes comfortably to earn their first FA Cup, sending Leeds home empty-handed.

The team was given an overwhelming reception when they arrived back in Leeds. Thousands were on hand when their train chugged into City Station and 60,000 lined the route to the Civic Hall for a reception in the Banqueting Hall.

Reynolds told the attendees, 'This is only the start. We all hope we will be back at Wembley next year and we will also win the league championship … For years we have struggled. Now we have achieved a little success, but we can do better. Our aim is to top not only the English but European football.'

Leeds had come closer in one year to winning a major trophy than they had in the preceding 45. Collins thoroughly merited his Footballer of the Year award and a recall to the Scotland side after six years in the cold. No player had a bigger influence on his team.

It was difficult to set aside the disappointment of failure but the young men of Leeds United left for their summer holidays in the knowledge that they were now members of football's elite.

Welcome to Europe

'He who wishes to fight must first count the cost.'

2 June 1965: Don Revie hums to himself as he drives the few short miles to Harry Reynolds' house in Bramley to discuss his plans to strengthen the Leeds squad.

The previous day Reynolds spoke to the Evening Post about United's nomination as one of the English representatives in the Inter-Cities Fairs Cup. Revie is determined to give his team every chance to compete effectively.

The club has never experienced anything to match the excitement of the season just ended. Revie hopes for success in the new campaign, though the popular opinion is that Leeds will be one-season wonders.

Reynolds greets Revie warmly and the men quickly settle down to discuss Revie's plans.

'We know our youngsters are the future,' begins Revie, *'and I've been very careful with the cash.'*

'You have that, Don,' beams Reynolds.

'Bobby Collins had a brilliant season, but he's 34 and can't go on for ever. I see John Giles as his long-term replacement, but that will leave us short on the right.'

'What about Greenhoff or Lorimer?'

'I wanted to bring them through slowly. I think we need to get someone in who's ready to do the business.'

'Okay, you're probably right. Who d'you have in mind?'

'I'm thinking of Alan Ball from Blackpool. He's only 20, but he's going to be a star.'

'But ... but he'll cost us a fortune, Don. He's already in the England side and everybody's after him.'

'Yes, I know, but Paul Reaney and Norman Hunter rave about him. You saw what he did against us. He would really make a difference. We can't afford to penny pinch. You get what you pay for and we have to think big. John Charles was thinking big, Alan Peacock was thinking big.'

'I know, I know, but Charles was a mistake. How much do you think he'll cost, Don?'

'Ball's not Charles, he's young and hungry. I'll try to get him for 90, but I might need to go to the ton.'

There is a sharp intake of breath from Reynolds. 'That'll take everything we've got. Are you sure about this?'

'I've never been more certain, Harry, never more certain.'

'I'm not sure how the board will react, Don.'

'If anyone can persuade them, it's you, Harry.'

Reynolds sits back and sips his tea, deep in thought. He is considering how the others will react. Roberts and Woodward may be difficult to budge but Cussins and Morris will lap it up and Bolton and Simon will go with the majority. It seems like an age to Revie before Reynolds speaks.

'Okay, let me see what they say.'

It took Reynolds a good hour to talk his colleagues round but the progress made clinched their support. Another year like the last one would cover the £90,000 that Reynolds requested.

He rang Revie with the good news and the two men agreed that, whatever the board said, if they had to go the extra £10,000, then so be it.

Revie travelled to meet Blackpool manager Ron Suart, suspecting that it would be a hard sell. Suart was unwilling to deal at any price. Revie's famous powers of persuasion could not prompt a change of heart and he skulked back to Yorkshire empty-handed. He was thoroughly downhearted but Roberts and Woodward were openly delighted.

The press got wind of the interest and the newspaper talk unsettled Collins. He was quoted as saying, 'If there is any transfer talk, I would definitely not dismiss the idea of moving on.' Revie reassured Collins, and in the end the Scot relented.

The manager was determined to get his man and sustained a long-term campaign to entice Ball to Leeds. For the moment, he consoled himself with the promise of his young reserves.

Many had been used sparingly, but some were ready to have a bigger say. Indeed, Jimmy Greenhoff was so certain of himself that he asked for a move to get first-team action elsewhere, joining keeper Brian Williamson on the transfer list.

United returned to action with a warning from Revie echoing in their ears. 'Because of that dirty tag given us by the FA and the effect on other teams and their supporters, our players will have to behave, to play like perfect gentlemen this coming season … They must steel themselves against retaliation.'

He also outlined the directors' plans for Elland Road. The idea came from Reynolds, who had been the driving force in setting the aspirational direction when the West Stand was built in 1957. He was determined that the club should have a 'super stadium' in which to play, one befitting his vision of where they aspired to be as a football club.

He had introduced the subject at a board meeting and pushed for a full-scale redevelopment to create a 'home fit for heroes'.

'We are aiming for the stars, chaps,' Reynolds told his colleagues. 'Everything has to be first-class. We have sorted the travel and hotels for the players, we are sorting the team. Now we need to sort the stadium. We cannot have this antiquated cattle shed. It might have been okay before the war, but it's a disgrace in this day and age. We need to think big.'

'But, Harry, how can we afford it?' asked Woodward.

'How can we afford not to? The way we pack them in, one day there'll be a tragedy at Elland Road, mark my words.'

Woodward wasn't convinced, and some of Reynolds' colleagues quailed as he listed the improvements he wanted. Bob Roberts was smirking at the thought of all the additional work his building firm would get out of the development. He should have formally declared his interest then and there and stood aside from any vote, but he was in there arguing on Reynolds' side for a change. Thanks to the force of his personality and the support of Roberts, Reynolds got his way.

Reynolds told the *Evening Post* that there would be a phased plan of improvements over the next decade with the first stage to be completed in 1966. That included turning the pitch round and building a new stand on the site of the present Spion Kop.

The board also discussed the 'hooligan element' and how they could avoid it getting hold. Within the first month of the season there were reports of missiles during the derby against Sheffield

United. Keeper Alan Hodgkinson reported that a bottle had been thrown at him when Leeds were denied a penalty after he caught hold of Lorimer round the waist.

Police went into the crowd to prevent further trouble, ejecting a youth from the ground. In the *Yorkshire Post*, Eric Stanger suggested, 'Someday, somewhere a ground is going to be closed because of the activities of a few hooligans.'

Leeds launched the season with victories against Sunderland and Aston Villa but got their comeuppance when they lost at West Ham. Against the run of play, Peacock scored after 12 minutes, but Leeds were undone by mistakes from Sprake.

The defeat blew away any trace of complacency and Leeds lost just one of their nine September fixtures. The first of those games saw Rod Johnson making Leeds' first ever substitute appearance as he replaced Charlton during the return with Villa.

By the end of the month, United were level on points with Burnley at the top, owing much to the sparkling form of Peacock. Seven goals in 11 appearances saw him recalled by England after three years in the international wilderness.

Peter Lorimer offered Peacock sterling support, while Terry Cooper proved an able deputy for Johanneson and Bell. Their absence gave Paul Madeley his chance and he was at left-back when United made their European debut.

United's fans were delighted when they were drawn against Torino in the first round.

The Italians were under new management: the redoubtable Nereo Rocco had deserted AC Milan after leading them to the European Cup in 1963. He was a renowned coach, the inventor of the legendary Catenaccio formation.

Torino were keen on British imports and Denis Law and Joe Baker had come and gone. Another Brit, Gerry Hitchens, took Rocco's men to third spot in Serie A in 1965. It was Torino's best finish since 1949 and they also reached the semi-final of the Cup Winners' Cup. They were hot favourites to beat Leeds.

Revie's men went into the first leg at Elland Road fresh from victory against Blackburn. They raced into a 3-0 lead within 28 minutes before deciding to close up the game and save their best for Torino. The crowd greedily demanded more and the players were subjected to a slow handclap in the second half. It emanated from only a few, but Revie was livid.

'It greatly upset my players,' he snapped. 'I have never heard anything so unfair about what must be the hardest trying set of players in the league. These are men and boys who in the last three-and-a half years have given Elland Road something to shout about at last.'

The directors increased ticket prices for European games with rises of 2s 6d for stand seats and 1s for standing. Such a move was common among the other English clubs playing in Europe, but supporters bristled at the indignity.

An Italian reporter told Phil Brown that the price increases 'will undoubtedly be markedly cheaper than those that Torino will ask', thought to be about 6s as a minimum.

For all United's lack of familiarity with the subtleties of continental competition, they took to the new challenge like a duck to water.

Revie sent his forwards out with mixed up numbers to confuse the Italians' marking plan – Peacock was at 7, Collins at 8, Cooper at 9, Lorimer at 10 and Giles at 11. The trick was quickly rumbled by the Italians, who resisted United's opening lunges. They could not hold out for long and Bremner opened the scoring after 25 minutes with a speculative curling shot from the left wing.

The Whites continued to press but it was the 48th minute before Peacock doubled the advantage. He had already seen a goal disallowed with the referee ruling the ball had not crossed the line, though Peacock was adamant that it was a good 18 inches over.

Opting to go for a killer third rather than sitting on a 2-0 lead, United's inexperience betrayed them. Orlando pulled a goal back 12 minutes from time.

Nevertheless, Revie was delighted, telling Brown, 'The team has never played better since I became manager. They were splendid in their skill and determination. They had not a thing left when they came in. How they maintained the pace on a poor night and soft pitch I do not know. I would like respectfully to remind our critics and our doubters that seven of last night's

United side were only 22 or under. The experience they gained last night should be most valuable to them.'

The away goals rule had yet to be introduced, so it would take a victory by two clear goals in Turin to put Torino through, but most experts believed their greater experience would tell.

In between legs, Peacock won his first cap for two years, playing alongside Charlton in a goalless draw at Cardiff. Hunter had only been kept out of the game by Alf Ramsey's loyalty to Bobby Moore.

'Without the continued help of such as Les Cocker and Syd Owen I might never have got back to peak fitness,' said Peacock. 'Now I feel better than I've ever felt. I have now got back some of that old edge to my game.'

'I couldn't have been more pleased had I been selected myself,' smiled Revie. 'It is tremendous compensation for the courage and determination which Alan has shown in his fightback to fitness when people were saying he was finished and that we had bought a boner.'

Peacock ploughed a lone furrow in Turin. Openings were scarce as United protected their slim advantage.

Collins was the heartbeat of a fiercely defiant display, but he would not see out the hour.

Norman Hunter recalls, 'I can still remember the tackle that put him out of the game. I saw a big defender coming towards him. Bobby was extremely quick over five to ten yards and he knocked the ball forward and accelerated after it but the big guy didn't pull up. He kept on running and his knee went right into Bobby's thigh. When I got to Bobby, his leg was waving around at the top. It was horrendous.'

Bremner was incensed and the guilty man, left-back Fabrizio Poletti, needed no interpreter as the Scot hissed, 'I'll kill you for this.' Bremner said later, 'That foul was just about the worst I have ever seen. When I realised what had happened, I lost my head completely, and I snarled at the opponent who had felled Bobby. Tears were spilling from my eyes; tears of hot anger and rebellious resentment. I don't imagine that the player knew what I had said, or that he even understood one word; but there was no doubt that he got the message, for he never came within a mile of me during the remainder of the game.'

United's ten men were left to withstand 40 minutes of all-out pressure from one of Europe's best attacks. Substitutes had been introduced in the Football League but were still some way off for European competition. What followed was possibly the greatest rearguard action that Revie's Leeds ever fought.

They played disciplined, controlled football, laying down an ironclad wall across the pitch, denying their opponents time and space and harrying them out of their poise. The absence of Collins seemed merely to reinforce their resolve.

It was one of United's finest half-hours. Torino grew more anxious as they struggled to impose their will. Their football became ragged and the crowd whistled in disapproval as the Leeds tentacles gripped tighter. The Italians could find no chinks in the United armour. Sprake made a couple of decent saves, but his colleagues shielded him from danger.

As the end approached, the Italians' football grew frantic. United came close to snatching a remarkable victory at the death when Bremner burst clear from midfield, beat the defence and saw his shot scrape the post.

The goalless draw sent United into the second round.

It was a memorable evening, and the triumph in adversity proved a turning point in the history of United. Their football, reviled in England, was perfectly designed for the European game and they were generously praised by the Italian press.

For Collins, there was a fear that, as he neared 35, his playing career might be at an end. 'The doctors told me that in 15 days I shall be able to get up and walk freely,' said the Scot. 'In three or four months I should be able gradually to resume training. But I will hardly ever be the same player again.'

Life After Collins

'Just as water retains no constant shape, so in warfare there are no constant conditions.'

Sunday, 10 October 1965: Don Revie is on his way to Harry Reynolds' house to discuss the loss of Bobby Collins.

'It's awfully sad, Don,' says Reynolds, 'but your plan has always been for Giles to take his shirt when Bobby retired.'

'That's not my problem, Harry. I'll do that soon enough, but what do I do to fill John's place on the right? When we didn't get Alan Ball, it scuppered all my plans. I've got to do something.'

'What d'you have in mind, Don?'

The two men spend most of the afternoon engrossed in conversation about Revie's plans.

Shorn of Collins, Revie gave Giles his head as playmaker, thereby creating a midfield partnership with Bremner that would light up the decade that followed.

The *Yorkshire Post*'s Eric Stanger suggested that 'it may be that in light of events they will have to go into the market and get a top-class replacement for Collins.' He hinted that Revie might renew his quest for Alan Ball.

'It was often said that Don Revie had it in his mind to groom me for Bobby Collins' midfield role when he bought me,' recalls Giles. 'I took it for granted that I would be switched to inside-left but it was not to be. Rod Johnson was drafted into Collins' position for the league match at Sheffield Wednesday four days later and kept his place for the following game against West Bromwich Albion in the League Cup. I was bitterly disappointed, and after brooding over the matter for a few days I decided to have a heart-to-heart chat with the Boss. Our conversation lasted little more than 30 seconds, for as I stepped into his office he looked up, grinned knowingly, and said, "I know what you've come for. You'll be pleased to know that I've put you down at inside-forward against Northampton on Saturday!" I don't think I have ever been as determined to put up a good show in a match as I was in that one. Luckily, the other Leeds players made it easy for me ... Whenever I received the ball there was always a colleague in a perfect position to receive a pass.'

United's style was transformed, with Giles' creativity emphasising their elegant side and slowing down the hurry scurry. It brought difficulties for Jim Storrie. 'My game was based on speed off the mark – the ability to lose a defender for a split second, or so. Bobby's style of play suited me because as I ran into an open space, I knew he would immediately put the ball into my path, no matter what position he was in. Johnny, however, liked to hold the ball more, so I was often caught in two minds, whether to run forward to receive a pass or move to the side so he could play a one-two off me.'

It took a while for Bremner and Giles to gel properly but by January, *The Times* was moved to remark, 'The two are now linking with the panache of Bremner and Collins, but with a difference. Collins tended to dominate his attack and to mark him tightly was to upset his team. Giles relies more on clever positioning, giving expression to his forwards rather than dictating their lines.'

The two men had contrasting approaches. Peter Lorimer recalled, 'Johnny was our brains and organiser. He kept us together as a team. Billy was totally different and undisciplined in the respect that he would tear about all over the pitch believing, "There is only me who can get us out of trouble."'

To fill the void on the right, Revie settled on Huddersfield wide man Mike O'Grady. On 13 October Revie made the 20-mile trip across the West Riding to sign O'Grady for £30,000.

The Leeds-born winger scored twice on his England debut in 1962, before illness forced him out of the next match, after which he slipped out of the picture.

He was a winger of the traditional school, though at 5ft 10in he was taller than the stereotypical outside man. He could play on either flank and had the happy knack of being able to drift in off the wing to contribute the odd goal, mostly with powerful drives from the edge of the area.

Andrew Mourant: 'In full flight, Mike O'Grady cut an impressive figure ... O'Grady had a great appetite for taking on defenders and would obey instincts to do so even if sometimes it meant losing the ball. It was not his way to search round for a team-mate to pass to, having run out of nerve or imagination. Mike O'Grady could be as potent a winger as any when fuelled with such self-belief. He would play with the attitude that no one was good enough to take the ball off him and was sometimes frustrated by Don Revie's strictures on the need for caution when … the opposition was there to be taken apart.'

Don Weston, transfer-listed at his own request, made the reverse trip, quitting United for Leeds Road.

O'Grady debuted against bottom club Northampton with Giles at No 10. Leeds won at a canter, 6-1, equalling their best in the division since hammering Leicester City 8-2 in 1938. It was reported that 'Giles was an instant success in Collins' berth at inside-left,' though Bremner's afternoon was even more memorable, heading the equaliser after a shock opener from the Cobblers but going on to receive his fourth caution of a still fledgling season.

Bremner was in constant trouble with officials and Revie pleaded with referee Ray Tinkler not to record the caution.

Revie admitted his transgression and the FA's disciplinary committee considered the matter on 19 January. Revie was ordered to give an undertaking not to repeat such a request.

An unchanged side took the field at Stoke a week later and won 2-1 to reclaim leadership of the First Division.

Stoke City were functional opponents, but Burnley, who United faced at Elland Road on 30 October, were title challengers, a tasty team packed with potential match-winners.

Revie was in hospital with appendicitis. In his absence, Leeds were led by Syd Owen. Weeks later, to relieve some of the pressure on Revie, the directors promoted Maurice Lindley to assistant manager.

Many were mystified that it was Lindley rather than Owen who became Revie's right-hand man.

Revie missed a splendid contest, fought out by two well-matched teams. Phil Brown described Burnley as 'the best side at Elland Road this season by far'.

United took the lead after 47 minutes when O'Grady outpaced full-back John Angus to pull the ball back into the centre. Storrie slammed it in off the post.

The lead lasted barely 30 seconds before Burnley equalised with a goal which 'will be remembered at Elland Road for many a day', according to Eric Stanger. 'Morgan swung over a centre which Irvine headed down without any great power and Sprake was left to collect a rolling ball rather than make a save in the accepted sense. Unhappily for Leeds he committed two cardinal sins – he took his eye off the ball and when it slipped through his hands was caught with his legs wide apart. A fourth-form schoolboy would have got a roasting from his games master for such elementary error. Unhappily, Sprake, though a super saver of a shot, remains prone to these sorts of slip and until he can eliminate them he will not be the complete goalkeeper.'

Despite bombarding Burnley, United were outmanoeuvred by the Lancastrians and dropped a point.

Icy weather resulted in postponed games against Manchester United and Newcastle. After Liverpool's win at Stamford Bridge on 4 December, the Reds led the table with 29 points, six clear of Leeds.

The spell was not totally barren with United meeting Leipzig in the Inter-Cities Fairs Cup.

There had been six inches of snow overnight, but there was never any question of the match being called off. The ground staff packed the snow and marked blue lines on it and an orange ball was used to aid visibility. Revie ordered his staff to shave the bottom layer off the players' rubber studs, with the exposed nails improving grip on the ice. Cardboard tips were applied to hide the nails while the boots were checked. The players kicked off the cardboard as they came onto the pitch. Within minutes blood was oozing from the East Germans' legs. Their furious complaints were waved away by a referee who insisted that he had already checked the boots.

There were no goals until the final ten minutes, when a low shot from Lorimer and a header from Bremner gave Leeds a comfortable two-goal advantage. Frenzel almost immediately got a consolation goal with a deflected effort, but United emerged with a priceless 2-1 victory.

A week later, the teams met again on another snow-covered pitch. Leipzig played above themselves, causing several scares, but there were no goals and Leeds were through.

United's league fixture backlog was up to three, prompting fears of congestion. Leeds faced a hard slog in the New Year, though the season had been extended to the end of May, thanks to the hosting of the World Cup finals. The extension offered some leeway.

Not everyone was kicking their heels. During the week that followed, Norman Hunter won his first full England cap.

He had been reserve for the side that played Hungary in May but had to withdraw because of a knee injury sustained in the Cup final.

Hunter's first appearance created history as he became the first England player to make his debut as a substitute. It came in a friendly against reigning European champions Spain in Real Madrid's Bernabeu Stadium.

The game marked the introduction of Alf Ramsey's 'wingless wonders'. It confused the Spaniards, their full-backs left with no one to mark. England took an early lead through Joe Baker. Hunter came on to join Jack Charlton but was deployed in midfield to free up Bobby Charlton and Alan Ball for more attacking roles. England continued to dominate but could add only one more goal.

Leeds stormed back into action on 11 December, hammering third-placed West Bromwich Albion 4-0. Giles (2), O'Grady and Storrie got the goals, but it was a superb team effort, prompted by Giles and Bremner.

Then came the frustration of another postponement, away to struggling Northampton – Leeds now had four games in hand.

'Northampton were willing to play and so were we,' said a frustrated Don Revie. 'I feel that where the desire of both clubs is to play then the referee should let the match go on.'

Christmas week brought a double header against Liverpool. It was a summit to savour, which could make or break United's season. Two defeats and Leeds' challenge would be dead in the water, while maximum points would build momentum.

Leeds were on defence for fully three-quarters of the Anfield clash but were always dangerous on the counter-attack. One such break brought the only goal. From a Storrie centre, Reaney forced goalkeeper Lawrence to parry and Lorimer netted the loose ball.

The points gap down to five, optimism was high, but Leeds fell for Liverpool's own counter-attacking game at Elland Road. Milne's goal in the 48th minute was enough for the Merseysiders to earn their revenge.

United could have been excused if their challenge had wilted, but, with 17-year-old wing-half Eddie Gray slamming home a 25-yard shot in his debut, they stormed back to win 3-0 on New Year's Day against Sheffield Wednesday. They followed up with victory at West Brom, before dropping points in home draws with Manchester United and Stoke City.

The FA Cup brought an easy 6-0 win against Bury before a league defeat at Sunderland, during which United lost Peacock with damaged knee ligaments. Despite hopes that he might miss three weeks, Peacock's season was over. In fact, dodgy knees would restrict his Elland Road career to nine more games.

Their season in the balance, United entered February with a Fairs Cup-tie against Spanish giants Valencia, winners of the trophy in 1962 and 1963.

Revie knew he faced a battle but hardly anticipated the full ferocity of the encounter.

Leeds dominated the opening half of the first leg at Elland Road but could not find their normal rhythm and struggled to make headway. Young Belfitt looked out of his depth up front. They failed to carve out a clear-cut opening.

Valencia were a knowing and cynical force, their possession football, spoiling tactics and heavy tackling disrupting United's play. They were far less wasteful of the possession they had and took the lead after 16 minutes, exploiting a misunderstanding in the Leeds defence. After pushing forward in numbers, the Whites were caught short at the back and Hunter and Reaney each left things to the other when a speculative long ball dropped into their half. There was no such hesitation from left winger Munoz and he was on the ball in a flash, rounding Sprake with a deft swerve to slip the ball home.

Content with a 1-0 lead, Valencia pulled everyone back, allowing United's frenetic assaults to crash against a wall of red shirts, packed in and around their own penalty area.

In charge was Leo Horn, a renowned Dutch official, who offered the Spaniards enormous latitude. They exploited Horn's tolerance. *The Times*: 'Mr Horn called up Roberto, the Valencia captain, after Mestre had made one scything late tackle on Bremner, very much a target for the Spaniards. What the referee said to Roberto made little difference. Valencia still piled in, and Leeds were not slow to respond.'

If the referee had been stricter, the match might not have developed as it did. Leeds were no angels but Valencia's tactics smacked more of the bullring than the football field.

'They were the roughest continental side I have ever seen,' reported Eric Stanger. 'They never hesitated to bring down the man when they could not get the ball, and they had no need to resort to such tactics, for in the few flashes of football there were they seemed themselves to be a clever, resourceful side ... Leeds were never afraid to give as good as they got, but they would have done better not to have tried to mix it quite so much ... for Valencia were just as strong as they were.'

The game restarted peacefully after the interval but things soon heated up as Vidagany flattened Bremner when he tried to make space on the right. The referee beckoned the Valencia captain for another warning but took no further action.

United finally developed some momentum and fashioned an equaliser when Lorimer drove home a Giles cross.

That was the prelude to the evening's descent into chaos, as recalled by Jack Charlton.

'15 minutes to go, and I raced upfield to add my weight to one of our attacks. As I challenged an opponent in the Valencia penalty area, I was kicked ... Before I knew where I was, I found myself having to take much more ... One of my opponents slung a punch which would have done credit to Cassius Clay. Right there and then my anger boiled over ... I chased around that penalty area, intent upon only one thing – getting my own back. I had completely lost control of myself ... Neither the Spaniards nor the restraining hands of my team-mates could prevent my pursuit for vengeance. Suddenly players seemed to be pushing and jostling each other everywhere. Police appeared on the field to stop this game of football from degenerating into a running battle. And Leo Horn walked off with his linesmen, signalling to club officials of both teams to get their players off, too. I was still breathing fire when I reached the dressing room – then I got the word that I need not go back. For a moment I thought the referee had called off the match ... Then it sank home that it was only Jackie Charlton's presence which was not required any longer. For 11 minutes the teams remained off the field, to allow tempers on both sides to cool down. By that time, I was beginning to feel sorry for myself, and not a little ashamed of the way I had lost my temper. The only consolation I had was that ... Vidagany had been told he need not return to the fray, either.'

The conflict continued to simmer. Seven minutes from the end, Valencia inside-forward Sanchez-Lage was dismissed after felling Jim Storrie. That finally calmed the atmosphere.

In the last quarter of an hour, either side might have gained a precious lead with Sprake having to stretch to tip Guillot's header over the bar and Bremner missing narrowly with a header at the death. In the end, the draw was about right.

The controversy rumbled on; Leo Horn claimed Leeds were on a £1,500 bonus to win. 'Money was the cause of the trouble ... I was reminded of South American cup finals I have taken, where players were on a bonus of $3,000 ... These games have become too important for the players. When Leeds lost a goal this nervousness spread ... I understand professional players, but they have changed. Money has made them too eager ... I have always regarded Charlton as a fine man. He was the cleanest player on the field, until he lost all control. I saw a Spanish defender kick him, and if Charlton had given a reprisal kick, I could have understood it and let it pass, because it happens so often. As captain of Leeds, and an international, he should have been the first player to exercise complete self-control.'

Horn accused Don Revie of asking him to let Charlton off, saying, 'Do you know what you are doing? This is an international.' Horn replied, 'Do you think this is the first time I have refereed a game? I don't care if Charlton is an emperor, he is not coming back on the field tonight.'

'Valencia didn't play football, they waged a war,' stormed Revie. 'It may take two teams to start a fight on the field, but at the same time it is a brave man who would not retaliate after being constantly kicked, shoved and body-checked. The Leeds players became frustrated and angry, not because Valencia scored first, but because of their niggling tactics. No player on earth would have kept his temper amid some of the things that were happening.'

The papers focused on the fisticuffs and there were calls for United to be thrown out of the competition and Charlton given a lengthy ban.

The Fairs Cup committee delayed their response, choosing to meet the day after the second leg. It was public knowledge that they would have observers present for the game in Spain and that behaviour there would colour their final judgement. They had already banned Roma for three years after crowd trouble and were ready to impose strict sanctions.

Horn was criticised for slackness. He had hoped to take the World Cup final but kissed goodbye to that hope. Switzerland's Othmar Huber took his place for the second leg. From the start Huber punished the slightest indiscretion and his fussy approach did the trick.

Despite sporting the No 9 shirt, Paul Madeley played deep, shielding the back four. Storrie, Lorimer and O'Grady shuttled between attack and midfield in a flexible formation that Revie had been using between legs. Shorn of Peacock, Leeds happened upon the perfect counter-attacking formation, with defenders as likely to pop up in the opposition penalty area as in their own. This was Revie's first great United side.

United set their defensive stall out in sweltering conditions, June-like in February. They gave a stereotypical stonewall display with Charlton at its heart. They were content to play on the counter and 15 minutes from the end took the lead from a break. Madeley freed O'Grady on the edge of the area with a 30-yard ball. Valencia clearly thought he was offside and pulled up, allowing the winger to pick his spot and fire a low cross shot into the net.

It was Valencia's turn to be incensed when their appeals were rejected. Goalkeeper Nito and left-back Toto were outraged. They jostled the linesman for not flagging and tore the flag from his hand. Nito made little attempt to save the shot but was more active in manhandling the linesman. His team-mates mobbed the referee, persuading him to consult his colleague. It made no difference – the goal stood.

Leeds hung on grimly for the victory that secured passage into the last eight.

The Fairs Cup committee declined to take any disciplinary action, with Sir Stanley Rous noting, 'The match last night was a model of good football. As far as the Fairs Cup is concerned, both clubs have exonerated themselves. If either qualify again, they will be welcome.'

Charlton was fined £50, with £30 costs, at an FA disciplinary hearing two months later but no Spanish player suffered any sanction.

Leeds struck a rich vein of form, thrashing West Ham 5-0 and turning in one of their best performances of the season in the FA Cup at Chelsea. They lost 1-0, but totally dominated the contest.

Leeds then triumphed 4-0 at Nottingham Forest, building on a goal from 18-year-old debutant Terry Hibbitt. When Madeley sustained knee ligament damage, Revie opted to restore Storrie to the role of spearhead, with Terry Cooper recalled on the wing as United drew 1-1 at Sheffield United on 26 February. Liverpool's defeat at bottom club Fulham, their first league reverse of 1966, saw the gap at the top shrink a little.

Thoughts swung back to Europe and a quarter-final with Hungary's Ujpest Dosza.

United were no respecter of reputations and blitzed Ujpest on a mud bath of a surface. Despite the presence of two world-class forwards in Ferenc Bene and Janos Gorocs, the Whites hammered Ujpest. It was not so much a victory as a rout.

Heavy rain from five o'clock left the ground waterlogged. The referee declared it playable, enraging the Hungarians, who were unused to such conditions.

Leeds pushed hard for a breakthrough and got it after six minutes. The Ujpest goalkeeper parried Bell's drive from the left and Cooper bundled home the loose ball. In the last ten minutes of the prolonged first half, Leeds made victory certain with further goals from Bell, Storrie and Bremner.

The Hungarians stormed back and Dunai netted a rebound in the 74th minute when Sprake spilled an effort. However, the 4-1 score made the outcome of the tie a foregone conclusion.

United lurched from the sublime to the ridiculous, stumbling to an inexplicable defeat at lowly Northampton. They put together back-to-back victories against Leicester and Blackburn, but then suffered two defeats in as many days against struggling Blackpool. If United's championship hopes were not quite extinguished, they were as good as over.

United improved their position with wins at home to Chelsea and away to Fulham on Good Friday but crashed 1-0 to the Cottagers at Elland Road on Easter Tuesday. Liverpool suffered their own blip with two successive draws, but even though Leeds hammered Everton 4-1 on 16 April, the Reds' win against Stoke City secured the title. Their triumph was not mathematically certain, but it would have taken an astonishing chain of events to deny them.

A draw in Budapest against Ujpest secured United's place in the last four of the Fairs Cup where they would face Spain's Real Zaragoza, winners of the trophy in 1964. They were a wonderful side, spearheaded by their 'Magnificent Five' – Canario, Santos, Marcellino, Villa, Lapetra. The first leg took place in Spain on 20 April.

Revie set out to contain his opponents. O'Grady's strained thigh kept him out of the game and Revie rested Lorimer, drafting in Greenhoff and Gray. He used Storrie as lone striker with the fit again Johanneson on the left. Sprake and Charlton enjoyed outstanding performances and were rallying points for a steadfast defensive display.

Around the hour, Zaragoza took the lead when the referee awarded a penalty for Bremner's handball. Lapetra's spot kick was placed to Sprake's left. The keeper anticipated the direction and got his hands to the ball but it trickled in off the post.

That was the only goal of a frantic game that ended with Giles and Violeta taking early baths.

The second leg provided another wonderful display as Leeds proved how perfectly equipped they were for the European game. Surely they had no chance of surviving on a firm pitch designed for the style of the Spaniards! Three times in the first 20 minutes Santos came close to extending Real's advantage.

Bremner pushed forward and after 23 minutes transformed the complexion of the tie. Hunter received the ball just inside the Spanish half and fed the overlapping Bell, whose square pass found Giles. His chip was nodded down by Charlton and the onrushing Johanneson and Bremner forced the ball home.

Canario half-volleyed Real back into the aggregate lead but as the game ticked into its final 30, Charlton headed home from Hunter's cross to level matters.

Captain Jack, who gave a peerless display, called correctly at the toss to decide which team would enjoy home advantage in the play-off. Revie leapt to embrace his skipper and United spirits soared. They felt that home advantage must tell.

Back in the league, Leeds beat Newcastle 3-0 while Liverpool saw off Chelsea to formally confirm their championship. Winning 19 of their previous 28 games, they had looked certain champions since January.

There was still second place to chase. United were hot on the heels of incumbents Burnley, trailing by three points but with two games in hand. They made no mistake with the first, winning 3-0 at Arsenal. The game was witnessed by only 4,544 spectators, clashing as it did with the televising of the Cup Winners' Cup final – it was Arsenal's lowest crowd since they moved to Highbury in 1913.

The victory narrowed the gap to a single point and the weekend brought Leeds and Burnley together for a decisive confrontation at Turf Moor.

With so much at stake, it was inevitable that there would be fireworks. It was no surprise that the first 45 minutes brought 21 fouls. After a clash early in the second half left Storrie and Willie Morgan writhing on the floor, referee Jennings called all 22 players together for a lecture. The mood heightened again when Leeds took the lead on the hour.

Storrie chased down Alex Elder on the touchline. The defender could have turned the ball out easily enough but attempted to find keeper Adam Blacklaw with a lofted pass. The custodian had come off his line and watched helplessly as the ball sailed into the open net.

The incident sapped Burnley morale and United had the best of the final 30 minutes to emerge with the points.

The victory put Revie and his men in great heart for the showdown with Zaragoza on 11 May. The directors gave a further boost by announcing they planned a £750,000 ground improvement scheme and there was hot newspaper speculation that Leeds had reactivated their pursuit of Alan Ball.

The devious Revie, mindful of earlier European triumphs in the Elland Road mud, decided on some insurance. Assuming the Spaniards would struggle on heavy ground, Revie persuaded the fire brigade to soak the pitch for hours beforehand. The move backfired spectacularly with the Spaniards appearing to relish playing in the mud.

They stroked the ball around with assurance and took the lead inside the first minute. Villa tricked Bell, Hunter and O'Grady before sending over a driven cross which Canario helped on to Marcellino, who scored at the back post.

Before Leeds could recover, they were two down, Villa scoring with the defence all over the place. After 14 minutes it was 3-0. Sprake was at fault when a 25-yard swerving shot from Santos flew past him. Unsighted he may have been, but he was certainly flat-footed as the ball found the net.

Shell-shocked by the opening salvo, United never looked like recovering. Greenhoff limped off with an ankle injury after 22 minutes and remained on the sidelines for a quarter of an hour, a passenger when he did return, eventually retiring altogether with 20 to go.

Zaragoza slackened the pace and settled for keeping ten-man Leeds at a safe arm's length. Charlton and Bell were thrown forward in a desperate attempt to save the game, and Big Jack managed to net a consolation goal with a low shot after 80 minutes, but it was nowhere near enough.

A marvellous adventure was over but there was the runners-up spot in the First Division still to secure.

Burnley's victory at Wednesday took them a point clear but their season was done. Leeds required one point from two games to secure second place.

The 2-0 defeat at Newcastle on 16 May heightened the stakes for the final game of the season, three days later at Old Trafford. Leeds recalled Bobby Collins.

Chelsea's defeat at home to Aston Villa left Man United needing only a draw to replace the Blues in fourth and give themselves a chance of qualifying for the Fairs Cup.

Both teams were disrupted by England's World Cup preparations. Alf Ramsey rejected the pleas of Revie and Matt Busby to release the Charlton brothers, Norman Hunter and Nobby Stiles from preparations for a tour of Europe in June.

Revie's selection against Manchester was bizarre, with Bremner as sweeper, Greenhoff at left-back, Bell at centre-half and O'Grady at left-half. Collins was restored amidst the chaos, despite having played two games in four days.

Terry Lofthouse in the *Evening Post*: 'The most interesting aspect was the return of Collins, who with Giles forged a fascinating partnership as dual schemers. He came back with all his old skill, canny ball distribution and confidence. The fact that the match was played in such an easy manner helped him to ease back into the swing of things. It was the Master (the Leeds fans' accolade) who provided the pass to Storrie from which Reaney scored with one of the finest headers I've seen.'

The goal restored equality, cancelling out Manchester's opener. Hearts were in mouths when David Herd gave the home side the lead.

There were suspicions that both sides were happy to play for the draw that gave them both European qualification.

'Don't take any notice, Don, people will always moan about these things,' Reynolds told Revie at the finish.

'It doesn't bother me, Harry, they can say what they bloody want. It wasn't tonight that settled things, it was the previous nine months.'

Revie and Reynolds celebrated a second successive runners-up placing with the season marking the transition from 'up and coming' to 'pre-eminent' for Leeds United.

In Need of a Cutting Edge

'Bravery without forethought, causes a man to fight blindly and desperately like a mad bull.'

1966: Moods across the United Kingdom are contrasting sharply.

Manchester has a sombre air with Moors murderers Ian Brady and Myra Hindley sentenced to life imprisonment for serial infanticide while South Wales mourns the loss of 116 children and 28 adults in October's Aberfan disaster.

Merseyside revels in its dominance of English football with the capture of both league title and FA Cup and Ray Wilson and Roger Hunt lifting the World Cup. London's East End does even better with three West Ham lads in the England side.

Swinging London parties for all it is worth; Twiggy, Carnaby Street and the miniskirt mark the city as a fashion hotspot while the Who, the Kinks, the Small Faces and the Rolling Stones threaten the Beatles' dominance.

Sectarian tensions grip Ireland with the IRA obliterating Nelson's Pillar in Dublin to mark the 50th anniversary of the Easter Rising and the re-established UVF launching its campaign in Belfast.

Johnny Speight's Till Death Us Do Part, set in London's East End, parodies the bigotry and racism which hold sway across the country; a BBC documentary, Smethwick: A Straw in the Wind, captures Birmingham barbers refusing to let immigrants into their salons while landlords refuse to let houses to them. 'They should live in a district by themselves. They're not clean,' one young mother tells the crew while a man complains, 'They're a nuisance when you've got to walk past them in the street, they won't move. They're a nuisance.'

The entire nation (outside Scotland) was united in joy by England's World Cup win. It was a once-in-a-lifetime moment and the involvement of Jack Charlton, Norman Hunter and Les Cocker in Alf Ramsey's triumph allowed Leeds United to bask in the reflected glory. Paul Reaney was included in the provisional list of 40 but missed out on the final selection.

Don Revie sought to enhance the association by pursuing another World Cup man. For more than a year, he sought to persuade Alan Ball that his future lay in Leeds.

Ball claimed that Revie slipped him sweeteners to influence his decision. He kept the secret from both his father and Blackpool manager Ron Suart and said he felt uncomfortable with the whole affair, although he kept the £300 proffered.

It had been obvious for some time that Blackpool would struggle to hold on to their prize asset with a clutch of predatory clubs in dogged pursuit. They had done so in 1965 despite a big-money bid from Revie but Blackpool's directors bowed to the inevitable and agreed to sell. Suart, revealing that Everton and Leeds both met the record asking price of £110,000, left the final choice to Ball.

Revie got wind of Everton's interest and tried desperately to convince Ball but got nowhere. He described the failure as one of his greatest disappointments as a manager.

Harry Reynolds confirmed that the Leeds directors had been happy to bankroll Revie's sortie into the transfer market. 'My board and I have never for a moment lost sight of the fact that what Leeds need first is a good, successful and well-founded team, and we stick to that.'

The outcome Revie feared for weeks was confirmed on 15 August when Ball opted for Everton. He had to amend his plans for the new season, his only involvement in the transfer market the £9,000 sale of Ian Lawson to Crystal Palace.

Responding to a 'team before ground?' enquiry from Phil Brown of the *Yorkshire Evening Post*, Reynolds confirmed that the redevelopment of the stadium was 'now inevitably somewhat clouded over by the national economic situation'.

The incoming Labour government had introduced the Building Control Act, which prioritised housing construction and made the outlook for other projects uncertain with a six-month wage and price freeze.

Reynolds confirmed that broad plans had been submitted to the various authorities, but that the board was concerned about raising the funds, even if building wasn't postponed by legislation. 'The national financial and economic situation has altered matters a great deal, apart from building restrictions. At present we just do not know when we can start.'

The plans had been adapted, but the intention was still for incremental, long-term improvement.

'The revised plan ... will not satisfy those who were hoping for a new stadium which would hold 70,000,' reported the *Evening Post*'s Terry Lofthouse. 'They have decided not to turn the pitch round. Instead they are to concentrate on remodelling the Kop, the Scratching Shed and the Lowfields Road stand side.'

According to Reynolds, the original plan would have cost almost £1m. While the new scheme would cost £230,000 less, 'there will be no change in attitude towards providing first-class amenities. Covered accommodation all round is the major move.' Reynolds envisaged a capacity of 50,000, with a minimum of 17,000 seats.

'This is sound policy,' noted Lofthouse. 'How many times would there have been a 70,000 crowd?'

After his pursuit of Ball proved fruitless, Revie recalled Bobby Collins, ranging him alongside Giles and Bremner in midfield. Giles had slotted smoothly into Collins' playmaker role and there was conjecture as to how the two could be accommodated without disturbing the overall shape.

After a friendly against a Glasgow Select XI in August, the press declared the combination ineffective. The *Yorkshire Post*'s Eric Stanger reported, 'I doubt whether the Leeds manager will finally settle for this combination. Collins and Giles are of a muchness in style, and at times they were liable to slow down operations in midfield.'

There were other concerns. The forward line lacked cutting edge and the hamstring strain suffered by Charlton was the first setback of an injury-ravaged campaign. Big Jack swelled the numbers in the treatment room and missed the opening game, away to Spurs.

Spurs' starting XI cost half a million and the club branded the country's wealthiest was tipped for a title push.

On a sweltering day, tempers boiled over in the opening minutes. The troubled centred on Dave Mackay and Bremner,

Scotland squad mates but now at each other's throats. Mackay went in unfairly on Bremner, who kicked back hard in retaliation. Mackay lost it and took the law into his own hands. The moment was captured for posterity, creating an iconic image of football in the 1960s: an enraged Mackay strides angrily over to Bremner, hoists him by his collar and prepares to give him what for, 'like Desperate Dan on steroids'.

Two years earlier, Mackay had broken the same leg for the second time within twelve months. Bremner's assault on the vulnerable area enraged Mackay, who said later, 'He could easily have broken my leg for a third time. I lost my rag and was temporarily capable of breaking his neck in return. Our faces almost touched as his legs dangled in the air.'

Referee Norman Burtenshaw lectured both men, but booked neither, merely awarding a free kick to United. Seconds later the two men clashed again as Mackay scythed Bremner down, but the incident brought the teams to their senses.

Giles, limping from an injury sustained in the first minute, nodded a low centre from Collins in off the post to give Leeds the lead. They were forced back into their shells by some concerted Tottenham raids and Mullery equalised after 27 minutes when Leeds failed to clear properly.

Giles was replaced by Cooper at the break and while Leeds were still sorting themselves out, Spurs went ahead, Gilzean heading home a Mullery cross that Sprake could and should have dealt with.

United responded manfully, with Collins' snapshot coming back off the bar. The restored skipper was in fine form, as reported by *The Sun*'s Peter Lorenzo. 'On a day when most came to applaud the £585,019 skills of Spurs, they were caught in mid-cheer and left to marvel at the stamina, snappy aggression and superb skills of Collins, a pocket-sized dynamo, a player small in everything but heart and ability.'

Tottenham took both control and a 3-1 lead after 61 minutes when Greaves' shot on the run beat Sprake. Greaves and Venables both struck the woodwork, but there was no further score. It was United's first opening-day defeat for six years.

Giles recovered to face West Brom four days later and he and Collins dominated affairs after Bell gave Leeds an early lead.

Giles added a second after 27 minutes but lack of precision and cool heads up front saw United waste countless opportunities and Jeff Astle pulled a goal back.

Collins was forced off at half-time with an ankle injury which kept him on the sidelines for several weeks. With him went United's dominance and they paid for their dallying, left hanging on in the second period. The two points were welcome and they added two more from a 3-1 victory against Manchester United as they got their season up and running.

There was no denying that the dominance and steamroller momentum of previous campaigns was missing – Leeds won just once in the next eight league games and a 3-0 defeat at Aston Villa on 8 October left them 13th.

The game did have a positive feature in marking Jack Charlton's 400th league appearance, thus making him the fifth Leeds player to reach that milestone, but he was struggling to find his World Cup form.

United had yet to field the same team in consecutive games and had already tried five different centre-forwards – Belfitt, Lorimer, Madeley, Peacock and Gray. The versatile Madeley was the only one who had netted; Giles was top scorer and two of his four had come from the penalty spot.

A burgeoning injury list and the lack of a proven goalscorer forced Revie to rely on reserves in nearly every game. When United drew with Burnley in September, the forward line included 21-year-old Madeley, Lorimer (19), Bates and Gray (both 18). The youngsters had proven their worth but Revie was resigned to going into the transfer market with Peacock struggling to recover from the effects of a summer knee operation. He had played just two league games since January.

Many expected Revie to sign a forward in the summer, but he wanted to give Peacock every chance to recover. The shortcomings in front of goal forced his hand and he put out the feelers for a proven hit man. Leeds were linked with big money moves for Aston Villa's Tony Hateley, Bolton's Wyn Davies and Norwich's Ron Davies. They came close to signing Hateley, but Revie baulked at the asking price.

He reiterated his commitment to developing homegrown talent, insisting that he would not buy big, 'I have no regrets about not getting Hateley, not at £100,000. I should not have served United well by having them pay a fee like that.'

He claimed that he had no objection in principle to inflated fees 'but there is a right price and a wrong price for every player.'

Reynolds echoed his words, reminding 'these people who blithely ask us to throw big money around that compared with several clubs we are still a long way from being rich.'

Both men reflected that a move into the market would hold back the younger players. Revie settled for the promise of Jimmy Greenhoff, who had done enough to convince that he was worth persevering with.

Greenhoff wasn't an immediate success, although he topped off the scoring in a 3-1 victory away to DWS Amsterdam when United kicked off their Fairs Cup campaign.

In the Elland Road return, Albert Johanneson netted a hat-trick in a 5-1 win. It was the highlight of an inconsistent season for the South African, who missed almost half the games. His was a typical experience as player after player succumbed to knocks and bruises.

Charlton's first goal of the season secured victory at Arsenal on 5 November. United were working their way up the table and had made it through to the fourth round of the League Cup where they faced a difficult trip to West Ham.

'Difficult' was the understatement of the decade; the Hammers blew United to the four winds. Two days earlier they had put six past Fulham and they carried on where they left off. They were irresistible, romping to a 7-0 victory.

The last time Leeds had conceded seven goals in a game was February 1929 when the self-same West Ham won 8-2.

It was a nightmare for David Harvey, making a rare appearance between the posts. *The Times* reported, 'He played bravely and at times brilliantly … his nerves must have been shattered by the sight of men like Charlton, Hunter, Bremner and Reaney being taunted mercilessly.'

Young Johnny Sissons played the game of his life, grabbing a hat-trick in the first half-hour. Geoff Hurst also scored three, but Johnny Byrne, 'Britain's Di Stefano', was man of the match. He didn't score but figured in five of the goals.

Revie paid the price for maintaining the formational switch he used against Arsenal. He used Bell in a man-marking role while Hunter switched to left-back, where he was tormented by flying winger Peter Brabrook.

Revie was not best pleased, though the result seemed a mere blip when two goals by Giles and a third from Greenhoff brought victory against Leicester. Leeds went to Anfield on 19 November in good spirits to face third-placed Liverpool.

Lightning struck twice – Leeds were blitzed 5-0. It was never as clear-cut as the scoreline suggested; three goals in the final 15 minutes gave the scoreline an unrealistic look.

There were fears that United's rise to prominence was built on sand. There was speculation that the Elland Road edifice was about to crumble, the *Yorkshire Post*'s Eric Stanger pondering whether United were 'about to sink into the mediocrity which all too often has been their lot'.

He reported that 'United's current weaknesses' had been 'ruthlessly exposed ... There has been a suspicion that the defence which has carried them so far is not as tight as it was ... In midfield there have been several games ... when the Leeds passing has been too slow, the build-up altogether too laboured with an over emphasis on playing the ball back in order eventually to go forward'.

United gained retribution for their Upton Park disaster when they beat West Ham on 26 November, though it was 83 minutes before Giles scored the decisive goal.

Collins was recalled for the trip to Sheffield Wednesday but the game ended goalless. Even the visit of Blackpool, adrift at the foot of the table, brought no solace. The Seasiders were down to ten men yet came away with a 1-1 draw.

There were searching questions at the club's annual general meeting on 12 December.

'We are improving and intend to carry on with the progress we have already made,' insisted Reynolds. They had tried to buy 'but the position is the same as if anyone came for our players. They would get the same answer as we have received – we don't want to sell.'

Revie conceded that 'we have just not clicked so far', citing injuries to experienced players. He was clear that the younger players needed old heads around them.

Stanger agreed that some of the youngsters would come through in the long term, though none of them were yet oven ready. United might have to 'settle for a transitional period and be content with a safe but unexciting place in the table'.

On a happier note, Reynolds announced that a profit of £59,028 had taken the club out of debt for the first time in its history. Three years previously the club was £250,000 in the red. Reynolds beamed, 'It is very nice to be straight across at the bank, after all these years. People think we are rolling in money, and forget we had large debts from years back to shift. We are doing all right as football clubs go in these days of increased charges for almost everything, but ... we are only breaking even as we go along.' The club needed average gates of 38,000 to balance the books.

As December drew on, United got their act together, beating Tottenham and pulling off a double against Newcastle, 2-1 at St James' Park on Christmas Eve and then 5-0 on Boxing Day.

Collins excelled on Tyneside but was out injured when United hammered the Magpies. Bremner, captain in his absence, led the rout, ably supported by Gray, O'Grady and Cooper. The 40,000 crowd revelled in the improvement and celebrated Leeds' return to title contention. They had sneaked their way quietly up from 13th at the beginning of October to sixth, three points behind leaders Liverpool after 22 games.

Their form was still patchy and they turned the year with a draw at Old Trafford, victory against Burnley and a single-goal defeat at third-placed Forest. It was a tetchy, fractious affair with Bremner dismissed 17 minutes from time.

Though he was the victim of some rough treatment, Bremner should have known better. The referee booked him for retaliation after a foul by Lyons, then read him the riot act. When the official missed a Forest player tripping Bremner it was the last straw for the Scot, who took a reckless kick at Forest keeper Grummitt and was sent from the field.

Bremner faced an FA disciplinary committee for the fourth time in three years. In 1964 he was suspended for 14 days; in

1965 for seven days with a £100 fine; in March 1966, seven days and £100. Now he was banned for a fortnight and fined £100. The flaw in his temperament was chronic. His appointment as captain improved things but the flash of temper at Forest demonstrated that he was not yet fully reformed.

Bremner was free to play on while he awaited judgement, back in action on 18 January as the Fairs Cup resumed with Valencia at Elland Road. Recalls for Collins and Giles seemed certain to provoke more animosity between the two sides.

Newspapers speculated about a potential bloodbath. The fears proved groundless – there were just 15 fouls, though there were a couple of torrid incidents.

Just before half-time, Charlton, chasing a high ball, felled goalkeeper Pesudo, who was replaced by Abelardo. As the second half began, Cooper hacked at the ball in Abelardo's arms and was confronted by furious Spaniards.

By then, we had seen all the goals. Greenhoff's scorcher from 15 yards gave United a 12th minute lead, but it was nullified by Claramunt after 39 minutes.

Leeds were happy to settle for the draw, as Valencia fashioned enough chances to have won. Having failed to exploit the early advantage, Revie conceded that it would be difficult in the massive Mestalla Stadium. The recently introduced away goals counting double rule meant that Leeds would need at least one in Valencia to get through.

United's injury crisis made the second leg a daunting prospect. Reaney was out with a calf injury suffered days earlier at Everton, and joined Greenhoff, O'Grady, Johanneson, Cooper, Peacock and Johnson in the treatment room.

Revie took a party of 13 to Spain, omitting both Collins, in discussion with Bury about a prospective move, and Jim Storrie, also looking for a new club. Seven of the party were 21 or under, including David Harvey, who turned 19 during the trip.

Within seven minutes of kick off, Giles forced a breakthrough. He seized on the ball when left-back Tota lost possession near halfway and resisted challenges by Paquito, Mestre and Roberto to home in on the area. He coolly drew out the keeper before netting with an unstoppable left-footed drive.

Leeds looked capable throughout of getting the result they required. Valencia's play became ragged as the clock ran down, while United's poise grew. Valencia tried all they knew, but Leeds fashioned the clearer opportunities.

Three minutes from time, United got the second goal their display merited, Lorimer lashing home from close range. It was an impressive exhibition of how to prosper in European football. An elated United party flew home in high spirits.

Between legs, United embarked on the FA Cup trail by beating Crystal Palace 3-0, then battered West Brom 5-0. Their league form stuttered: a hammering of Fulham was forgotten as Leeds contrived to lose at Everton. They then beat Stoke, the game lit up by a 35-yard piledriver from Lorimer.

Stoke was a happy curtain call for Collins: 11 days later he severed a five-year association by joining Bury. His was a virtuoso performance, pulling the midfield strings in the manner that had won him renown. 'I played a blinder,' he said.

Collins insisted that Revie had dropped him 'quite out of the blue ... I didn't particularly like that. At least when it happened at Everton, Harry Catterick gave me some warning.' Revie informed Collins that Blackpool wanted to sign him and then promptly dropped him. 'I couldn't understand it. I didn't want to go to bloody Blackpool.'

That move came to nothing and it was at his own request that Collins was granted a free transfer.

'They said to me, "You're not the player you were" ... I didn't like the way it was all done ... But Leeds had a lot of good players coming through and somebody had to go. Johnny Giles and Billy Bremner had teamed up in midfield and you could see they would be superb together.'

Leaving almost simultaneously was Jim Storrie, off in search of first-team football at Aberdeen. He had fallen out of favour, appearing just eight times all season.

Given the impact of injuries (there had been almost 100 positional changes in 37 matches by the time of Collins' farewell), it seemed a perverse decision for Revie to dispense with the services of two of his more experienced campaigners.

Bridesmaids Revisited

'If he sends reinforcements everywhere, he will everywhere be weak.'

10 March 1967: As the season ticks into its final two months, Don Revie is considering how best to attack the home straight.

United's league form is inconsistent, with eight defeats in 30 games and they are in a mediocre sixth position, but they have shone in the cups, through to the last eight in the Fairs Cup and about to face a tasty FA Cup fifth round clash against Sunderland.

There had been bad blood between Leeds and Sunderland for years and the pairing augured ill. Trouble was delivered in spades.

The first game at Roker Park was tense, ending 1-1 with Charlton quickly equalising Neil Martin's 22nd minute opener. The football was eclipsed by bitter personal vendettas. Jim Baxter and Johnny Giles were at each other's throats and both were booked; Bobby Kerr was badly hurt in a tackle by Norman Hunter and taken off on a stretcher with a fractured tibia. Referee Ray Tinkler was criticised for not taking a firmer grip when he saw the warning signs.

The replay was not as stormy, but nearly spawned a disaster. A record number of spectators – 57,892, some 5,000 above normal capacity – flocked to Elland Road with thousands more locked outside. Harry Reynolds had made much over the previous couple of years of plans for a premier stadium, but his words rang hollow as steel and concrete crush barriers on the Lowfields Road terracing collapsed with five minutes gone.

A thousand men, women and children spilled onto the pitch. Play was halted and the players were shepherded off, leaving police and ambulance men to launch a rescue mission.

Reynolds appealed for calm and the Leeds Chief Constable took control from the centre of the pitch. The injured were ushered back to sit, two and three deep, along the touchlines.

There could have been an absolute tragedy but only 32 people were taken to hospital and comparative order was restored after a 17-minute break.

After the resumption, Leeds had the best of matters, though they struggled to find a way through a defence bolted expertly by George Kinnell and Colin Todd. When they did make a chance, they found goalkeeper Jim Montgomery in sharp form.

Against the run of play, John O'Hare gave the Wearsiders a 35th minute lead. Giles slammed the ball through a ruck of players to equalise almost immediately. United could not find a winner, Montgomery performing more heroics to deny Charlton and Hunter in extra-time.

The evening was momentous for Big Jack, his 475th first-team game, breaking the previous record set by Grenville Hair.

The drawn-out tie meant playing six games in 11 days. After facing Manchester City on the Saturday, Leeds would meet Sunderland on Monday and then Bologna on Wednesday, before Blackpool on Saturday and then on to a double header with Sheffield United over Easter. United's plea to Bologna to delay their meeting by a fortnight fell on deaf ears.

Unbelievably, if there was another draw with Sunderland, Leeds would be forced to replay against the Roker men the same day as they faced Bologna.

Revie took 24 players to the replay in Hull, saying that, if necessary, he would field a second XI in Italy. 'We certainly would not scratch,' he promised, 'Not after going all that way in the Fairs Cup, and you never know with our reserves.'

Unable to find any hotel accommodation in Hull, the United party would travel to Bridlington, rise at 5am to fly from Brough to Luton, then on to Italy by chartered flight. They were due to arrive at Forli, some 40 miles from Bologna, about 1.30pm. The journey back would be just as arduous; up at 4am for the return flight, one night's rest and then off to Blackpool on Good Friday before returning home to face the Blades.

It was ridiculous.

For once, United could field something akin to a full-strength side against Sunderland. Revie included Charlton, Hunter and Reaney after withdrawing them from the Football League squad.

Sunderland came close to taking a first-minute lead but United assumed control. While Belfitt missed two clear chances, the pressure brought them the lead for the first time in the 221 minutes played so far in the tie.

Montgomery punched away a free kick but it came back to Lorimer, whose shot rebounded off the inside of the back post, where Belfitt was on hand to nudge home.

The lead seemed decisive, given Leeds' capacity for protecting slim advantages. A rare mistake by Bremner 12 minutes from time offered a way back. His poor header sat up for Allan Gauden to half-volley home. Sprake had the original shot covered but was deceived by a deflection.

Three minutes remained when Leeds were awarded a questionable penalty.

Peter Lorimer recalled in his autobiography, 'Don said out of the blue: "If anybody gets anywhere near the box, get down." Jimmy Greenhoff ... set off on one of his jinking runs and was fully five yards outside the penalty area when he was brought down. By the time he had stumbled, fallen and rolled over a couple of times he was inside the box, and the referee, Ken Stokes, pointed to the spot so quickly that it was almost embarrassing ... I remember thinking in the dressing room after the game, "That was a funny statement of Don's." Maybe he thought that Ken had not so far given a penalty and might do so at the next debatable incident, maybe there were other factors.'

The incensed Sunderland players lost their cool. Some bickered with the referee while others squared up to Leeds players. Baxter and Bremner exchanged heated words and at one point Bremner grabbed Baxter by the throat, an assault which prompted a Sunderland fan to intervene.

Something was said between Albert Johanneson and Sunderland skipper Kinnell and the South African sped off with Kinnell in hot pursuit. The referee and his linesmen were engaged with trying to calm down the other Sunderland players and had no time to pursue Kinnell.

Order was finally restored after five minutes of mayhem and George Mulhall was dismissed for protesting too vigorously. Ignoring the chaos, Giles calmly stroked the ball past Montgomery. That sparked George Herd into further complaints and he was also dismissed. Referee Stokes was forced to add more than five minutes of injury-time as the police struggled to maintain order. He was given an escort to the dressing room at the final whistle.

There was an ugly fracas in the tunnel as the players departed, and Bremner tangled again with Baxter, who was rumoured to have punched the Leeds captain.

Charlton tangled so fiercely with Martin that they had to be physically dragged apart as they traded insults. When the referee arrived to help calm things down, Charlton snapped, 'I don't know what you've come out for. If any more of this continues, we won't need a referee, we'll be after a priest!'

The result sent the United party off in good heart to Italy. This was a team whose resilience under stress was becoming legend. The adrenaline rush of victory carried them through the pressure cooker atmosphere.

Bologna, featuring World Cup finalist Helmut Haller, were dominant, scoring after 63 minutes. Charlton headed a free kick from Fogli against Hunter's back and in the ensuing scramble Danish international Harald Nielsen crashed the ball home.

United refused to surrender and fought hard to prevent another score. They even pursued an unlikely equaliser in the final quarter with Bremner and Giles driving them on, but to no avail. They returned to Yeadon Airport with heads held high.

The defeat damaged neither morale nor form and United won the next four league games. Moving inexorably towards a potential hat-trick of major trophies, Leeds had suffered a single defeat in ten of the most punishing games one could imagine, all in the space of four short weeks.

They beat Manchester City in the Cup quarter-final, despite being outplayed. Peacock limped off after 25 minutes, frustrated by Heslop's dominance. Substitute Greenhoff turned the game Leeds' way.

The only goal came after 50 minutes from a corner earned by Greenhoff when he beat Heslop in the air. Charlton nodded Gray's inswinging centre into the net. City claimed a foul on goalkeeper Harry Dowd, but referee Eric Jennings confirmed the score.

A goalless draw at Leicester kept Leeds fourth, six points behind leaders Manchester United but with a game in hand.

Shortly afterwards, the Yorkshiremen lost Charlton with a toe broken in England's defeat to Scotland at Wembley. The injury ended Charlton's season though he had already done enough to be voted Footballer of the Year, having been in almost non-stop service since August 1965.

Bell deputised in the second leg against Bologna. United were again without O'Grady and Johanneson. The two were limited to 36 league games between them due to a series of niggling injuries.

United feared it would be a frustrating night but were back on level terms after just nine minutes. When Belfitt headed Hunter's long cross down at the back post, defender Janich flattened Greenhoff as he went for the kill and Leeds were awarded a penalty. Giles kept his cool despite goalkeeper Vavassori's premature move and he put the ball into one corner as the keeper dived to the other. Giles nearly got a second with a fierce cross drive but the keeper turned it past the post.

United had the best of things but snatched at their openings. There was the constant threat of being caught by a breakaway.

It was nip and tuck the entire night; not even a gripping 30 minutes of extra-time could settle the outcome and the decision came down to the spin of a disc, which went the way of Bremner.

On 22 April a Lorimer scorcher brought United victory at West Ham, but Manchester United's defeat of Aston Villa left fifth-placed Leeds nine points in their wake. The Whites had three games in hand, but Manchester needed only two points from their two remaining fixtures to confirm the title.

Leeds faced Tommy Docherty's accomplished Chelsea side in the FA Cup semi-finals, offering the chance of retribution for fourth-round defeat in 1966.

62,378 fans were at Villa Park, the receipts of £32,490 a record for the stadium outside the World Cup. The two sets of fans cheerfully goaded each other across the packed terraces – the clubs did not get on and a bitter enmity had developed.

The Londoners had the better of the first 30 and Chelsea were unlucky not to be awarded a penalty when Sprake's extended boot caught Boyle in the face as the keeper jumped for a ball after seven minutes. It was symptomatic of the antipathy between the players.

Chelsea continued to force the play and the game was condensed into the Leeds half. Gray, Cooper and Bremner had some decent efforts but Leeds could develop no momentum.

A brutal first half looked set to end in deadlock, but with moments to go the Londoners took the lead. Charlie Cooke, Chelsea's best forward, slipped past Bremner and Belfitt, took a return pass from McCreadie and drove his centre at Hateley, whose flicked header beat Sprake.

United threw Bremner forward and the tension rose as crunching tackles flew in. Greenhoff had to come off for attention on the hour and ten minutes later Belfitt was withdrawn. Lorimer had an immediate impact when he joined from the bench with Leeds posing some difficult questions and Chelsea ready to settle for what they had.

Leeds built a head of steam as they laid siege to Bonetti's goal. With seven minutes to go, they looked to have scored. From a long punt to the edge of the area, Bremner nodded through Chelsea's square back line. Cooper strode onto the ball and thrashed it home. Just as Leeds began to celebrate, referee Ken Burns ruled Cooper offside and the goal void.

United rallied and with seconds to go Hunter was impeded by Tambling and the referee awarded a free kick 25 yards out. He marched the Chelsea wall back the required ten yards. Giles took what he considered the signal from the official to proceed and rolled the ball sideways to the waiting Lorimer, who slammed a shot unerringly past Bonetti.

The Leeds players leapt in the air while the Londoners hung their heads in despair; but pandemonium broke out as Burns signalled for the kick to be retaken. Ruling that the wall had encroached within ten yards, he perversely denied the offended team what seemed a perfectly good goal. The decision sparked mass protests and violent argument, but Burns would brook no debate.

Inevitably, the retaken kick came to nothing and Chelsea survived. Seconds later, Burns whistled for time and the distraught Leeds players collapsed in anguish.

Still, who were United to argue? It was the same Ken Burns who awarded them a dubious late penalty against Sunderland. But the Leeds perspective, like that of most teams, has always been one-eyed.

A 2-1 victory over third-placed Liverpool kept United's slim title hopes alive. The win came courtesy of a second-half goal from Greenhoff and a Giles penalty in the 81st minute but the result was overshadowed by trouble from a small, unruly element in the crowd. Referee Jack Taylor was attacked during the match and duly reported the matter to the FA. Harry Reynolds appealed for the crowd to behave when the game was stopped at the start of the second half.

Three days later, Manchester United wrapped up the title by slaughtering West Ham 6-1 at Upton Park. The same evening Leeds drew with Chelsea. Defeat at Manchester City was followed by a 2-0 win at Sunderland, confirming fourth place and a European spot.

United had one game to go, a meaningless local derby against Sheffield Wednesday. With nothing at stake, Revie rang the changes, retaining only three of the players who had won on Wearside. He gave a first-team debut to Dennis Hawkins and a first league start to Jimmy Lumsden, with Rod Johnson getting a rare outing and Alan Peacock appearing at centre-half.

Hibbitt scored the 11th minute decider as an XI with an average age of 20 despatched the Owls. Leeds finished five points off top spot, desperately regretting their poor start. The problem was obvious: Leeds had managed 62 goals in 42 games. Only eight teams had managed fewer.

With European qualification in the bag, Revie's men could relax a little as they prepared for a Fairs Cup semi-final against Kilmarnock.

The first leg at Elland Road marked a personal triumph for Belfitt, indeed the peak of his career. His dream night began in the first minute when he gave United the lead; three minutes later he added a second, diving spectacularly to head in an O'Grady centre.

Convinced that Kilmarnock had little to offer, United grew complacent. Killie needed little encouragement and Bertelsen and Queen went close before McIlroy turned a centre past Sprake.

Belfitt settled mounting nerves by sliding home his third goal in the 31st minute, following a clever dribble from Giles and Gray's neat cross. It should have been enough, but United were in casual mood. They abandoned defensive discipline, and Gray's back pass to Sprake held up in the mud, allowing McIlroy to pull back a second goal.

Belfitt's endeavours were driving Killie to distraction. After 38 minutes he earned a fourth when McGrory handled the ball in the area to keep it away from him and Giles calmly stroked home the penalty. There the score stayed, despite United hitting the woodwork three times and Killie once.

It was a flattering scoreline, but O'Grady had led the Scots a merry dance and United were clearly the better side. Revie pronounced himself satisfied, though behind the scenes he made it clear that he was far from content.

For the second leg, United were back to the mean defensive display that had frustrated so many over the preceding four years. The good football came from Leeds and long before the end they had shown themselves tactically superior, pulling back everyone but Belfitt at any sign of danger.

Job done, United took their summer holidays with the prospect of silverware when action restarted in August. Fixture congestion delayed the other semi and UEFA deferred the final against Dinamo Zagreb until the start of the new season.

Leeds went into the first leg in the 40,000 capacity Maksimir Stadion on 30 August with precious little chance of playing themselves into form. Their three league games yielded no victories. They drew 1-1 with Sunderland, then lost without scoring at Manchester United and promoted Wolves.

Bell, Madeley, Johanneson and Giles were on the injured list and Revie set his stall out for a defensive display in Zagreb; he opted for Belfitt as lone striker and 19-year-old Bates on the right.

The game was played in oppressive heat. United were well used to the sedate pace of the European game and settled well. Committed to containment and allowing their opponents to pass the ball around in their own half as they wished, United contented themselves with deep defence, allowing Dinamo the preponderance of first half possession.

Just when it seemed that United would make it to the interval on level terms, they fell behind. Cercek came barging through to head a Piric cross past a helpless Sprake. Leeds remonstrated in vain that Charlton had been fouled but Spanish referee Adolfo Bueno Perales waved away all protests.

The United players were furious but recovered their equanimity. Defeat by a single goal would be a decent outcome and they reached the break with no further scares.

The interval gave them time to reorganise and they carried the game to Dinamo. O'Grady shot but from too far out to trouble the keeper and Hunter's free kick was marginally wide.

It was a wake-up call for the Slavs and they went 2-0 up on the hour. Zambata, granted too much freedom on the right, fired the ball across the area. Rora half-volleyed past Sprake to send the 40,000 crowd wild. It was the first time that Leeds had conceded more than once away from home in Fairs Cup football, and they were rocking.

United did well to come out of a torrid evening with a two-goal deficit; they could easily have fallen apart, as many of Dinamo's previous visitors had.

It was disappointing, but in the cold light of day Leeds could console themselves with the knowledge that an early goal at Elland Road would throw everything into the melting pot. United had fought back from desperate positions before and were determined to do so again.

As was the wont of a United board made up of sharp businessmen, they announced a hike in ticket prices for the return leg.

'We hope they will accept the increase,' said Reynolds. 'Any profit will go back into the club to help pay its running costs and the ground improvements we are undertaking.'

The price rise and a 35,000 crowd boosted receipts to £20,177, a new stadium record, beating the £16,000 for the Sheffield United-Leicester City FA Cup semi-final in 1961.

There was speculation that Peacock would be recalled, thanks to a notion that if the Slavs were to be undone it would be by dint of aerial bombardment. Instead, Revie opted for Greenhoff and

Belfitt operating in tandem and sprang a surprise by playing Reaney on the wing, a selection which betrayed his caution. It may have been prompted by the away goals counting double rule; a goal conceded would leave Leeds needing four.

The players had expected kitchen-sink attack. 'Instead, he was really cautious,' recalled O'Grady. 'He filled our heads with the opposition. I was a winger yet he was warning me about the other winger ... expecting me to operate defensively as well as up front. You'd be sitting there thinking, God, just let us play!'

The tone was decidedly low key; the *Evening Post*'s Phil Brown, stood at the Gelderd Road end, noted that 'There are things to learn about an Elland Road crowd. It's divided firmly into us and them. We on the Kop were on the side of the angels. They were the fans packed into the echoing corrugated iron-covered Scratching Shed at the opposite end of the ground. But the us and the them became a communal we during the game. In fact, the angels take their lead from the Scratching Shed. From the opposite end of the ground, this now notorious enclosure resembles an assembly of puppets. They act as one, raising their scarves in parallel lines, and they speak as one. There's nothing ragged about a Scratching Shed chant heard across the ground. It comes over as a kind of choral shouting. In the main it was the plainsong of "United! United!" and sadly plaintive it became as the match went on and the goals didn't come. We picked up their chants but our efforts were sadly ragged in comparison.'

Despite United's defensive line-up, they took the game to Dinamo and made some decent chances. Greenhoff flicked on a centre from Giles but his subtle header bypassed the far post. The miss set the tone for the evening.

The return of Giles for his second appearance of the season was a distinct bonus, bringing poise to Leeds' work. He dominated affairs, operating in smooth tandem with Bremner, though United failed to exploit the full width of the pitch.

Dinamo were content to vacate midfield and park the bus. Wave after wave of white shirts beat like breakers against impregnable blue rocks. The visitors focused doggedly on retaining possession, their deliberate play stymying any serious Yorkshire impetus.

The game was played in and around the Dinamo area, the disappointing thing a lack of imagination rather than the number of United chances. The towering defenders made easy meat of the high balls lumped metronomically into the penalty area. Had Peacock been playing, the tactic might have been reasonable – Charlton spent more time in the Zagreb area than his own, the target for a glut of corners and free kicks. The full-backs stopped his header and a shot by Bremner on the line.

Leeds were guilty of over-elaboration when they tried a more cerebral approach, thoughtless and unlovely, 'like automatons,' wrote Geoffrey Green in *The Times*, 'crushing themselves against an iron defensive fortress, with no effective methods to break down the citadel'.

In the closing minutes of the first period, Bremner looked to be getting somewhere with a neat dribble from halfway before unyielding defenders blocked his path. With depressing predictability, the free kick came to nothing.

Just after the interval, Charlton forced the ball past Skoric from a corner, but was denied the goal for impeding the goalkeeper.

United could not make the vital incision. The blue Yugoslavian wall shuffled across the pitch as circumstances dictated, too knowing, too assured, simply too refined to break under the incessant waves of one-dimensional attacking. Out-Leeds-ing Leeds, indeed!

Dinamo blinked a couple of times like a drunken man when the physical power of Leeds threatened to sweep them aside, but they held out.

After the final whistle, Albert Morris wished the visitors well and applauded sportingly as FIFA president Sir Stanley Rous presented them with the trophy. He looked longingly at the Fairs Cup and then sadly at Don Revie.

Harry Reynolds was thoroughly downcast when Revie met him at his house a couple of days later. His arthritis was playing him up like never before and he was forced to rely more and more on crutches to get around. He wasn't in a good way physically and the defeat to Dinamo had left him depressed.

'I'm not sure whether we'll ever win owt, Don,' he said as the two men settled down for a cup of tea.

'You might be right, Harry. I don't know what else we can do. We just get so far every year and then can't do it. The lads are great, we play so well, and then something buggers it up. I despair, I really do.'

Reynolds, Revie and all of West Yorkshire could only look on enviously and wish that one day it might be their turn to sample some glory.

It was a sad conclusion to the most exciting of campaigns. United were starting to earn an unwelcome reputation as big-time bottlers, of being the bridesmaid but never the blushing bride. However, Leeds United were very soon to have something of substance to show for all their efforts.

Beliefs and Bad Habits

'The end and aim of spying in all its five varieties is knowledge of the enemy.'

Late February 1967: 19-year-old Terry Hibbitt is furious with Don Revie for dropping him. He tells Revie so in no uncertain terms. Impulsive and struggling to hold his tongue, Hibbitt is one of the few players prepared to answer the Boss back. To Revie he is a liability and a luxury he cannot afford.

'Blummin' heck, Hibby lad, you could whinge for England.' Revie collapses into his chair in exasperation. Hibbitt is testing his patience to the maximum.

'How could you drop me, Boss? I've let no one down and you know I'm better than a lot of them out there.'

Hibbitt announced himself with a fanfare when he made his debut in February 1966 against Nottingham Forest. Within minutes of coming on as a second-half sub, he scored a stunning goal, lobbing Peter Grummitt from 20 yards.

He had to wait a year for his second appearance, against Valencia in the Inter-Cities Fairs Cup, but then enjoyed a run of games due to an injury crisis. He had impressed but Revie dropped him as soon as his senior players were available.

Revie shifts uncomfortably as he sips his tea. Hibbitt is one of the biggest moaners at Elland Road and is quickly back on the offensive.

'What's so special about Eddie Gray? You treat him like a son. Always in Daddy's good books. It was the same when we were in the apprentices. You took him off the ground staff after a year – me and Jimmy Lumsden, we had to do the whole two years, cleaning out the bogs and weeding the pitch, while Eddie was swanning about. It's just not fair.'

Revie has heard enough. He slams his fist on the table. 'That's enough, lad, I'm the boss. I do what I think is in the best interests of Leeds United and that's the end of it.'

Hibbitt doesn't bat an eye, but takes a softer tack. 'I understand that, but where does it leave me, Boss?'

'You're still in my first-team plans and you know you'll get another chance, touch wood. You'll just have to bide your time and not break any mirrors.'

'Why are you so superstitious, Boss?'

'Drummed into me as a boy, it was. My mother warned me never to turn a gypsy away from the door without buying something. I only got in the Man City side for the Cup final in 1956 because a gypsy gave me a bit of tree bark to carry as a charm. It certainly worked for me.'

Hibbitt knows he can come back to his future when he gets Revie in a better frame of mind and decides to play along.

'Talking about gypsies, Boss, what's this I've heard about a gypsy curse? Any truth in it?'

Revie sits up in surprise. 'You've heard about that, have you? I guess it's all round the club then?'

'If Hibby knows about it,' mutters Revie to himself, 'then he will be winding up the others.' He shoots him a sideways glance, knowing that he has to do something. He decides to give Hibbitt a version to spread round the dressing room.

'The year after I was appointed manager, I got a letter from a supporter. He said that before the stadium was built, a bunch of gypsies were thrown off the land to make way. They weren't happy and one of them put a curse on the place, said nobody who made his living there would ever enjoy any success. At first, I just dismissed the notion as nonsense. But these last five years, we've had so much bad luck that I'm worried there might be something in it ...'

Revie is lost in his own thoughts now, talking as much to himself as to Hibbitt.

'Apparently, only a practising gypsy can remove the curse and the vicar's given me a contact.'

Revie's local clergyman had pointed him in the direction of Gypsy Laura Lee, 37-year-old daughter of Gypsy Rose Lee. He hadn't done anything yet but had decided that enough was enough. What was the harm in playing along? If she could do something, it might be the making of the club.

A few weeks later Revie sent a car to fetch Lee from her home in Blackpool to free the ground from the curse.

She asked for all gates and doors to be locked before going to the middle of the pitch, scratching the grass and throwing down some seeds, then repeating the act at each corner. There were even lurid stories that she urinated in all four corners of the pitch.

Nothing was said publicly at the time, although a few of the players heard the tale. Hibbitt openly scoffed at the stupidity of it all and thought Revie had been taken in by a charlatan.

Rumours began to develop and eventually the *Yorkshire Evening Post* tracked Lee down for an interview in June 1971, by which time she had upgraded to a luxury caravan in a farmyard at Cayton near Scarborough. Relishing the publicity, she insisted that she had known Revie for six years and had carried out many readings for him. Gullibility and gossip were constant fuel for the Revie myth.

Whether there was anything to the curse or not, within 12 months of Lee's intervention, Leeds had begun winning silverware, convincing Revie that his actions were merited.

Hibbitt had observed first-hand how preoccupied Revie was with his little rituals and pet phobias: he had a morbid fear of ornamental elephants and the colour green and just could not bear the use of birds in pictures or emblems, something which would see the owl badge on the players' shirts replaced.

Revie insisted on wearing the same lucky blue mohair suit to every game, before which he would take the same short walk from the team hotel wearing the 'same lucky tie, one or two lucky charms in my pocket. I walk to the traffic lights every morning, turn round and walk back to the hotel.'

He wore out the pants in his suit through continual wear but refused to don anything else, fearing the consequences.

Another of Revie's peculiarities was an interest in Freemasonry. It had come to the fore a couple of years earlier as Revie did everything he could to secure favours from authority. In 1965 he joined the Leodiensis Lodge in Leeds and remained an active mason for the rest of his life, although he never spoke publicly about the association.

Revie first happened upon Freemasonry while a player at Manchester City, a club long associated with the movement. City, founded in 1880, were rescued from bankruptcy in 1894 by local masons; the price for their patronage was that the club changed its colours from red and black to the light blue and white which were the chosen favours of a master mason.

Revie's Maine Road manager, Les McDowall, was a mason and many of the City players were inducted when they retired.

Revie, who would do anything to safeguard the financial well-being of his family, was given food for thought when colleagues whispered in his ear about the benefits of allegiance to the brotherhood. He spent some time in conversation with former United director John Bromley, an active mason who was a director of Leeds Masonic Hall Co Ltd. Revie's conviction that the Establishment were persecuting his beloved Leeds when they gatecrashed football's top table set him thinking.

Revie was a fiercely religious man who always said his prayers before retiring at night, so it might be considered odd that he should throw his lot in with the movement. However, Freemasonry's bad press only came to the fore in the 1980s when the Church of England revealed its 'significant concerns' about Christians becoming Freemasons amid renewed controversy about the presence of the secretive organisation at the heart of the British Establishment.

It was widely said that Freemasonry paved the way to the England manager's job for Alf Ramsey. He joined the Waltham Abbey Lodge in Essex in 1953 and saw allegiance as a means of accessing favourable treatment from the powers that be.

Revie's membership might have been down to a sense of altruism, but it was more likely to be in the interests of family and club. He would seek out any help he could to further the cause of Leeds, no matter how unlikely the notion.

His planning and preparation for games were meticulous and he was determined to build a footballing family. His pursuit of a family atmosphere gave birth to his insistence on personally hand-soaping his players after training and he was obsessed with getting close to the players' wives and families and United's cleaning ladies. The nod was more in the direction of the Weasleys than the Corleones, no matter what the views of Revie's critics.

From the outset of his management career, Revie introduced radical new ideas around exercise, nutrition and team bonding. In addition to regular games of bingo and carpet bowls, he hired ballet dancers to teach the players better balance and movement. But no list of Revie's beliefs would be complete without the infamous dossiers.

He revelled in the story of how the documents became a way of life at Elland Road, revealing that near the end of the 1963/64 season he had sent Syd Own to take a look at a young player whom he had heard good things about. 'The report that landed on my desk the following Monday was a masterpiece! I had never before seen such a detailed breakdown of a footballer. Syd had left nothing to chance. He outlined how good the player was on his right and left side; the angles or lines along which he tended to run with the ball; the shooting positions he favoured, and so on.'

Revie was convinced that such reports could be invaluable if they focused on the teams Leeds were due to meet each week. It soon became routine that either Owen, Maurice Lindley or Revie himself would go to observe United's opponents for the following Saturday. Their handwritten notes were typed up by secretary Jean Reid on the Monday morning and used throughout the week to prepare the players for the next match.

'On many occasions,' recalled Revie, 'we held practice matches in which the reserve players adopted the same style of play as the team in question, and the first-team lads had to try and break it down.'

One example from August 1964 when Liverpool drew 2-2 with West Ham included the following:

'Liverpool took the field first and proceeded towards the Spion Kop end, this being the end they prefer to defend in the first half, an advantage may be gained by getting out first when we play there. Use the right-hand goal for warm-up and should we win the toss elect to stay as you are at KO. Shankly has devised his team tactics to cover some deficiencies in his playing strength. Both full-backs lack pace and our wingers must seek the ball behind them.

'Liverpool depend a great deal on centre-half Yeats, who sticks like glue to the centre-forward and clears his lines decisively at all times. In this game both wing half-backs played a very stereotyped game and should one go on attack, the other stays back, even when an opportunity may arise to move with ease into a position to change the point of attack. The majority of Milne's service goes towards outside-right Callaghan, and usually consists of a short crisp pass.

'The Liverpool defence play square with both full-backs endeavouring to keep close to the wingers even when a strike is made through the inside positions. It was noticeable that West Ham's inside-left, Hurst, was on to a number of balls behind the Liverpool right-back in the first 15 minutes and I could not figure out why this approach was not sustained because it proved highly dangerous in the early period. Balls into this area will probably be more productive because of the two wing half-backs. Right-half Milne tends to advance more than Stevenson. It was Yeats who was having to move out to challenge Hurst on most occasions.

'After this early period I consider West Ham played to Liverpool's advantage by building up attacks slowly, and neither Sissons nor Brabrook would seek the ball behind the full-backs or attempt to run without it to enable colleagues from behind to carry the ball into an attacking position. Once West Ham had gained possession Bobby Moore, playing in a position between C-H and L-B, was usually served with the ball by his colleagues, to distribute elsewhere.

'Thompson at O-L has speed and ball control, and invariably takes on anybody in line with his striking runs. I feel there are times when he had the chance to cross balls from the wing but even so he elected to take on his opponent to get in on goal. Thompson tends to go inside or across the front of his full-back because he favours his right foot.'

The full report went on for pages and pages and pages and offered meticulous analyses of all the individual players. Some of the reports were particularly scathing in their criticism of individuals: 'His whole attitude is wrong. He lacks courage, has no desire to work and appears to treat his profession as a big bore!'

Revie's pre-match ritual of reading out selected snippets of information on the strengths and weaknesses of the players they were about to take on was light years ahead of his rivals.

Although such research wasn't entirely new, nobody had attempted anything as thorough and systematic as Revie. The dossiers contained reams of information, covering shooting and dribbling skills, how strong players were in the tackle and how well they used the ball in possession.

It was said that opposing clubs so feared the power of the dossier that they would go to any lengths to stymie the process. 'You heard stories that sometimes Maurice and Syd found it difficult to get into away grounds,' recalled Eddie Gray. 'I think there were occasions when they had to pay to enter through the turnstiles to get into grounds.'

The reports contained forensic analyses of the pros and cons of each player. Revie was obsessional about the detail but some of the squad were less appreciative. Norman Hunter thought Leeds paid opponents too much respect though he knew better than to voice his concerns to Revie.

Peter Lorimer found the dossiers useful, particularly when Leeds were playing unknown foreign teams in Europe. 'Nowadays if a British club is playing a European side, they're able to get films of the opposition so that they can sit and watch them during the week. But we didn't have that available to us at that time,' said Lorimer. 'Thanks to the dossiers we were able to build up a good mental picture of what to expect before we got on the pitch, so they were really important.'

Lorimer felt, however, that there was a risk of building up too great a respect for opponents. The players should have been thinking about their game, not worrying about teams who were simply not in Leeds' class.

'Sometimes we would play a team in a cup match that were maybe two or three leagues below us, but we would still have the dossiers,' he recalls. 'Are we playing a non-league team or Real Madrid?'

There was never any public protest about Revie's fastidiousness at the time, but not everyone was a convert. Hibbitt derided the dossiers and Gary Sprake referred to them as 'mind-numbing … Syd Owen would pass them on for Revie to read out, they would last about an hour, by which time the lads would be bored silly. I was – although nobody would dare tell any of the coaches this, and certainly not the Boss.'

Billy Bremner sometimes struggled to maintain his concentration and often only skim read the material. 'I wasn't taking a lot in,' he admitted, 'but I thought I'd better pay attention because if he said to me, "What was I saying there?" and I wasn't paying attention, he wouldn't be too pleased. Yet if we played Arsenal on the Saturday and then again on a Tuesday, three days later, we'd have the same dossier. The only time I would listen was when he was talking about continental players I didn't know.'

'Sometimes you had dossiers on players you'd played against two or three weeks earlier,' recalled Norman Hunter. 'You already knew them inside out, but you'd still sit there and listen because there might be a bit of information in there about set-plays that had slipped your mind. If we had to sit there for three-quarters of an hour listening to a dossier that may have been boring because we already knew the contents, then we were all prepared to sit there and listen. It was how Don was as a manager and we got used to it.'

'To be honest I think the role the dossiers played in our success was exaggerated,' recalls Johnny Giles. 'With every successful team, people want to know the secret, so they look for superficial things like the dossiers, or what players had for their pre-match meal, or even the playing bingo before matches when we were away from home. But what made Don so successful at Leeds was years of good practice. Getting the best players in, and then providing the right environment for good players and good characters to flourish. It wasn't the dossiers, it wasn't the pre-match meals and it wasn't the bingo. They weren't the reason for Don's success at Leeds and they weren't the reason for his failure at England.'

Bremner recalled other aspects of Revie's management: 'He was never a tough disciplinarian despite his outward image. If you stepped out of line you knew you were for the chopping block, but he never had to rant and rave. He commanded respect because he gave respect and treated his players as men. Though we were allowed to dress in casual clothes for travelling away, we always had to remember that we were representing the club and had to be presentable. We were not allowed to have very long hair. We didn't have to look like convicts but we were expected to look neat.'

Revie's approach to discipline and his obsession with fate eventually got to Terry Hibbitt.

After he made just three appearances in 1970/71, taking him on to 62 games in five years for Leeds, Hibbitt's patience was exhausted and he asked Revie for a transfer, eventually moving to Newcastle in a £30,000 deal.

Geordie boss Joe Harvey was delighted with his bargain capture, though he did acknowledge that 'he'd cause trouble in an empty house!'

When Norman Hunter was chatting after one match to Newcastle striker Malcolm Macdonald, who became the beneficiary of Hibbitt's passing abilities, he confided the reason why Revie had let him go for such a pittance.

'He had to go, he definitely had to go … We'd done a training session, and at the end of it we were having a bit of a five-a-side, with the goalkeepers playing out. All five-a-sides here are pretty competitive, and Gary Sprake and Paul Reaney have tackled each other, neither liking the way the other has gone in. So they are on their feet now with fists clenched, squaring up to each other.

'At that point, little Hibby's come running straight over to them and gone, "Yak, yak, yak, yak." So Paul's turned to him and said, "Terry, this hasn't got anything to do with you. Piss off!" The warning falls on deaf ears, because Hibby's gone "Yak, yak, yak" again and given Paul a mouthful. Then Gary has a go. "Terry," he says, "you've been told once. It's nothing to do with you. Keep your nose out of it!" And Terry's turned to Gary and said, "Talking of noses, what about your wife's!" As I said, he had to go.'

The First Trophy

'Security against defeat implies defensive tactics; ability to defeat the enemy means taking the offensive.'

1 September 1967: Don Revie is driving over to see Harry Reynolds, clear that it will be a solemn discussion. In the early hours of the previous day Revie flew back into Britain from baking Zagreb after losing to Dinamo.

The hollow echo from the trophy cabinet seems to have no end. The club has only the Second Division trophy and a couple of West Riding Senior Cups to show for the last few years. Revie worries that the team will never realise its potential.

Revie's mood is low, but not as low as that of Reynolds. As his mentor opens the door to admit him, Revie can see that Reynolds has been crying.

'Whatever's wrong, Harry?'

Revie thinks it might be down to the defeat in Yugoslavia, but he quickly realises there are more serious issues.

'I'm weary, Don, I've had enough.'

'Eh? What d'you mean?'

'I can't go on, it's too much. I'm going to resign the chair.'

Revie staggers back. He had not expected this. Over the last month, Reynolds has shown no lack of energy and Revie came to Bramley looking for Reynolds to lift his spirits. That is no longer an option and Revie switches from mentee to mentor in double quick fashion to offer comfort to a tired old man.

'Is it really that bad, Harry? It's only one match. And we've still got the second leg to come ...'

'It's not that.'

'Well, what is it then, Harry?'

'D'you remember what Sam Bolton said about being tired? This job takes it out of you, Don, and I'm not as strong as I used to be. I'm feeling the strain. My arthritis is getting to me and everything is an effort these days.'

'But you're so important to the club, Harry, you're so important to me ...'

'And that's why I was crying. I'm letting you all down.'

'You're not, really you're not. Your health is more important. We'll survive.'

'I know you will, Don, and that's why I'm resigning. We've built a club that will outlast both of us and you don't need me holding you back.'

Reynolds had been planning for the redevelopment of the stadium and he had written to users of club car parks warning that large sections would be unavailable. They would be needed to store building materials so that there could be a rapid start when the final game was over.

He had announced that £60,000 had already been spent on ground improvements, better floodlights and new turnstiles. 'Frankly, our ground badly needs improving,' he said. 'Parts of it were in a shocking state.'

If everything went well, he said, 'the club would get about £25,000 out of the Fairs Cup and television rights, which was at least a start towards paying for the many improvements to come.'

United's financials had improved markedly under Revie's stewardship. The club declared a profit in the year to July of £64,174, topping the £60,000 level for the second successive year. Five years previously there had been a six-figure overdraft. Directors' loans of £40,000 had been cleared and the bank overdraft stood at a meagre £453, a rosy picture indeed.

There were tears of sadness in his eyes as Reynolds made his decision public, disappointed that he had not seen Leeds secure the silverware that their advance deserved.

The relationship between Revie and Reynolds had been the cornerstone on which United's advance had been built. The manager's relationship with the other members of the board had never been as warm as that with Reynolds and the chairman's colleagues envied Revie's standing with the supporters. They supported him because of the success he brought to the club, but they did not worship him in the way that Reynolds did.

The two men continued to remain close and Revie would often drive over to see his former employer and seek his advice, not because he needed it but because Reynolds was a good sounding board, despite his physical infirmity.

Albert Morris was elected to replace Reynolds and was stiff and standoffish by comparison. Revie's relationship with other chairmen was never as strong as that with Reynolds. The influence of the board dwindled noticeably following Reynolds' retirement, and Revie was now omnipotent. None of the directors would dare question his authority. It played to his ego and he took the club on to a new and very impressive level.

United had made a slow start. After three league games, they had one point and one goal to their credit and were rock bottom. It seemed that the upstarts had had their time in the sun.

Revie spent much of 1967 chasing a new centre-forward, resigned to the fact that Peacock's knees could no longer withstand the rigours of First Division football. Revie was reluctant to pay the going market rate and persevered with the potential of Greenhoff and Belfitt, but it was clear that Leeds needed a proven goalscorer if they were to seriously compete for honours.

As they entered the new season, Greenhoff had scored 15 times in 74 appearances across five seasons; Belfitt was more productive with 16 goals from 39 games over three campaigns, three of them coming in the Fairs Cup semi-final against Kilmarnock in May.

To really mix it at the top, however, Leeds needed someone who could regularly contribute 20 goals a season. The last Leeds player to achieve that feat had been Storrie with 25 in 1963. Since then, the highest league total had been Storrie's 16 in 1965.

Liverpool had Hunt and St John, Manchester United Best, Law and Charlton, Chelsea Osgood and Tambling and Tottenham the incomparable Greaves.

Where would Leeds be if they had 37-goal Ron Davies of Southampton or the 29 goals of West Ham's Geoff Hurst?

However, Revie's target was not a goal getter; his priority was someone with the raw physical strength and ability to hold the ball up and create openings for those coming from deep.

The paucity of goals from United's front men was mitigated by those from elsewhere. Over the three seasons since promotion, Lorimer had scored 33 goals, Giles 31, Johanneson 26, Charlton 26 and Bremner 22. Revie saw this as a key strength and worried that a big-name striker would disrupt the outstanding team spirit. What he was looking for was a target man to lead the line, one who could play with his back to goal and resist robust pressure from towering defenders to allow those behind to come onto the ball.

After defeat at Wolves on 28 August, Eric Stanger commented, 'So bankrupt is their attack that they must be wondering where the next goal is coming from.' Revie played down any talk of crisis, saying, 'They have surprised me before and they are quite capable of doing so again. While it is nice to get off to a good start, don't forget the Football League is decided over 42 games. Last year we got only 19 points from the first 17 games, but we were still there at the finish.'

Lorimer got United's season on the move with eight goals in five games; three straight victories left them eighth at the end of September, reassuring supporters that the problems had been a mere blip.

On 22 September, Revie finally bagged his quarry, smashing the club's transfer record by paying Sheffield United £100,000 for 22-year-old Mick Jones. The holder of two full England caps, Jones had scored 63 goals in 149 games for the Blades.

But it was not his goalscoring prowess that attracted Revie, it was the ability he had to shield the ball, to keep possession when the ball reached him, no matter what the pressure exerted on him. The ball would stick no matter how it came and how fierce the challenge and Jones would lay it off smartly to oncoming players as they joined him. Jones was the type that Revie had wanted but never got when he bought John Charles in 1962.

Revie had stalked Jones for a year despite no encouragement from Bramall Lane. When the Blades bolstered their midfield by buying Willie Carlin from Carlisle for £40,000, the sale of Jones was a quick way to balance the books. Revie was delighted to have got his man, though Albert Morris claimed it was 'a heck of a lot of money to pay for a player'.

Jones himself confided, 'I cannot say that I am glad to leave Sheffield, but it was too good an offer to refuse. I don't want to leave my colleagues or the loyal supporters at Sheffield. I hope the Leeds crowd will be as good to me.' It was a muted commitment to the Elland Road cause, but Jones' hard work quickly won him a fan base in the West Riding.

This time it had been Revie securing the commitment of the board to a huge outlay, rather than Reynolds. The manager had asked Morris permission to address the board and laid out the reality of things.

'We have a team of great young players,' Revie told them. 'We've done far better on a shoestring than could have been expected. Everyone else is spending big and we have to match them if we want to compete. Liverpool have taken Hateley, Everton went for Ernie Hunt, Man City Francis Lee ... God save us, even Stoke City with Banks, Elder and Eastham.'

'We have to balance the books, Don,' responded Morris.

'I know, Mr Chairman, but if we'd had a 20-goal man last season, think what we'd have done, what we'd have won, how much we would have made.'

'Speculate to accumulate, that's what they say,' blinked Cussins through his large glasses.

'How much are you thinking?' asked Simon.

'We agreed a ton for Alan Ball and we'll need about the same for a top-class goalscorer.'

'You better get someone worth it ...' grumbled Bolton.

Revie's first negotiation without Reynolds had convinced him he could do it. Revie the manager had come fully of age. 'I just tell them the truth and give them the facts, they're businessmen. Speculate to accumulate, I'll have to remember that one.'

'There were no agents in those days,' recalled Jones, 'and I was the world's worst financial negotiator. Don asked what I was earning at Sheffield and I told him £35 a week with a £4 win bonus and £2 for a draw. He said, "I'll double it", and I was signed and done and a Leeds player ten minutes later. He said they had been watching me for two years but you weren't aware of such things. The club you played for had a bind on you and matters like that weren't openly discussed ... When I'd signed, my brother-in-law, who was a mechanic, wanted to know the details and I suppose it put it all into context when he said he was on £12 a week. I think that was about the national average then, so I was on good wages.'

Jones' debut came during the 3-2 defeat of Leicester the next day, and he received this tribute from Richard Ulyatt in the *Yorkshire Post*. 'Mick Jones did not find his new distinction of being Yorkshire's costliest footballer too burdensome ... he looked to be far and away Leeds United's best centre-forward since John Charles.'

In an attempt to keep their finances in order, United agreed two departures, with Willie Bell moving to Leicester for £40,000 and Alan Peacock to Plymouth Argyle for £10,000.

Bell grew restless when an early-season injury saw him lose his place to Cooper. Fearing a lengthy stay in the reserves, he was granted a transfer.

Peacock had made only six starts in the previous 18 months after a succession of serious injuries. He came close to selection for the 1966 World Cup squad, but his fragile knees let him down just at the wrong time. Peacock's first goal for the Pilgrims came in his fifth match, but his was not a long stay. Following his 11th appearance, on 20 January against Derby, the former England man was given medical advice that he should retire from playing, aged just 30.

The two men had given sterling service to United and Revie was sad to see them depart. It was clear evidence, though, of his commitment to youth.

The development programme that Revie had nurtured was a conveyor belt of Britain's finest young talent. One could sense Revie's pride whenever he spoke about his young gems. It had taken six years of hard work and late nights, but he was now reaping a wonderful harvest.

The signing of Jones represented the final piece in the jigsaw. The defensive old firm of Sprake, Reaney, Charlton and Hunter was boosted by the flair of Cooper and the use of two overlapping full-backs offered new options. The formation was generally 4-3-3, though it could fluctuate between 4-2-4, 4-4-2 and even 4-5-1, thanks to the flexibility of Lorimer, Greenhoff and Gray. Bremner and Madeley provided the key midfield platform for launching attacks. Despite being deprived for many months of the wide men, Johanneson and O'Grady, and playmaker Giles, United's fluid approach was more than a match for most of the teams they faced.

Leeds' passage through the autumn was like a veritable juggernaut in pursuit of every trophy on offer.

After beating Leicester, Leeds had to be content with a goalless draw at West Ham, but then went to town as the Fairs Cup campaign began. Spora were limited opponents and United turned in a stunning performance in the first leg in Luxembourg, winning 9-0 with four from Lorimer. It established a new club record and set Leeds up for a home match with Chelsea.

The encounter was inevitably seen by Leeds as a chance of avenging their recent FA Cup defeats by the Blues. Chelsea's disarray following the resignation of manager Tommy Docherty the day before the game made them lambs to the slaughter.

Docherty resigned within hours of being given a 28-day suspension from all football activity following incidents on Chelsea's tour of Bermuda in June. Docherty shouted his mouth off once too often to the referee and to officials of the local association. They reported him to the English football authorities. The FA took time to deal with the matter, not convening until mid-October.

Docherty arrived for training to discover that the FA had banned him from all football for a month. He was ordered by Blues chairman Charles Pratt to attend an emergency board meeting that afternoon. Pratt and Docherty had been at loggerheads for years. Knowing his dismissal was imminent, Docherty asked to be momentarily excused. He returned with a crate of champagne to announce his resignation.

On the morning of the match, Chelsea were 19th in the table, without a win in a month. In sharp contrast, United were unbeaten since 30 August. They had conceded only five goals in the nine games since then.

The only cloud on the Elland Road horizon was Bremner's 28-day suspension, which meant he would miss six games for United plus a European Championship match for Scotland. He received the ban for his dismissal at Fulham in September. It brought his disciplinary sanctions over recent years to 68 days' suspension and £350 in fines. He was determined to sign off with a bang.

The referee issued a mild rebuke to both men when Bremner clashed with Fulham's Mark Pearson. Pearson took his medicine quietly but Bremner spat it out. He refused to accept any fault and insisted that the referee should know as much. He continued protesting and instead of a ticking off he received a booking. He was still seething and continued to give the referee lip, the inevitable consequence being a dismissal.

He knew that he was in the wrong and so did Revie, who gave him both barrels later, telling him that he was letting his team-mates down.

'When Bobby Collins retired,' recalled Revie. 'Jack Charlton became skipper for a while. He's a superstitious devil and always likes to take the field last. So I turned to Billy Bremner. At that time he was constantly in hot water with his temper. I had it out with him with a warning that if he did not mend his ways he'd be hounded out of the game as a thug years before his time. I told him that whatever happened on the field he must pick himself up and walk away. He had to set a good example to others.'

In the knowledge that he would be cooling his heels for the next month, Bremner took out his frustration on Chelsea. The game was marked by his phenomenal performance.

Johanneson broke the deadlock after five minutes, ensuring that any brittle confidence remaining after Docherty's departure would come under the severest of examinations. Chelsea were found badly wanting as matters tottered from bad to worse.

After 11 minutes, Greenhoff made it 2-0 with a fierce drive and then Charlton headed home a third. There was a lull in affairs for the next 20 minutes as United drew breath but they went four ahead shortly before the break courtesy of Lorimer's fierce shot from the angle.

The game was over as a contest and Leeds were on autopilot after the interval. Gray beat Bonetti with a magnificent shot from the edge of the area on the hour to keep the score sheet ticking over, but United were content to play within themselves now at a comfortable half-pace.

Ten minutes from time, Marvin Hinton had the misfortune to deflect another Lorimer power drive past Bonetti, but that was a mere appetiser for the coup de grace.

Bremner had been outstanding, having a hand in five of the six goals, and signed off from football for a month with a spectacular bicycle kick to make it 7-0.

Phil Brown described it as 'one of the greatest games of his young life' in the *Evening Post*. 'His passes flowed like pieces of silk unrolling, prompting the taker into an opening perfectly, and his reverse pass, the best in the industry for me, and given to very few of my time, flashed several times to cut out a third of the defence.' His goal, Brown reported, was 'a final stroke by an artist on a masterpiece'.

United won four of the six games played during Bremner's absence and continued to prosper when he returned; they were fourth when they faced second-placed Liverpool on 9 December, a point behind Shankly's men and three shy of leaders Manchester United. They had reached the last eight of the League Cup and the third round of the Inter-Cities Fairs Cup.

That spell also included Jack Charlton's 500th first-team appearance for the club in the 7-0 defeat of Spora at Elland Road on 17 October.

The wheels came off when they played Liverpool at Anfield in December, and particularly for one man.

On occasion a player's entire career is defined by a single incident in a single match. This was the case for Gary Sprake that day.

There was an inch of snow on the ground, but it was soft underneath and World Cup referee Jim Finney had no hesitation in declaring the pitch fit to play.

Liverpool adapted the better to the conditions, moving the ball directly whenever they had the opportunity. United played a more circumspect game, often making more passes than was advisable and seeing the ball stick on the pitch or skid past its intended target.

There was little surprise when Liverpool took the lead after 18 minutes. Tony Hateley rose to beat Charlton and fed Roger Hunt down the middle. Reaney and Hunter converged on the England man, but both misjudged things. Hunt made no mistake, swerving round them to slide the ball home.

As half-time neared, Leeds were holding their own when tragedy struck.

Gary Sprake had the ball in his hands and was about to throw out towards Terry Cooper when he noticed Liverpool anticipate the pass and prepare to intercept. As he started considering his options, his concentration let him down and the slippery ball evaded his grip as his arm swung and the ball went sailing over his shoulder and in the direction of his goal. He could do nothing to stop it and it nestled gently into the net behind him in an iconic moment of footballing legend.

Sprake stood transfixed with despair for seemingly an eternity as the enormity of what he had done dawned on him. It was one of the most memorable own goals of all time and Sprake wished that the Anfield turf might open up and swallow him whole as he hung his head in despair.

Bremner consoled his distraught keeper as the teams went off, but Anfield was less generous. During the break, the home club's disc jockey waggishly featured Des O'Connor's No 1 hit of the time, *Careless Hands*, in sarcastic 'tribute'.

The result brought an unceremonious end to United's good run, but the lasting memory was the forlorn figure of Sprake, pitifully asking himself 'Why me?'

History seldom deals in shades of grey and Sprake was pilloried for his habitual mistakes, but at the time he was accorded more generous consideration. Eric Stanger: 'It was not a silly mistake but a freakish happening caused by the slippery ball on the snowbound pitch ... I doubt if Sprake could repeat it if he tried. I did not blame him for a moment, nor did his colleagues or manager ... Sprake, to his credit, turned the ribald jeers of the notorious Spion Kop to cheers by his second half display.'

Sprake himself was philosophical. 'It is an inevitable part of being a goalkeeper. I have read lots of comments that I was nervous and that I somehow lost my confidence due to the mistakes but this was never the case. I openly admit that before a game I would be terribly nervous and sometimes be physically sick but I had been like that since the start of my career. Once I started the game I would be fine and, although I would be angry at myself and disappointed if I made an error, I can honestly say it never affected my confidence.'

Down the years, the criticism of Sprake has been overplayed, but that day at Anfield wouldn't be the last time that he made a high-profile error on the big stage.

After the defeat Leeds quickly recovered momentum – they went undefeated until April, carrying all before them in the hunt for four trophies. After despatching Fulham 5-0 at Craven Cottage on 6 January, Revie remarked, 'Leeds United have never played as well ... It was terrific.'

A week later another five-goal victory against Southampton took Leeds second. This was the prelude to a period of cup activity, with three games in three weeks against Second Division Derby County, managed by Brian Clough.

The Rams boss was 32 and would go on to be a fierce critic of Revie and Leeds. In 1967, though, he purred with admiration during an interview with the *Yorkshire Post*. 'It would be silly to underestimate Leeds, who are such a good professional side with a top-class manager ... They can teach my lads a lot – how hard they have to work, how much effort and dedication is required – in short, a complete picture of what we have to aim for in the future. Leeds must be the envy of nearly every club in the country with their spirit and running power and large pool of good players. People tend to underestimate their individual ability but make no mistake about it – these lads can play.'

The clubs were paired in the two-legged League Cup semi-final and the FA Cup third round, with the first match in the League Cup at the Baseball Ground on 17 January.

Leeds were sternly tested and required a classic away performance and a second-half Giles penalty to secure victory. They never looked like conceding, too experienced in the black arts of defensive play, but there were some hairy moments with Leeds-born Kevin Hector several times going close.

Ten days later, United repeated the feat with a 2-0 FA Cup victory at Elland Road. Charlton and Lorimer's second-half goals secured a scrappy victory.

The long-running saga came to an end on 7 February as Leeds sought a place in the League Cup final.

The Rams took the game to Leeds in the opening exchanges and tied the aggregate score on 12 minutes when Hector headed past Sprake. The advantage lasted for little more than a minute. Lorimer was fouled on the edge of the area and took the free kick himself. His chip was met by Madeley who nodded down for Belfitt to score off the post.

Leeds took the lead in the final minute of the half. Giles dribbled past three men and shot home despite the best efforts of goalkeeper Matthews. In the 60th minute Giles missed a penalty, but seven minutes later Belfitt snatched his second from a Bremner free kick.

Stewart netted a consolation for Derby a minute from time, but it was too little too late – United were through to the final.

When Leeds took a 2-1 lead against West Ham on 10 February, they retreated into their shells, earning the wrath of supporters, as reported by Eric Stanger: 'Strange things happen in football but surely nothing more strange than Leeds United having to suffer boos, whistles and the slow handclap from a large section of the crowd ... For a full three minutes Leeds kept the ball in an area of a few square yards near West Ham's right corner flag.'

When Leeds repeated the feat as they protected another 2-1 lead, at home to Forest in the Cup, the fans' reaction was less critical. With minutes to go, United held the ball deep in the corner but there was no booing or slow handclapping this time, only cheers of relief from a 50,000 crowd who had been on a knife-edge. Entertainment was secondary.

The contest was bitter. Forest used every method, fair and foul, to disrupt the Bremner-Giles partnership, committing 26 fouls against United's eight.

The Guardian's Eric Todd described referee Jack Taylor as 'extravagantly tolerant' for overlooking Lorimer's punch to Winfield's stomach and ignoring a clash between Hunter and Baker. He took no names and 'subscribed to the optimistic view that players are terrified by a wagging finger, or that a soft answer will turn away wrath'.

Leeds enjoyed two weeks off before the League Cup final at Wembley on 2 March. There were doubts about the fitness of Charlton, Sprake, Giles and Greenhoff, but all were in Revie's selection, though he was deprived of the cup-tied Jones and opted for the versatile Madeley at No 9.

There were two schools of thought regarding the outcome. The Doubting Thomases looked back on two lost finals, a couple of league runners-up spots and two defeats in semi-finals since United's return to the top flight and declared Leeds bottlers.

More positive voices boasted of United's status as the team of the season, still in the running for four trophies.

Leeds were eager to wipe out the memory of the 1965 Cup final, a sterile occasion that raised no one's blood pressure but the priority was victory to end the silverware famine. The League Cup was the least significant of the majors but Leeds cared not – a trophy was a trophy.

Defences were on top with Charlton and counterpart Ian Ure gobbling up the aimless high balls that came their way but United broke through after 18 minutes. And they owed it to a tactic they had made much of over the previous two years.

From the second of two consecutive corners, Gunners keeper Jim Furnell had both Madeley and Charlton to contend with as he flapped at the ball. It fell to Cooper who moved in eagerly to volley it straight back into the middle of the goal.

Arsenal protested that Furnell had been impeded but referee Hamer adamantly awarded the goal. Even Bremner admitted in later years that it should have been a free kick, but no one of a Leeds persuasion cared.

Charlton's goal-line antics had unintentional roots. One day while Big Jack was training with the England squad, he set about winding up brother Bobby. The younger Charlton had always fancied himself as a goalkeeper and at one corner kick Jack decided to annoy him by standing directly in front of him, blocking him from coming out to catch the cross.

'What are you doing? Get out of the way.'

Jack just laughed and began nudging the kicks on so they eluded Bobby. Pleased with his trick, Jack recounted the tale to Revie and suggested trying it out for real.

When Charlton tried the move on an unsuspecting Sprake, the keeper couldn't handle it, lashing out with his fists. Revie and Charlton exchanged knowing glances as Bremner hauled Sprake away. The tactic was quickly added to the United repertoire and proved remarkably successful.

Charlton didn't get it entirely his own way, of course.

'This tactic was highly controversial,' wrote Jimmy Greaves. 'Jimmy Hill echoed the thoughts of many, saying that although taking up a position on the goal line in front of the goalkeeper was not in breach of any rule, Jack's action was not in the spirit of the game. Arguments raged, but Jack continued with this tactic and to some effect. The fact that Leeds scored several goals off the back of Jack's legal obstruction of the opposing goalkeeper only served to make this tactic even more controversial. The tactic finally came unstuck at Goodison Park when Jack came up against Gordon West. He was determined no member of the opposition was going to dictate to him in his own penalty area and devised a tactic of his own to counteract Jack's presence on his goal line. Big Jack trundled upfield to take his by now customary position on the goal line. Only Gordon West didn't do what all the other goalkeepers had done. Instead, much to the surprise of Jack, West took up a position just beyond his far post. When Eddie Gray floated the ball just under the Everton crossbar, Jack thought he was going to be treated to an easy "good morning" goal, but as soon as Gray crossed the ball, Gordon West took off from his position by the far post and launched himself at the flighted ball. Having gained the necessary momentum and height, West reached over the top of Jack and punched the ball clear, in so doing embedding his knees in Jack's back. The ball sailed towards Row G, while Jack went down like a bag of hammers. "I guess that's the end of that," suggested West, as Jack lay on the Goodison turf in some considerable pain.'

After taking the lead against the Gunners, Leeds petered out as an attacking force as they settled for a containing game even this early. Frustrated by an inability to convert their possession into goals, Arsenal tried to turn United's tactics against them shortly before the break. McLintock charged Sprake as he caught a corner, sparking an untidy set to. Ure was surrounded by Leeds men pushing and pulling him in concerted rage. The referee calmed things quickly, but the mood had become decidedly ugly and the half-time whistle was opportune in giving tempers time to cool.

Leeds came out of their shell at the resumption and Bremner chased a loose ball into the box. He nearly took Furnell's head off his shoulders in his eagerness to get in a shot, provoking anger in the Gunners ranks, but the incident was quickly over.

Chances became scarce with Madeley withdrawn into an auxiliary defensive role and Belfitt coming on for a limping Gray with 15 minutes to go.

Sprake was forced into one save, diving to turn away a shot from Radford, and Arsenal found the net once, but Armstrong's effort was disallowed for an infringement on Giles.

United held out to register a fifth clean sheet in nine matches, breaking the trophy duck that had haunted the club. It was a job well done rather than a thriller.

Revie insisted that injuries forced Leeds to abandon the attacking game he had promised. 'Under the circumstances, we would have been foolish to attempt to do this. We were playing with virtually nine fit men … It was impossible for us to look upon this as just another match. All players are nervous at Wembley, but this was particularly true as far as Leeds were concerned as it was so vital for us to win.'

Each club pocketed £30,000 plus TV fees, considerably better than their take in 1965 against Liverpool – £21,000.

The game was drab, worse even than 1965, but no one at Elland Road cared a jot. Harry Reynolds' desperate desire to 'win summat' was the driving force and few could deny that Leeds deserved their moment of glory.

Even amidst the triumph there was disappointment. Reynolds missed the game, taken ill overnight. Revie gazed forlornly at the empty seat where his benefactor should have been and sighed. He arranged for the players to go and visit Reynolds with the trophy as soon as they returned to Leeds.

The onset of arthritis had curtailed Reynolds' activities. 'It was almost unbearable, I could no longer move around, or even sit down, without this terrible pain. I was no longer enjoying life. There was nothing I liked better than going down to the pub to meet my friends but even that became a burden. Instead of having my usual five pints or so, I was struggling through two and the beer began tasting awful.'

Two years later, Reynolds told Richard Dodd of the *Yorkshire Post*, 'I went in for this operation on my right hip. I can't begin to describe to you the difference it made. I was a new man and my friends say I look ten years younger … Anyone who has my complaint should have this operation. I've cause to be extremely grateful to the surgeons. You are bound to miss it when you give up, but I still see all the home matches.'

European Success

'He who is prudent and lies in wait for an enemy who is not, will be victorious.'

7 March 1968: Don Revie is putting the finishing touches to his weekly column in the Yorkshire Evening Post. Five days ago, he was full of pride when Leeds lifted the League Cup. The victory is hugely symbolic.

Leeds waited an age to win a major trophy and Revie is convinced, as he told Eric Todd before the game, 'victory would be a springboard to even bigger things.'

The silverware confirms that Leeds are no bottlers. Revie uses his column to fire back at the team's critics.

'Now we have won this trophy, we feel that a great weight has been lifted off our shoulders. At last Leeds has cast away that champion runners-up tag – and are now in a good position to win more honours. I am positive we will take another title before the end of the season.'

Revie lays down his pen and sits back in his chair, smiling with grim satisfaction. 'That'll show the bastards ...'

There was a new feeling of confidence about Elland Road. Days after their Wembley win, Albert Morris revealed as much when he announced plans to develop the stadium.

'The board was unanimous that we should go ahead,' said Morris, as he unveiled an architect's model of the new covered accommodation that was planned for the Gelderd Road end of the ground. He confirmed they had decided to build a new stand to replace the Kop at an estimated cost of £200,000.

The development was partly in response to safety concerns which had been amplified by the problems experienced when the stadium hosted Sunderland the previous March. Then the crush barriers on the Lowfields Road terracing collapsed in a dangerously overpopulated ground and there was a near tragedy. The changes were also partly to silence the grumbles of supporters about having to stand out in pouring rain on the uncovered open terrace.

The existing Kop held up to 17,000 and was separated from the Lowfields Road stand by a flimsy fence. It was known that on some occasions the stand had housed an incredible 19,000 people, though in practice it was full with 14,000. The northern boundary of the stadium and the area's capacity would be unchanged by the plans but the required footprint of land would be significantly smaller. The new accommodation would be steeper and less deep, replacing the huge, mounded terrace that would be flattened. The front of the stand would be withdrawn 75 feet from its existing position, allowing the playing area to be shifted north eventually. The work would entail the removal of 45,000 cubic yards of the embankment, making room for further development at the Elland Road end where the anachronism of the Scratching Shed lurked like the gaping maw of some ravenous beast.

It was hoped that many from the Shed would shift to the new stand. One regular there told the *Yorkshire Evening Post*, 'We think we will be able to make more din and get more people to join the clan under the bigger stand.'

Work would start on the new stand and its cantilever roof as soon as Leeds had played their final league match in May with completion anticipated by September.

The stand would house a 60-foot licensed bar, two snack bars, two cigarette kiosks and a new gymnasium. Two 150-foot high floodlighting towers would be erected at the Gelderd Road end, each 'carrying 75 powerful lamps'.

Morris agreed a stand with seating would bring more financial gain, but the board were determined to preserve the identity of the Kop. The scheme originally put forward would have cost £150,000, but the amenities would have fallen well short of what was now planned.

'We have confidence that the team will continue to succeed,' said Morris, 'so we should be able to see our way clear in the next few years to tackling other ground improvements.'

Many criticised the changes as piecemeal; it was a decade since the last major development at the ground, the construction of the West Stand following the fire in 1956. But the directors reasoned that slow, incremental change was the only way to go without disrupting the playing season.

Within a month, 67-year-old Morris was gone, dying suddenly in Leeds General Infirmary. He was replaced by vice-chairman Percy Woodward, initially in an acting capacity. After the loss six months earlier of Reynolds and the retirement of Harold Marjason, the board was suddenly down to five but showed no intention of taking on fresh blood.

The club had already had to deal with other sad news in the week following the League Cup final.

Grenville Hair, who appeared almost 500 times for Leeds, collapsed and died of a heart attack on 7 March, aged just 36. He had taken over as manager of Bradford City in 1967 and had steered them to a promotion chase. They were three points off top spot in the Fourth Division as Hair suddenly collapsed whilst taking training.

United issued a memorial tribute plate and a minute's silence was observed before the FA Cup fifth-round clash with Bristol City the following Saturday. The Lord Mayors of Leeds and Bradford were guests for the day.

Goals from Jones and Lorimer in the 11 minutes before half-time put Leeds in control, but the game finished in ugly fashion with Sprake dismissed. Chris Garland brought Bremner down and as referee Dimond rushed over to book him, all hell let loose with Sprake punching Garland after he spat in his face. Lorimer took over in goal for the last few minutes and was not troubled in a routine victory.

The next three games brought only draws but the points were enough to take Leeds top, level on points with Man City and Man United, but ahead on goal average.

Jack Charlton's appearance in the draw with Forest on 13 March was his 448th in the league, setting a new club record as Big Jack moved past the total set by Ernie Hart in 1936.

Ten days later, the Whites hosted second-placed City in a crucial fixture. The importance of the occasion drew a crowd of 51,818, the best of the season.

City's recent displays had been breathtaking, punctuated by the contributions of Francis Lee, Mike Summerbee and Colin Bell. Their clever combination play gave Lee a shot which

Sprake saved before making a point-blank stop as Bell followed up. Bell later hit the bar and then had a goal disallowed.

Leeds improved after the break, with substitute Madeley partnering Jones up front. Giles stroked the ball home after 52 minutes to open the scoring after Jones got the better of two defenders and played him into space on the edge of the area. 15 minutes later, Charlton plunged at the back post to nod home Giles' cross. He ended up sprawled in the net but emerged with a wide grin and celebratory punch as Leeds secured a 2-0 victory which extended their unbeaten run to 22 matches.

The season was at its business end as United returned to Fairs Cup action, meeting Rangers at Ibrox in the first leg of their quarter-final.

Rangers, backed by an 80,000 crowd, tried everything to secure an advantage, but got little change from a magnificent back line – when they did get through Sprake's handling was immaculate.

The goalless draw was 'the result we came for', admitted a delighted Revie.

A fortnight later, United completed the task at Elland Road. They took a while to settle but went ahead through a Giles penalty after 25 minutes when Alex Ferguson handled. Five minutes later, Greenhoff fluffed an opening manufactured by Giles but Lorimer made no mistake when the ball ran loose.

United were never going to surrender a 2-0 lead. The Scots had several decent chances, but the biggest danger to substitute goalkeeper Harvey was the missiles thrown by Rangers fans.

In between the two legs, United gained straightforward home victories over Sheffield United in the Cup and the league. The league game ended 3-0 thanks to two penalties from Giles.

Leeds were now in an extraordinary position – with the League Cup already in the bank, they were in the last four of both the FA Cup and the Fairs Cup and led the First Division. It was rare indeed for a team to hold such a strong hand in the closing weeks of the season.

The Easter period kicked off poorly at Tottenham. Leeds conceded their first goals in seven as a 26-game unbeaten run came to an end. The same day, Man United regained the leadership by beating Fulham 4-0 at Craven Cottage. Man City closed up in third by beating Chelsea while fourth-placed Liverpool surprisingly lost at home to Sheffield United.

Victories against Coventry, Spurs and West Brom left Leeds well placed, though Man United retained supremacy by beating Sheffield United. Man City dropped a point at Wolves and it looked like the title lay between the two Uniteds. The Reds had 54 points from their 39 games; Leeds (53) and City (50) each had a game in hand. Leeds had easily the best goal difference, having conceded substantially fewer than either of their rivals.

Their match in hand was away to a Stoke City side rooted in the bottom two. It should have been an easy two points, but things were not straightforward.

Stoke were fighting for their lives and could have been two ahead inside ten minutes. United were lethargic and soon trailed to a Peter Dobing goal, the same player adding a second before the break.

Given a rocket by Revie, Leeds came out fighting. They were soon level, with Greenhoff getting the first and Charlton heading home from a corner.

Slackness allowed Dobing to complete his hat-trick, but United continued to pound away. They threw everything at Banks' goal, with Hunter hitting the post, Jones forcing the keeper into a tremendous save, a penalty appeal turned down and Greenhoff blasting wide with the goal at his mercy. The home fans were living on their nerves, but City held out to send United's hopes plummeting.

Revie's men had no chance to catch their breath; four days later, they faced Everton in a highly charged FA Cup semi-final.

It was immediately apparent that the encounter would be fiery as keyed-up players launched into some fierce tackles. Within three minutes, Tommy Wright was the first to need attention, followed quickly by Colin Harvey.

Neither side was prepared to give anything. At one stage Reaney passed back 40 yards to Sprake and his Everton counterparts were just as focused on safety first. There was a series of scrappy fouls and even scrappier play, with Jones suffering robust treatment from Brian Labone. United were no angels and after 25 minutes there had been 13 fouls, ten of them by Leeds players. Sprake suffered most, getting a thorough going over from Joe Royle. A foul was given for one heavy charge, and after a second clash, Sprake was left on the ground needing lengthy treatment for a badly damaged right shoulder.

The game became bogged down in an untidy midfield stalemate and it was clear that it would take a flash of brilliance or a misfortune on somebody's part to break the deadlock. Jones thought he'd made the breakthrough when he was left in space in the goal area but his shot came back off the far post and was gathered by a relieved Gordon West.

Sadly for Sprake, he was the day's victim. His movement was badly restricted by his damaged shoulder and he was unable to throw the ball out. Royle took every opportunity to harass the Welshman into error and eventually his persistence paid off.

On the verge of half-time, Sprake gathered the ball and looked to move it on. Royle harried him and Sprake, furious at the treatment he had been getting from Royle, lost it. He was forced to use his weaker foot and in his anger he attempted to follow through into Royle's midriff. The distraction led to him scuffing his clearance and the ball fell limply to Husband. The forward seized on the opportunity and the ball came looping back and on its way in. Charlton used his hands to turn it away, hoping that Sprake would save the inevitable penalty.

Paul Reaney recalled later: 'I'm going across the line towards it but Big Jack's coming back and handballed it. I'm yelling at him, going, "What you doing?" I could have got it off the line, I gave Jack some stick for that.'

Jonny Morrissey did the business from the spot. Charlton and Morrissey had a bitter rivalry and the defender was furious when the Scouser spitefully goaded him afterwards. 'I won't forget this, you bastard,' Charlton promised.

The second half was more open. Both sides had chances but Leeds had the better of things as Giles started to exercise some influence and Greenhoff replaced the limping Gray. Leeds threw Bremner and Charlton into attack as they chased equality. It was a predictable tactic and easily thwarted by a defence which resorted to time wasting and spoiling tactics.

Revie's men made plenty of openings but could not capitalise – in the space of four short days they had seen their challenge for both league and Cup come a cropper.

United's critics rejoiced at their demise, stinging Revie. He used his Saturday column to issue a defiant message.

'I do not care what the general soccer public feels about Leeds United so long as we are still held in high esteem among our own fans … On grounds all over the country, I understand that the fans cheered heartily at the news that United would not be back at Wembley … that our downfall was a victory for attractive, attacking football.'

Revie was 'heartily sick of denying that we are an uninspiring, ruthless and unethical side with little or no individual flair'. He insisted that people were too easily swayed by what was written about Leeds and blamed the FA for the Dirty Leeds tag that dogged the club's footsteps.

The games were coming thick and fast now; Wednesday brought the first leg of the Fairs Cup semi-final, away to Dundee, as United went for a hat-trick against Scottish opposition.

Dundee never managed to threaten in the manner that Hibs and Rangers had but Leeds had to be content with a 1-1 draw. They could be excused for taking their foot off the accelerator – it was the 62nd game of a marathon season.

Elland Road played host to the match of the day on 4 May, Leeds v Liverpool. United were a point behind the two Manchester clubs but had a game in hand. Needing a win, Leeds went into the game without Sprake and Charlton.

The Kop's capacity was reduced for the game, cut by 4,000 as the builders had already moved in to begin their work. Nevertheless, there was an attendance of 44,553.

Leeds started well, taking the lead after a quarter of an hour with a splendid goal. Giles intercepted from the edge of his area and sent Lorimer haring through down the left. He raced towards the goal before laying it across the area for Jones to finish off smartly.

Leeds had other chances but did not enjoy the best of luck. They were still ahead with six minutes to go and fell back on defence, inviting Liverpool onto them.

From a Callaghan corner, Harvey punched the ball clear only for Thompson to nod it back into the safety zone. Yeats' header found the post and Lawler scored at the second attempt.

Seconds later Lawler repeated the trick, bundling home his second from deep within the Leeds area.

It was ironic that when they needed it most, United's ironclad defence, 'their pride and joy these many months,' according to Eric Todd in *The Guardian*, should be found so wanting.

With both Manchester clubs winning handsomely, the defeat left Leeds' title hopes in shreds. They needed both of their rivals to lose their final game.

The Whites had a match in hand, which came during the week at Arsenal. Leeds continued without the injured Sprake and Charlton and had to play without Hunter and Cooper, both on England duty. The defence was in tatters – even Reaney was played out of position, with Nigel Davey at right-back.

Arsenal scored four times, but Leeds equalised on three occasions and pummelled the Gunners for the last 15 minutes – the Londoners' winner came seconds from the end.

That ended even mathematical improbabilities. For the final game, a meaningless trip to Burnley, Revie included Belfitt, Bates, Hibbitt, Davey, Sibbald, Yorath and Lumsden, with Madeley and Gray in central defence. United lost 3-0 to end the season fourth after five defeats in six games.

By the time Leeds faced Dundee in the second leg of the Fairs Cup semi-final, the stand behind the goal at the north end had been flattened – the open space between the massive banks of the east and west stands brought an eerie feel to proceedings. There was a crowd of 23,830 in a stadium whose capacity had been slashed from 53,000 to 33,000.

Revie recalled all his regulars, save Charlton, still out with the ankle he jarred in the first leg. United struggled, only getting their attacking act together in the final 30 minutes, during which they struck the woodwork twice.

For long periods it seemed that they would have to rely on the away goal to progress but after Sprake made a decent save from Scott, Gray drove in an 80th-minute winner to ensure a place in the final for the second year in succession.

As with the previous final, fixture congestion saw the two-legged tie held over to the autumn, bringing relief to United's weary warriors. They had played 66 times in a momentous season and were fit to drop.

Their opponents in the final were Ferencvaros, reckoned by both Matt Busby and Bill Shankly to be the best across the whole continent.

The home leg was played on 7 August. With no league action to get their eye in, Leeds warmed up with a posthumous testimonial for Grenville Hair on 30 July against Bradford City, the club Hair managed. The proceeds went to his widow. Leeds won 4-0 at Valley Parade.

Preparations continued with a friendly against Celtic at Hampden and Leeds gave an impressive performance. Celtic took a first-half lead but the Whites came out fighting after the break. Giles smacked one goal home from 35 yards and then Lorimer got the winner with a sublime chip.

The game drew a crowd of 75,110, dwarfing the pitiful 25,268 who came to Elland Road to watch Ferencvaros. The attendance was impacted by the clash with a local bank holiday with live television coverage being another factor.

With a splendid new stand at the Gelderd end, two new ultra-modern floodlighting pylons to keep it company, and the beautiful condition of the pitch, the stadium finally resembled a place fit for heroes. It was a shame it should resemble a graveyard on this important evening.

Revie had a full squad available but omitted his natural wingers, Johanneson and O'Grady, both available again after protracted injury problems. He opted instead for Madeley as a midfield anchorman.

There had been a stream of propaganda coming out of Elland Road over the summer months that United would opt for a more attacking style in the new season, but the first signs were not encouraging. Revie knew that if he threw caution to the wind, Ferencvaros would pick his men off.

Scouts had identified the Hungarian keeper as a potential weakness. During the 1966 World Cup, the national team's custodian had struggled with the high ball.

Leeds set out to test Geczi and it was soon obvious that he, too, was tentative under aerial examination. He spilled one early cross straight to Hunter, ten yards from goal but the defender was taken by surprise and fired wide. The nervy Geczi struggled throughout with crosses.

Leeds had much the better of things as the Hungarians allowed them to pass the ball round in their own half. United penned Ferencvaros back for long periods, though their final ball was poor.

When Jones forced a corner after 41 minutes, United, renowned for their dead-ball routines, gleefully capitalised.

Charlton took up his familiar position on the goal line and as the kick looped across, Geczi struggled to get above him and could only get his fingertips to the ball. It dropped towards the line and Jones was on the spot to bundle it home.

Ferencvaros later complained bitterly that Charlton impeded Geczi, but there were few protests as the ball entered the net.

After 65 minutes, Giles went off with double vision. He was barged into from behind by a Ferencvaros player as he tried to get his head to a long ball. Out cold for two or three minutes, when he tried to get back to his feet he felt so dizzy that it was obviously pointless carrying on. Greenhoff replaced him.

Five minutes later, Leeds had to use their second sub. When Jones bore down on goal, Geczi flattened him as he entered the penalty area. The whistle went before Jones set off on his run, so it was all in vain. It was an appalling foul and Geczi was jeered repeatedly while the hapless Jones was removed on a stretcher to be replaced by Belfitt.

The substitutions disrupted United's rhythm and allowed the Hungarians back into the game. Charlton did well to rob Varga on the point of shooting and Rakosi was foiled by a brilliant save from Sprake at the very end of a tight game.

Revie acknowledged that Leeds would face a difficult challenge in the second leg in Budapest. 'It is going to be tough in the second leg, but we have faced this kind of thing before. Ferencvaros played as well as we expected them to. The fact that we kept a clean sheet was a good thing. If we get a goal over there they have got to get three.

'A very difficult match is ahead of us. We know how formidable the Ferencvaros attackers are. We expect them to produce some fireworks. But Leeds has proved time and again that its defence can stand its ground at the hottest moments.'

Despite his rough treatment, Jones was fit to lead the attack when United commenced their league campaign against

Southampton at The Dell. The only change saw Greenhoff in for Cooper, with Madeley moved back to replace Cooper.

Leeds conceded a soft goal after 90 seconds from Southampton's opening salvo. It filled the Saints with ill-advised confidence and as they poured forward in search of a second, United picked them off. Bremner stepped over Jones' low cross, leaving Lorimer to hammer the equaliser from 20 yards. The Scot left the field soon afterwards with a torn muscle.

Jones gave United the lead five minutes before the break, beating two defenders to a long clearance by Sprake. After 63 minutes Hibbitt made it 3-1 with a brilliantly executed left-foot volley that dipped under the bar at the last minute.

A thumping 4-1 victory followed against promoted Queens Park Rangers, though a spirited west London side made United struggle for some time. A rare goal from Reaney two minutes from the end gave the scoreline a flattering touch.

Leeds ended the week by beating Stoke 2-0 despite the absence of Giles, Madeley and Lorimer. United were the only side boasting a 100 per cent record, the run lengthened by victory at Ipswich.

The qualities offered by Giles were evident. He brought something special to the Whites' game; in his absence the attack lacked conviction, cohesion and creativity. Giles was subdued through injury against QPR and missing completely against Stoke. United struggled on both occasions. He was on the sidelines until the beginning of October.

The match at Nottingham Forest on 24 August was abandoned at half-time with the score 1-1 after a fire in the main stand.

A blaze caused by an electrical fault took hold in the dressing rooms and spread rapidly, the whole stand going up in flames. Some of the Forest players said that they had to batter a door down to get out. There was no panic, despite a crowd of 31,126, and nor were there any casualties.

The players were listening so intently to Revie's tactical instructions for the second half that for a time they were completely oblivious to the smoke billowing through the door. When Sprake tried to tell Bremner that he smelt burning, the skipper snapped, 'Wrap up, the Boss is talking!'

The first point was dropped on 28 August in a disappointing home draw with Sunderland while the last day of the month brought a vital battle against title rivals Liverpool. United were still dogged by injury, with Giles, Madeley and Gray sidelined. Defences dominated and there were few chances worthy of the name. United took the one that came their way after 27 minutes to register the only goal. Leeds broke up a Liverpool attack and Bremner instantly sent a 40-yard ball curling through a square Reds defence. Ron Yeats slipped as he tried to clear and Jones outpaced him to collect the loose ball, round onrushing keeper Tommy Lawrence and slide the ball home.

Leeds built on the success by beating Wolves and were in great heart as they travelled to Budapest for the second leg of the Fairs Cup final. Popular opinion was that Ferencvaros would have the firepower to see off United in the Nep.

The game was in grave danger of being cancelled following the Soviet invasion of Czechoslovakia.

Cold War tensions were still rumbling between the United States and the Soviet Union. Earlier in the year, Antonin Novotny had lost control of the Communist Party of Czechoslovakia to Alexander Dubček, who launched a programme of liberalisation to revive the country's economic fortunes.

Soviet leader Leonid Brezhnev was concerned that Dubček's actions would weaken the Communist Bloc's position and decided on radical measures. On the night of 20 August, armies from five Warsaw Pact countries invaded Czechoslovakia. Tanks occupied the streets, followed by hundreds of thousands of troops. 72 Czechs and Slovaks were killed and hundreds more wounded.

There was widespread anger throughout the western world, but the reality of nuclear stand-off ruled out a challenge to Soviet military force.

To avoid disruption and boycotts, UEFA elected to segregate Eastern and Western clubs in their tournaments.

There was no doubt about United's willingness to travel to Hungary. They had come too far to be denied at this stage. Revie used his weekly *Evening Post* column to lay out his stance, accepting that Leeds would be condemned by many for not refusing to play.

'Sadly, soccer is being used as a weapon in the political arena,' he warned. 'Political opinion should not be allowed to interfere in any way with sport. Boycotting matches against Communist countries is the easy way out. Surely trying to beat them on the soccer field is a better way to show one's distaste.'

With Giles and Gray unavailable through injury, and Greenhoff now at Birmingham, Revie drafted O'Grady and Hibbitt into his starting line-up. His approach, as ever in Europe, was to dominate midfield with a smothering web, leaving Jones alone up front to forage. United had honed the style over three hard years in Europe.

The Leeds team strode into the magnificent Nep Stadium determined not to yield an inch.

Ferencvaros were straight onto the attack with all-out assaults on Sprake's goal. United adopted a rigorous defensive approach from the off, funnelling back behind the ball whenever danger threatened. For all that, the Hungarians struggled to pose any direct threat and it was 16 minutes before a real goal attempt was made, so tight was the United covering.

The Leeds defenders were all calm confidence, coolly averting attacks and taking pains to retain what little possession they had. The green-shirted Hungarians swarmed all around them, penning them into their area, but calm Yorkshire heads refused to yield – there were no panicky clearances, inviting Ferencvaros back onto the offence, and United grew in assurance.

They broke out in the 35th minute to earn a free kick on the right, giving Charlton the opportunity for a forward advance. The Hungarians had seen enough of the defender's aerial dominance in the first leg to appreciate the threat he offered.

With the attention focused on Charlton, Jones was given room to operate and his high looping header from O'Grady's free kick dropped onto the bar before going behind. When Ferencvaros lost possession, Leeds threatened again but O'Grady was just short of Hibbitt's smart ball to the back post. It was a clear demonstration that Ferencvaros dare not take Leeds lightly.

Such moments were rare as United defended in depth, though they had the measure of the Hungarian forwards, reading their intention almost before they made their move. Even with Novak and Szoke controlling the right flank and Varga and Rakosi the other, giving Juhasz the opportunity to join in, Ferencvaros could find no way through or round a white wall.

Rakosi fired wide from a Varga centre and then Sprake saved with his feet from Szoke. On the hour Ferencvaros sought fresh impetus, bringing on Karaba to replace Szoke. Eight minutes later, Revie responded, replacing the tiring Hibbitt with Bates.

Leeds had weathered the best of the Hungarians, but now Ferencvaros found a second wind and intensified their efforts to snatch an equaliser, forcing a succession of corners and hemming United into their own box.

Most of the chances fell to Rakosi, but he was found wanting. As the game entered its final ten minutes, the Ferencvaros attacks grew frenetic, thrusts coming from everywhere. But there was an icy confidence about United's defence, almost sneering, 'Is that all you have?'

In the 86th minute, the Nep rose as one as Varga cut in from the left to beat Sprake, but United were reprieved when West German referee Schulenberg ruled the goal offside. Then Bremner had to clear from Albert, Varga's overhead strike just beat the post and Sprake was forced to dive at Albert's feet to deny him a shot.

'It was probably my greatest performance for Leeds,' recalled Sprake. 'Near the end I made what I regard as my best ever save … The Hungarians were awarded a free kick outside the box in a very central position, to be taken by their dead-ball ace Novak. I lined up the wall to my right-hand side and stood just behind it to cover my left-hand post. He hit the ball as hard as he could and you could feel the crowd trying to suck the ball into the net … I had only a split second to see it as it dipped over the wall and I managed to dive full-length to my left and slightly behind me. It was important that I got a full hand to it as it was hit so hard it rebounded off me and ended up halfway up the stand.'

It was the finest moment of Sprake's career, earning him the tag of the Hero of Budapest, and it signified symbolically that Ferencvaros' challenge was done. They had thrown everything they could at United's stonewall defence for 90 enthralling minutes and had been resolutely denied.

The final whistle went and the neon scoreboard said it all – Ferencvaros 0 Leeds United 0 – the Inter-Cities Fairs Cup was won.

Bremner went up to receive the trophy from Sir Stanley Rous, president of FIFA. The United players gleefully embarked on a lap of honour to mark a historic victory.

Revie was the proudest man in the Nep. 'When we got into those final few minutes,' he said, 'my heart nearly stopped beating. Every minute as the final whistle drew near seemed like an hour. It was a real team effort here tonight … The way the boys kept their heads and their cool play was really tremendous … We are proud to be the first British club to bring home the Fairs Cup.'

He didn't say so, but Revie knew the victory would come as a slap in the face for United's critics, those who had written so spitefully following the dull-as-dishwater Wembley victory over Arsenal and had not even tried to hide their pleasure when Everton beat Leeds in the Cup.

This was poetic justice indeed, but Revie knew well enough not to gloat. He had won two of the four trophies that United had chased, but it was still the championship he craved, the true endorsement of Leeds United as a magnificent team.

Going for the One

'He wins his battles by making no mistakes. Making no mistakes is what establishes the certainty of victory.'

July 1968: Don Revie gives his annual brief to his squad ahead of pre-season training. He brims with confidence now that the club have broken their trophy duck.

'You are going to win the championship, lads, and what's more you are going to do so without losing a single match.'

Johnny Giles looks askance at Billy Bremner. 'I think he's serious, Billy.'

Bremner returns the glance. 'He wouldn't say it unless he believed it, John.'

A few feet away, Jack Charlton snorts his derision. 'Yeah, right, and look at them pigs flying past ...'

Norman Hunter, Paul Madeley and Paul Reaney nod their acceptance. 'Whatever you say, Boss.'

Revie was on a high, his ego stoked by rumours that his services were wanted by other clubs. Now that Matt Busby had finally lifted the European Cup, the gossips had it that he would announce his retirement any day and be succeeded by Revie. After Leeds secured the League Cup and the Fairs Cup, Revie decided to strike while the iron was hot and made a formal request for an improved contract. His existing deal, with an annual salary of £7,000, had four years still to run but Revie pushed for both a bigger salary and an extension.

Elsie and Don spent many an hour discussing the situation. She encouraged him to press his case.

'Now that Harry's gone, you'll never be in a stronger position. You're the biggest man in the club. They know they can't do without you. You've got a job for life.'

'I want to be fair to them, Elsie, and I don't want to be seen as a money grabber. A fair day's work for a fair day's pay. I promised Harry.'

Harry Reynolds was no longer there to argue Revie's case, but there was no need. 'We have the best manager in the Football League,' gushed new chairman Percy Woodward, 'and we want to keep him.' The directors offered a new contract that would take Revie through to 1975.

The document went unsigned for three months as Revie pursued a decent financial settlement. He told the *Yorkshire Evening Post*, 'I have had some generous offers from other clubs in the last seven years. Two months ago, I was approached by another First Division club to become their manager at double my current salary. They also included fringe benefits like a house and car.'

Revie's relationship with the old-school Woodward and the rest of the board had become strictly business rather than personal. It worked both ways: to the directors, Revie was 'just an employee', albeit one whose authority was absolute; to Revie, the board was a necessary evil, one which understood neither the club, nor the fans, nor the players. They were funders to whom he would table a business case for the investment he required. They paid just enough to keep him.

George Lascelles, the Seventh Earl of Harewood, became life president of the club in 1961. 'Once Harry Reynolds had left,' he remarked, 'Don wanted to run things on his own. Before too long, he was doing that very thing. He had the final say on everything and he was very much Leeds United. Whether some of the directors resented this, I don't know. But I did feel that there perhaps wasn't a true appreciation of just what Don was doing for Leeds United.'

The lessons of previous years had finally sunk in. In 1967, Revie sent his men out in scattergun pursuit of four trophies, declaring that he would be satisfied with 'any two of the four'. A marathon 66-game season left the Whites 'almost like automata,' according to *The Guardian*'s Eric Todd. 'Never again,' Revie promised himself. This time there was only brief distraction from the domestic cup competitions. Leeds' involvement in the FA Cup lasted two games, while the defence of the League Cup brought three unspectacular and poorly attended ties against sides from the lower divisions. Only the Fairs Cup saw a run worthy of the name.

Leeds' playing resources had been stretched to breaking point in 1968, but there were no new signings.

It wasn't because Revie didn't have the funds; the club returned a profit of £57,635. Revie was convinced his squad was strong enough if it only enjoyed reasonable luck with injuries. He was even prepared to lose one bright young star. Despite playing plenty of games, Jimmy Greenhoff was not guaranteed a start when everyone was fit. Desperate for regular first-team football, he left for Second Division Birmingham in a £70,000 deal.

The lack of a consistent goalscorer remained a concern. The arrival of Mick Jones had brought a focal point but his 11 goals from 36 appearances represented a ratio which could not match that of Rod Belfitt.

As if acknowledging the issue, Revie tabled an £80,000 bid for Willie Morgan. The Burnley winger had been negotiating a new contract but chairman Bob Lord refused his wages demand. It seemed to be a foregone conclusion that Morgan was on his way to Elland Road, but Lord blocked the sale and the winger moved to Manchester United instead for £117,000.

Revie was unperturbed, he could get by without Morgan. Even without him, he insisted, the approach would be more attack-minded, 'a policy of free expression,' according to the *Yorkshire Post*'s Dick Ulyatt.

Johnny Giles: 'We switched to a more attractive, open style of play in away matches. We took this latter step, not only to try to shrug off our "unattractive" image, but to bring us more away victories. We felt we were well equipped to win the championship the previous season but threw the title away through being over-cautious away from home. We were too easily satisfied with a draw in situations in which we should have aimed for victory.'

Preparations included a prestige friendly against Celtic. Leeds fielded the selection that dominated the campaign, an embryonic 4-1-4-1, with the classic rearguard of Sprake, Reaney, Charlton, Hunter and Cooper shielded by Madeley as a midfield anchor. Lorimer, Bremner, Giles and Gray ranged across the pitch in support of Jones. The approach was fluid, with overlapping full-backs and goals likely to come from anywhere. O'Grady, when restored from early season incapacity, was the one other player to feature with any regularity.

Greenhoff played the first three league games, Hibbitt nine of the first ten, Belfitt six and Bates three, while Johanneson managed one substitute appearance in the league to go with two starts in the cups. Apart from Terry Yorath, with a brief appearance off the bench in Europe, that was it, with the 12 main names monopolising matters.

United's defence of the Fairs Cup began within a week of beating Ferencvaros. They faced Standard Liege, formidable opponents in the Stade Maurice Dufrasne. A goalless draw made United favourites and they followed up by beating table-topping Arsenal 2-0 to leapfrog them in the league.

Giles, whose injury kept him out of the second leg of the Fairs Cup final, returned in the League Cup against Bristol City. Leeds won more convincingly than the 2-1 scoreline suggested. The Irishman made an immediate difference, bringing authority to midfield, but Revie chose to omit him for the visit to champions Man City, saying, 'I don't want to risk Johnny in this game ... I'm giving him a run in the reserves to give his knee lighter match practice.'

City were struggling, though a 4-0 win at Sunderland improved morale. Revie warned that while form is temporary, class is permanent, and his caution was well-founded – Leeds caught City oozing both.

Leeds had gone 15 matches without defeat but had not won at Maine Road for 32 years. The wait would go on for they were beaten convincingly, with Colin Bell's two goals crowning a 3-1 victory.

Revie said it all. 'Too many players off form.'

Single-goal victories at Newcastle and Sunderland at the beginning of October took United top as Liverpool dropped a point in the Merseyside derby and Arsenal drew at Man City. Goals from Lorimer and Giles secured a 2-0 win against West Ham in a bad-tempered clash on 12 October.

Then came a stumble: United lost at Second Division Crystal Palace in the League Cup, meekly surrendering the trophy they had been so proud to win the previous March. That was as nothing to the hiding that they took at Burnley. A young Turf Moor outfit won 5-1, United's worst defeat since they lost 5-0 at Anfield in 1966. Leeds weren't that bad, it was just that Harry Potts' side had an inspired afternoon.

In a season when United finally realised the rich potential they had hinted at for five years, the game stood out like a sore thumb, a very, very sore thumb.

Relations between United and Burnley had been fractious ever since Leeds returned to Division One. Autocratic Clarets chairman Bob Lord was blunt, opinionated and provocative; he went out of his way to rub Revie and the United board up the wrong way. He was later to say, 'We have to stand up against a move to get soccer on the cheap by the Jews who run TV.' The Leeds directors, several of them Jewish, were deeply offended by Lord, but their abhorrence only made him more spiteful. Sheer, bloody-minded malevolence was one of the reasons why he refused to allow Willie Morgan to cross the Pennines. The feud would grow so extreme that five years later he banned his own directors from attending games at Elland Road.

Lord could rub his hands with vindictive glee at the end of an afternoon when Leeds got a frightful drubbing, blown to the four winds by a team in peak form.

James Holland wrote in *The Guardian* of the Burnley youngsters 'impudently toying with the opposition. Time and again United's defenders were drawn out of position by the bewildering mobility of the Burnley forwards.'

Revie later revealed that Gary Sprake had suffered a close family bereavement on the eve of the match and struggled to cope during the game. The manager pointedly failed to reveal who decided the keeper should play. Unaware of the tragedy, Phil Brown commented, 'Sprake was right off form, and was completely unrecognisable as the hero of Budapest and Liege. He really must try to be more consistent.'

'While all five Burnley goals were excellently conceived, Sprake ought to have prevented three of them,' reported Eric Stanger, 'but it would be unfair to lay the blame for defeat entirely at his door. Charlton was often left stranded by Casper, Reaney found the lithe Kindon setting him more problems than most outside-lefts ... They were outthought, outpaced by these youngsters who ran, chased and never gave in in the manner that Leeds used to do before they reached maturity.'

The result was hard to take for United fans – there were several scuffles in and around the stadium afterwards and several arrests as supporters vented their frustration.

It was the clearest of warnings that there would be no procession to the title. Only time would tell whether the wound would prove fatal.

The tribulations continued with a difficult return match against Standard Liege at Elland Road.

A pre-game spat between the two clubs gave the evening an uncomfortable start. Standard had neglected to bring their customary strip of red shirts and white shorts and only had an all-white kit with them, though they must have known it would cause a colour clash.

Referee Gunnar Michaelson asked Standard to change colours while Revie and Liege coach Roger Petit argued in the tunnel about who should change.

The Leeds change strip of all-blue was offered to the visitors, but they insisted that it did not fit and ignored the officials' decree that they should change. Liege officials insisted that the rules were observed and United had to comply. Eventually, Leeds agreed to compromise and donned the blue kit with an irritable shrug. As a consequence of the argument, the game kicked off 20 minutes late.

If Liege's tactics were designed to unsettle Leeds, it worked – United let the frustration show as they threw themselves into haphazard kitchen-sink attack.

Leeds were without Giles, injured at Burnley, and they badly missed his subtlety and eye for the opportunity. Standard were in fine form, 'balanced, well organised in defence and quick to counter-attack' (Stanger). They appeared to have the measure of United, though O'Grady looked like he might force a breakthrough with his tireless probing and neat ball control. He came in for some heavy attention from left-back Thissen, who went into the referee's book after 27 minutes.

United were rushing their work and displayed none of their customary composure. They were a side better equipped to sit on a lead than chase a game. The gung-ho approach was always likely to leave openings at the back and Leeds were found wanting at the end of the half.

A minute before the interval, the worst happened. Standard had shown impressive speed on the break on several occasions, with Erwin Kostedde a constant threat. Charlton, guilty of a lack of concentration, coughed up a loose pass which was picked up by Van Moer, who fed Galic. With the United rearguard out of position, a fine through ball exploited the gap, sending Kostedde clear down the middle. He hurdled two strong tackles to get in a shot, which Sprake blocked. Kostedde reacted more quickly than the chasing Cooper and Reaney to fire home at the second time of asking.

Cooper had been nursing an ankle injured at Burnley and did not come out for the second half. He was replaced by Bates, with Madeley moving to left-back. The switch did nothing to calm their defensive anxiety and Leeds were suddenly facing an uphill struggle.

Six minutes had gone in the second half when the visitors launched another swift break. The Leeds defence was guilty of more slack marking and slow challenges when a ball through the left channel put Galic in the clear. He added the second goal with clinical efficiency, leaving Sprake clutching at air.

It was a devastating blow. With the Burnley debacle fresh in their minds, United could have been excused for accepting defeat gracefully. With away goals counting double, they needed three goals to stay in the competition and it was a mighty big ask.

Whether they would have been able to recover anything other than pride if they had been given pause to reflect on the size of the challenge is anybody's guess. As it was, they had no time to feel sorry for themselves and were back in the game almost immediately. Charlton made partial amends for his lapse by outjumping everyone to head home an O'Grady centre.

Suitably revived, Leeds committed even more furiously to attack and a succession of wild risks. They left themselves open to the distinct possibility of conceding a third, Depireux striking an upright and Reaney heading another effort off the line.

With the wave of attacks appearing to run out of steam, Gray was called from the bench after 70 minutes to replace Hibbitt. He brought fresh legs and suddenly Standard's assurance began to fray. The winger was fouled soon after taking the field and the free kick was ready made for Lorimer. He needed no second bidding and hammered the dead ball low and true from 35 yards to bring the scores level on the night.

Standard still had the advantage of the away goals and it appeared they would have enough, either nous or luck, to secure victory. But United had triumphed against the odds before and had a blinding conviction that things were never over until the final whistle. They battled on, pinning Liege back into their final third, seeking to roll them over by sheer force of will.

Barely two minutes remained when Leeds pressure won them a corner. Lorimer floated a cross to the near post for Charlton to flick goalwards. Bremner was in the perfect spot to stab home the winner. It was the most dramatic of goals, crowning one of United's more spectacular European nights.

The result eased the pain of the defeats at Palace and Burnley. To have gone out of the Fairs Cup in that same week might have done United's championship challenge irreparable damage. As it was, the high-octane thriller replenished their belief, a turning point in one of their finest campaigns.

Leeds' standard defensive routine brought three successive goalless draws as they stabilised.

After the scoreless run was extended to 337 minutes against Tottenham at home, Eric Stanger wrote, 'Sooner or later there will be a happy ending to this lean spell … but the signs say not yet … This present Leeds attack is overloaded with players who are happier in midfield. It is this lack of marksmen up front that makes Leeds United so dependent on their ploys from free kicks and corners and on the ability of Reaney and Cooper making the overlap by their strong running from full-back.'

United had a tasty Fairs Cup pairing with Napoli, a club that had figured in some tempestuous ties over the years. In 1967, the Burnley players and management had to be escorted out of the Italians' stadium by armed troops and mounted police at the end of the game.

United played magnificently to win the home leg 2-0, the goals headed by Charlton from dead-ball situations within three minutes of each other in the first half. United had three goals disallowed and a penalty appeal turned down, while Italian international Dino Zoff had an inspired night in goal.

'While Naples played a lot of good, clean football,' bemoaned Revie, 'their men also resorted to moves which upset me. Certain of our players … had fingers poked in their eyes … then there was the punch Mick Jones got while on the grass.'

Naples had been fined twice for crowd disturbances in the previous two seasons and United asked for special observers to attend the return leg, Revie flagging up his concerns in writing to Peter Joiris, the Fairs Cup secretary.

Joiris was one of two neutral observers at the game with the gates patrolled by troops and armed police. Considering the tie a dead rubber, only 15,000 were in the 100,000 capacity Stadium San Paolo, but the night air was rent by the sounds of firecrackers as the teams kicked off.

Despite missing five regulars, Napoli were unrecognisable from the tepid team that surrendered at Elland Road and took the lead after 14 minutes as United were forced onto the defensive.

Napoli drew level on aggregate after 84 minutes when Juliano converted a penalty after Charlton fouled Sala. United spent the final five minutes pushing hard for a decisive goal but could not find a way through. Extra-time made no difference.

The 2-0 defeat left the teams level on aggregate and the outcome came down to the flip of a disc. Bremner called correctly to put United through.

The victory was tinged with bitterness. A Napoli player butted O'Grady in the face with the ball yards away. The Italian then threw himself to the ground with both hands over his face, writhing in mock agony. He smirked as the trainer tended his 'injury', but the referee was completely taken in and issued a stern lecture to an incredulous O'Grady.

Revie refused to talk to the Italian papers 'because I just did not trust myself to speak … The three away legs we have played in the Fairs Cup this season have been the toughest we have experienced so far in Europe. There were times on Wednesday night when I was thinking of bringing them off. We have a young side and it's not fair to them. If that is the way they treat their guests, I hope we never have to play Naples here again.'

Woodward echoed Revie's views: 'We cannot go on, we dare not go on, risking games like that against Naples. The danger to our valuable players is too great ... We have had a very great deal of money from our Fairs Cup games ... but with players costing £100,000 nowadays, the risk of having one or more crippled has to be considered. The whole question of different interpretations of the law between British and continental football will have to be closely considered.'

In between the Napoli games, United beat Coventry and Everton, the Coventry display 'technically faultless' according to Geoffrey Green. The game was won by a 'thunderous volley' from Madeley 'a fine swerving shot, first time, from the edge of the penalty area to the roof of the net'.

Leeds beat Sheffield Wednesday 2-0 at Elland Road, with Lorimer scoring both goals. He had been ignored for weeks by Revie who preferred a formation with Madeley lying in deep midfield. Lorimer was recalled when Madeley replaced the injured Cooper at left-back. Unsettled by Revie's decision to omit him, Lorimer asked for a transfer. There were hints that he would be used as makeweight in a deal, with Joe Baker (Nottingham Forest), Peter Cormack (Hibernian) and Colin Suggett (Sunderland) mentioned as targets. He remained on the list for months but there were no takers.

Lorimer was quickly on the scoresheet again, netting another brace in the Fairs Cup against Hanover a week before Christmas. United had been profligate in front of goal for longer than they cared to remember but all that changed when they faced the lacklustre Germans.

Leeds took the lead within four minutes when Hunter combined with Giles and Gray before centring to O'Grady, who hammered home at the far post. After 34 minutes, Hanover fell further behind when Hunter fired home spectacularly from 25 yards with his supposedly weaker right foot.

Hanover were untried against opposition of such class, and Leeds revelled in the space they were given. Lorimer made it three from close range after 52 minutes, Charlton headed home a Bremner free kick on the hour for 4-0 and a couple of minutes later Lorimer added his second. The humbled Germans managed a late consolation effort.

Three days later, United did even better, hammering Burnley 6-1 to avenge the debacle at Turf Moor.

United went all-out for an early goal and got the start they wanted, Lorimer scoring after 90 seconds. He profited at the back post when Jones' header was blocked.

All Burnley's hopes evaporated – United had set their minds on annihilation and they were up and running.

All season long, the Leeds defenders had been ready to throw their weight into attack. For much of the first half they spent their time firmly on the offensive and Gray, O'Grady and Lorimer were constant adjuncts to Jones as Giles and Bremner secured a midfield stronghold. There was little that Burnley could do to stem the tide with United in such dominant form.

After 24 minutes, the siege bore further fruit. A long-range shot from Giles seemed to spell no danger, but the goalkeeper spilled it. Lorimer was on it in a trice to slide it home for 2-0.

Under normal circumstances, securing a two-goal lead would have tempted United to shut up shop. However, on this occasion, they continued to go for the jugular.

After 36 minutes, Giles crashed home a fearsome volley, and then Jones centred perfectly for Bremner to head home. Four-down, Burnley were shell-shocked.

The Lancastrians hinted briefly at a rally, coming forward on several occasions. Sprake had to save from Casper and then Thomas twice went close. They got the reward for their effort when Coates took a pass from Thomas and chipped Sprake from all of 25 yards.

Burnley were quickly disabused of any notion of a revival. United were back at them, like worrying terriers – Lorimer twice went close, first with his head and then with a typical long-range effort; Jones was felled in the box by the keeper, but the referee waved all appeals away.

Eventually, Leeds got a fifth, Jones breaking a long scoreless run by converting a simple chance. With two minutes left, Gray completed the scoring, the 6-1 final tally proving that anything Burnley could do, Leeds could do better.

It seemed a matter of professional pride that the wrongs of October should be righted.

The ghosts of Turf Moor laid to rest, Leeds pressed on with their pursuit of the championship. Nine victories from their next ten league games saw them overtake Liverpool. A 5-1 drubbing of Stoke City on 8 March put Leeds eight points clear, though they had played two games more than the Reds.

Almost as if confirming that the only target was the championship, United bowed tamely out of the FA Cup, beaten by Sheffield Wednesday in a third-round replay. Their run in Europe lasted till the fourth round when they lost both legs against Ujpest Dozsa.

'Some people said we played too many matches in the past,' said Revie. 'We now have the chance to prove whether they were right or wrong – but we still have to win our matches. We have got to buckle down and work for it.'

Following the defeat to Wednesday, Leeds' championship credentials were tested by European Cup holders Manchester United at Elland Road. O'Grady scored a cracking winner after 75 minutes. Giles chipped the full-back to find the winger, who made it 2-1 with a first-time piledriver.

The match was marred by crowd trouble and more than 50 spectators needed treatment after missiles were thrown. 2,000 fans were locked out and many had climbed the advertising hoardings at the Scratching Shed end to get in. A number of fans insisted that problems with the new stand made matters worse.

At the annual general meeting a couple of days later, Woodward, slumming it in the stand, claimed, 'There was no bottle throwing and no fighting. The police were not fighting with the crowd, they were stopping the crowd getting on to the playing area. I am not a young man by any means, and I'm only 5ft 5in tall, but if it's in the interests of the club I'll take my luck like everyone else and mix with the crowd just to see for myself what spectators are grumbling about … I am not being forced into this by the recent events, I merely want to look at things from the fans' viewpoint. It will prove enlightening and will help the board of directors in their deliberations over ground improvements.'

The board was acutely conscious of the grumbling from the fans in the Lowfields Road stand about conditions and prior to the game with Manchester City in April, Woodward kept his promise. According to Jon Howe, 'Woodward paid to get into the popular side for the first time in 30 years to see for himself why fans were complaining about queuing outside, poor viewing conditions and the lack of amenities. Entering at 2.15, he experienced first-hand the diabolical view in some areas and the frequent crushing. He then left by an exit and paid again to enter the Kop to do the same. By kick off he had seen enough and whilst leaving to watch the game in the directors' box he claimed the complaints had been justified.'

On a happier note, director Sidney Simon reported that the £135,000 liability shown in the accounts against the new stand had since been paid off. 'We don't owe a penny on the stands today,' he grinned.

The directors revealed that they had agreed with the local authorities to reduce Elland Road's capacity from 52,000 to 48,000. Woodward said, 'We are re-estimating all our various sections and when necessary will take steps to close them as our crowd indicator shows them to be filling up. It is a big relief to settle this worrying question. No club wants its crowd to be uncomfortable. Our long-term plan of improvements to be done in stages should make things a lot better for everybody.'

Woodward also revealed that United would be going ahead 'sometime in the next 12 months or so' with the building of an extension of the West Stand to fill the gap between it and the Kop. It would offer an extra 2,000 seats, which would compensate for the loss incurred by the reduction of the ground limit.

Champions ... Champions

'Supreme excellence consists of breaking the enemy's resistance without fighting.'

15 January 1969: With the club's annual general meeting out of the way, Don Revie is in conversation with Syd Owen and Les Cocker about what the next few weeks will bring.

The chances of an undefeated campaign have vanished but Leeds have recovered with six victories in the last eight games and an undefeated run of 11. That sequence has kept them in the top two since November and they are hunting down leaders Liverpool, two points in arrears with two games in hand.

When Leeds went out of the Cup to Sheffield Wednesday the previous week, Revie told the players, 'I am going to work you harder than ever.'

He has been true to his word, but they accepted the extra training without a murmur as Revie told the press, 'We have our best ever chance of winning the title because we can concentrate 100 per cent on the league. This last couple of years we've played so many important midweek games that we couldn't afford to drive the players as hard in training for fear that they would be jaded. We had to keep them pepped up with light work in the mornings and massages and sauna baths in the afternoons.'

Revie tells Owen and Cocker, 'We've been knackered these last two seasons, but we've only got the league to go for now, we'll never have a better chance, 17 matches, 15 weeks.'

'You're right there,' says Owen, 'just need to keep it going.'

'Aye, looking good,' offers Cocker, 'but you know Bill Shankly, he'll be geeing his lads up and looking to stuff us at Anfield. They're going great guns.'

Cocker was spot on, the Reds looked ominously strong, limiting goals conceded to nine in the last 22 games. Arsenal and Everton were still in the running, but it looked like a straight fight with Shankly's men.

Revie had already improved the odds, persuading the League to bring forward the Easter game at QPR to 24 January. Rangers were also out of the Cup and rock bottom, struggling for points and easy meat. Revie saw it as a smart move to reduce the Easter pressure, especially as Leeds would otherwise have had a blank week, after exiting the FA Cup.

Revie took a long, hard look at United's prospects. They still had to travel to Arsenal and Everton, as well as Anfield, but he was content.

He was not quite as happy come tea-time on the Saturday evening. Leeds dropped a point in a goalless draw at White Hart Lane, the result overshadowed by the double fracture suffered by Spurs full-back Joe Kinnear.

Liverpool had also been in the capital, but their 2-1 victory at fifth-placed Chelsea had been smooth and efficient and their points advantage clicked up to three.

Leeds were in the Smoke again the following Friday, with the rearranged fixture at QPR. They had to play in red shirts borrowed from their hosts, after the officials declared that there could be a colour clash with Rangers' blue-and-white hoops.

The Londoners needed a point to get off the foot of the table, but nearly got both, hammering United from the start. They almost took the lead when Roger Morgan's first-minute free kick beat Sprake, but Charlton had it covered. Thinking it was going wide, he allowed it to drop over his head. The ball found the post, sparing Charlton considerable embarrassment.

It was United who went ahead a minute later. Madeley brought the ball through and got in a shot. It came back off the keeper and Jones netted from 12 yards.

Rangers were quickly back and unlucky to be denied a penalty; early in the second half a second spot-kick claim was successful but Sprake dived to his right to save Keetch's effort.

United brought Belfitt on for the injured Giles as Rangers pushed hard. Rodney Marsh was having an inspired game and he and Mick Leach both came close to an equaliser before Frank Clarke missed a sitter. Sprake was then lucky to grab a glancing header by Clarke on the line. Shots continued to rain in on the United goal but somehow they survived to take both points.

Revie later identified the match as the turning point of the season, admitting, 'We could have lost 4 or 5-1.' He was baffled that Rangers were not near the top, pondering why all teams raised their game against his side.

The following day Liverpool beat Burnley in the FA Cup fourth round, meaning they would continue to be distracted by dreams of the Double. They continued to progress remorselessly in the league; Roger Hunt got the only goal against Sheffield Wednesday at Anfield on 1 February.

Leeds had the better day, thrashing struggling Coventry 3-0 at Elland Road to hold the deficit to a point.

The torn thigh muscle which Giles sustained at Loftus Road kept him out of action for a fortnight. He was not missed against Coventry nor when Leeds flew to Germany for the formality of their Fairs Cup-tie against Hanover.

United had the weekend of 8 February off, with the Cup fifth round taking precedence, but the snow and ice that saw all but four of the 38 games in England postponed brought an unexpected bonus. Leeds could bring forward another Easter fixture. The Easter Monday game against Ipswich was switched to 12 February, giving them the chance to overtake Liverpool.

Revie: 'We must get these matches in when we can, for you never know what the situation will be near the end of the season. We cannot afford to be faced with a backlog of fixtures, for we want a smooth run-in.'

The weather had a major influence on events that frostbitten winter and United pulled out all the stops to keep their pitch playable. With temperatures rarely getting above freezing, the ground staff turned to some primitive solutions. The surface was covered with tons of straw and braziers were used to thaw the ground. The plan worked admirably, keeping Leeds active while others were left kicking their heels. The Ipswich game was one of those that benefited.

A 2-0 victory took United a point clear, with they and Liverpool both having played 29 games.

In the weekend fixtures, Liverpool looked to have the easier option, at home to a Nottingham Forest side languishing in 20th, while United hosted seventh-placed Chelsea.

Revie acknowledged that Chelsea represented the most difficult of their remaining home games. The Blues had already won six away matches including those at Old Trafford and Highbury and lost only by the odd goal at Anfield.

With an early case of mind games, Bill Shankly rang Revie before the game to tell him he was certain United would only draw. Revie had the last laugh.

Leeds had to ask for special dispensation to allow their pitch clearing efforts time to succeed. Club secretary Keith Archer said, 'It was easy enough to get the straw off, even with a labour force that did not come up to expectations, but then we had to tackle the snow. We should not have done it had not a machine been called in and had not the League agreed to our putting back the kick off until 3.15. We wanted a half hour's delay, but out of consideration for Chelsea's travelling plans we agreed to a quarter of an hour.'

With the delay, Leeds were aware before the off that Forest had taken a fifth-minute lead at Anfield. They also got the news that Barry Lyons had made it 2-0 in the 62nd minute and were content to defend the single-goal lead given them by Lorimer.

'We had to win,' admitted Revie. 'They pulled back nine men into their penalty area and covered each other so well that we were unable to break through in the first half. One could sense the tension building up in the United players as they battled to overcome the problem. The most encouraging feature was that they did not allow this tension to interfere with the normal tempo of their game. They continued to attack patiently and skilfully, and reaped the reward ... In previous years, we would probably have panicked if we had failed to score earlier on, and fallen into the trap of hammering high balls into the Chelsea goalmouth in a frantic effort to drive the ball home by sheer force.'

The mood around Elland Road was buoyant. Jack Charlton, another regular contributor to the *Evening Post*, wrote, 'Everybody is cursing the snow and icy winds, but I shall always remember this as one of the most wonderful spells of weather. It has given us the chance to break away ... We are going to take some catching now.

'I saw Don Revie just before the Chelsea match, sitting exhausted yet happy in an armchair. He had been working on the ground since seven in the morning. He had called in all the staff who were not playing, as well as more than 100 people from the Employment Exchange. This is "Revie's Army". Its soldiers used to take a long time to do the job, but nowadays they can clear the pitch much more quickly, so that it hasn't frozen over by the time we get on it. It is an expensive process. Only the top clubs can afford the £500 or so it takes to make the ground firm but it's certainly worthwhile.'

The Chelsea result increased United's lead at the top to three points, prompting one bookmaker to make Leeds 6-4 on favourites, although they had twelve matches yet to play, with eight of them away. Liverpool had slipped to 7-2, behind Everton, 3-1 as they closed on their neighbours.

Leeds had been due to play at Goodison the following Tuesday but soon after lunch on Monday the referee announced a postponement because of the state of the pitch.

Leeds had asked for an early decision because they had intended to travel that afternoon.

United now had to find new dates for two matches as they had still to rearrange their game at West Brom, postponed on 28 December. There was soon another, with the weekend trip to Sheffield Wednesday off due to another frozen pitch.

Revie was committed to finishing the programme by 26 April, Cup final day. He was dismissive of offers to extend the season to 24 May as players would be required to join their national squads for the home international matches, now scheduled for a compressed week between 3 and 10 May.

Leeds were likely to lose Reaney, Cooper, Charlton, Hunter, O'Grady, Bremner, Gray and Sprake while Ireland skipper Giles would be needed for a World Cup game against Czechoslovakia on 4 May.

England candidates faced another call-up in late May for the tour of South and Central America in preparation for 1970's World Cup finals.

The postponement of Leeds' game at Hillsborough gave Liverpool the chance to close the gap at West Ham, but they had to settle for a point. The Hammers took a 33rd-minute lead but Roger Hunt headed a second-half equaliser.

267

There were fears that Leeds' rearranged fixture three days later at Nottingham Forest would also fall victim. This was the game postponed back in August.

'Really it all depends on the weather, but we are already doing all we can to keep the game on,' commented Forest secretary Ken Smales when asked about the prospects.

Work had begun in a slow thaw, with 60 volunteers helping to get three inches of snow off the pitch before it melted and there were ten-inch drifts in parts. A quick thaw would bring trouble just as surely as would more snow and frost, for the ground drained into the adjacent River Trent, which was swollen and expected to block the drain.

Forest, with only one home appearance in nine weeks, could finally christen their new stand when the referee declared the pitch playable. United gained an emphatic victory after opening the scoring five minutes before the break. Jones met Cooper's lofted centre at the far post to head past the keeper but Baxter managed to clear from inside the goal. The linesman insisted the ball had been over the line and a goal was awarded.

Leeds controlled the second half but had to wait until a minute from time to secure the points. Lorimer looked offside when he collected the ball 35 yards out, but there was no whistle and he raced on unchallenged to score. That left Leeds four points clear with 11 games remaining.

Phil Brown reported in the *Yorkshire Evening Post* on 'a relentless finish by a side which had had its determination tested in both attack and defence. I rate the win as one of United's soundest performances of the season.'

Leeds had the chance to extend their four-point advantage on 1 March with the Reds in Cup action at Leicester. Perhaps it was nerves, but they gave a scratchy, woeful performance against Southampton at Elland Road. A confident Southampton twice took the lead before United fought back to win 3-2.

Maybe as a distraction, a frustrated Revie focused on the attendance, apoplectic as he spoke to Phil Brown. 'We could have had 40,000 – there are over two million people within 15 miles of the ground. If we lost three matches in a row, I don't think we would get 25,000, and if ever we got a real slump, I can see us having to sell players to live. Here we are, top of the

Football League, having lost only two matches out of 32, and only 33,000 turn up to watch us play a side sixth in the table.'

Brown reminded readers that an average home gate of 36,000 was needed to pay the way. Out of the 18 games played thus far, there had been less than the required figure on ten occasions.

After Revie's outburst, the *Evening Post* received a string of complaints ranging from insufficient toilets to terraces too shallow for short people to see when there was a big crowd.

Terry Lofthouse met Percy Woodward for a question-and-answer session, beginning, 'When United met Sheffield Wednesday in a Cup-tie at Hillsborough there were receipts of £12,000 from a gate of 52,000. At Elland Road, receipts were £18,000 for a 48,000 gate. Doesn't this suggest you are charging higher prices?'

Woodward responded, 'We have got to charge economical prices or the club cannot pay its way … If we are to make improvements the money has to come from somewhere.'

When asked how much profit a 36,000 gate generated, Woodward commented, 'We only break even … We bring in roughly £10,500, but out of that we have to maintain the club, and that works out at about £5,500 a week. There are players' wages, staff wages, hotel bills, travelling expenses, players' kit and numerous other things. And don't forget electricity, rates, paying policemen and many more such items. Some of those stretch over 52 weeks, not just the football season.'

When Lofthouse asked when work would start on further ground improvements, Woodward indicated the summer of 1970 'if we have the money. The first stage is extending the West Stand and build at the corner of the stand and the Kop, level with the floodlight pylon. We shall have more standing accommodation there as well as more seats. Bearing in mind the vast amount of money the new Kop has cost, you can imagine how much this first stage will require. We've got a lot of plans, but I'm afraid none will be implemented in this close season because we won't have enough money to start the first stage. Don't be misled by the big profits we've announced in recent years; they've simply helped to pay for the £250,000 new Kop. And we paid out £100,000 for Mick Jones.

'We are not trying to milk supporters in any way. But without the money for Mr Revie to build his team ... we cannot do a thing. We've ploughed every penny back into the game.'

Revie had calmed down in time for the press conference for the Fairs Cup clash against Ujpest Dozsa. He recalled how well the Hungarians had played when the sides met in Budapest three years before.

He was wise to be cautious – United lost 1-0 to an outstanding team playing a classic European game of counter-attack.

All this time, Liverpool's pursuit had been on hold. Their last league game was on 22 February and their fixture with Arsenal on 8 March was postponed with the visitors having eight men sick. United thus travelled to struggling Stoke City with the chance of increasing their advantage to eight points.

In 1968 Stoke had scuppered Leeds' title hopes in an end of season tussle, but there was to be no repeat. City were only allowed to get as far as the United penalty area three times in the first half as the visitors raced into a three-goal lead courtesy of an opener from Jones and a Bremner brace.

Stoke rallied in the second half and pulled one back from the penalty spot but O'Grady added two goals to complete a 5-1 rout.

Leeds could easily have scored eight, so rampant were they. England manager Sir Alf Ramsey recognised as much, selecting Charlton, Cooper and O'Grady against France a few days later. Reaney and Hunter were non-playing subs as England won 5-0, their best victory for more than two years. Cooper and O'Grady were outstanding, with the winger opening the scoring after seven years in international exile. Perversely, Ramsey dropped him and he never got near the squad again.

United's game at home to Forest on 15 March was postponed because of snow, giving Liverpool the chance to narrow the eight-point gap, which they duly did with victory at Sunderland. There was a week to go to the big showdown with Leeds at Anfield and huge expectancy in the air.

Before that, United faced Ujpest in the Fairs Cup and flew out to Budapest without Reaney, Charlton and O'Grady, all in bed with flu. Hunter also had a high temperature, although he travelled and was expected to play. The manager called up reserves Terry Yorath and Jimmy Lumsden as cover.

Revie suggested that the bug was connected with an injection the players received on England duty. 'If we had six, seven or eight down, we would ask the Fairs Cup committee for a postponement but, with four outstanding league fixtures still to fit in, we can do without another postponement.'

There were further scares when Bremner, Madeley, Cooper, Jones and Hunter were rushed off to bed with high temperatures on arrival in Budapest. In the end all five played (Bremner at full-back) but Ujpest won 2-0 to end United's Fairs Cup hopes.

Shankly was beside himself with frustration as Liverpool's game at Newcastle was postponed. His mood was soon even darker. As United flew home, Maurice Lindley contacted the Football League to ask for the Liverpool-Leeds game to be postponed. Leeds had ten first teamers unavailable and the League had little option other than to accede to the request but the postponement was kind to United.

The decision was controversial, particularly with United already given leave to bring fixtures forward. Liverpool were furious, muttering about conspiracy, though Shankly would only comment, 'This is terrible … a great disappointment.'

Daily Mirror football writer Derek Wallis accused the League of favouritism, claiming that United had been guilty of 'expert juggling with the fixtures'. The League retorted that it hoped this would be the first and last time anyone would accuse it of favouritism.

Their support warmed Revie's heart, though it smacked of prickly self-regard. The League mocked Wallis' 'evidence' and accused him of smearing Revie for 'legitimately … keeping his team playing'. They described as irrelevant the fact that other clubs did not have blank dates because of commitments in other competitions, pointing out that it 'was similarly irrelevant in other years when other clubs switched dates and Leeds could not … Had he taken the trouble to check, he would have discovered that many other clubs switched fixtures from Good Friday … Holiday fixtures are classified as midweek fixtures and the rule is that if the two clubs agree to a switch of a midweek date the League generally make no objection.'

The next games for the title rivals came on 29 March, with Liverpool away to QPR and Leeds in Wolverhampton. Looking match rusty after their lay-off, United were slow off the mark and had to be content with a goalless draw while Liverpool shaved a point off the lead with a 2-1 win in London.

Two days later Liverpool faced Arsenal in a rearranged game. While the Gunners were eight points back on Leeds, they had not given up hope on the title themselves and offered Liverpool a severe test on a surface made treacherous by falling snow. Liverpool were in control until Jimmy Robertson gave Arsenal the lead two minutes before the break. A penalty at the start of the second half brought Liverpool level and there were no more goals.

United's advantage was down to four points, though 13 from eight matches would be enough. Leeds earned the first of those the following night in a goalless draw at Sheffield Wednesday.

Points were all that mattered and both sides achieved workmanlike single-goal victories on 5 April, Leeds entertaining champions Man City while Liverpool hosted Wolves.

The Reds sought to narrow the five-point gap with their game in hand, at Stoke the following Monday. They made their intentions plain with all-out assault from the first whistle. For all their effort and enthusiasm, Liverpool only drew Gordon Banks into serious action on one occasion, forcing him to tip over a long-range drive from Callaghan. At the other end, Stoke had strident penalty appeals turned aside when Thompson seemed to handle the ball.

Liverpool lost Hunt with a dislocated shoulder in the 50th minute. He had scored his 300th goal for the Reds at Wolves two days earlier and would be missing for several weeks, news that was as unwelcome for Shankly as the loss of another point.

Leeds kept ground with a draw at West Bromwich, fighting back after falling behind in four minutes.

Liverpool seemed to have the easier option at the weekend, away to struggling Leicester, while Leeds travelled to meet third-placed Arsenal in what promised to be a stormy clash.

Liverpool managed a routine 2-0 victory, but United had more trouble against opponents still smarting from losing a second successive League Cup final, going down to Third Division Swindon Town.

The match burst into ugly life after just four minutes with a fierce confrontation in United's area. A high ball was missed by both Sprake and Gunners centre-forward Bobby Gould as it hung on the wind. There had long been bad blood between the two men and Gould kicked out at the keeper. Sprake reacted furiously, flooring the striker with a vicious left hook. Both players were booked by referee Ken Burns, though most witnesses thought that Sprake should have been dismissed.

The keeper complained, 'He kicked me in the balls and called me a f***ing Welsh so-and-so. I lost it and decked him.'

Sprake was off on the walk of shame but Welshman Burns whispered in his ear, 'Everything will be okay, Gareth. I heard what he called you.'

There was suspicion that Burns felt he owed United one after cheating them in the Cup semi-final against Chelsea in 1967. He had not refereed them since. Burns claimed that in a case of retaliation, both offenders should get the same justice. 'From what I saw I did not consider the offences serious enough to warrant a dismissal.'

Thus reprieved, United opened the scoring after 14 minutes. With everyone but Ian Ure in the Leeds half, Mick Bates pumped a high clearance forward. Ure misjudged the flight of the ball at halfway and Mick Jones left him standing before beating goalkeeper Bob Wilson.

George Graham volleyed an equaliser 20 minutes later, but Leeds quickly restored their advantage. Ure was again at fault and this time with virtually a carbon copy of the mistake which allowed Swindon to score at Wembley.

Then, Ure, pressured by Peter Noble as he prepared to make a simple pass back to Wilson, waited until the keeper was no more than a yard away before releasing the ball. It rebounded to Noble off Wilson's knee and Smart added the finishing touch.

Against Leeds, Ure again seemed to have the situation under control as he took the ball back towards his own goal after cutting out an intended through pass. Giles, remem-bering the Wembley slip, kept the pressure on and Ure's pass was too far to Wilson's left. Giles got to it just before it reached the byline to walk the ball home for 2-1. There were no further goals and another valuable two points had been nabbed to keep the advantage over Liverpool to five.

The sides marched in time again on 19 April, Leeds beating Leicester 2-0 and Liverpool hammering Ipswich 4-0. United now needed four points from three games, though these included trips to Anfield and fourth-placed Everton.

Tension crackled the following Tuesday evening as Leeds travelled to Goodison and Liverpool were at Coventry. Radios were evident amongst fans eager to keep up with the scores.

Liverpool pressed hard and were denied by the woodwork but the dismissal of Alun Evans and Coventry's Maurice Setters for fighting lowered the temperature and the game petered away to a disappointing goalless draw.

Despite the absence of a flu-stricken Jones, Leeds were in collected mood at Goodison, satisfied with matching both Liverpool's point and their clean sheet.

The two teams sat out the following Saturday, Cup final day. The equation was simple: if Leeds drew or won at Anfield on the Monday, the championship was theirs; if Liverpool were victorious, then United could still secure the title by beating Forest at home two days later, though such last-ditch drama was unappealing. Revie had suffered too many disappointments to take anything for granted and refused to count any chickens.

Revie was able to select from strength; his only change was to recall the fit again Jones, with Lorimer dropping to the bench.

Liverpool were unchanged; they continued without Hunt, who had not played since dislocating a collarbone at Stoke on Easter Monday. Evans, who became Britain's first £100,000 teenager when he arrived from Wolves earlier in the season, led the attack despite his dismissal at Coventry.

The gates were closed with 53,750 passionate football followers inside and hundreds more locked outside.

Bremner complained of a sleepless night to Phil Brown. 'I even got up out of bed at four o'clock in the morning and smoked a cigarette to try and stop thinking about the game.' Winning the toss, he chose to make Liverpool play towards the Kop in the first half. It was a calculated risk, leaving Leeds to weather a fearsome opening burst.

Revie hinted that United would attack whenever they had the chance. Few who had seen them play over the previous six years gave those claims much credence and it was soon evident that Leeds would be content with a clean sheet.

The first few minutes were frenetic and United struggled to conceal their anxiety, rushing their work and launching into some rash challenges. Liverpool were just as wound up and there were some fierce clashes. United committed two fouls in five minutes and Liverpool retorted with four in five, all driven by nerves. In that period Tommy Smith, Tommy Lawrence, Cooper, Sprake and Jones required treatment.

As the initial storm started to ebb, Leeds established a calm rhythm and shape that Liverpool found difficult to fathom, let alone pierce. Cooler heads might have improved the Reds' effectiveness, but they were all set on overpowering the champions elect. In contrast, United stuck coolly to Revie's blueprint, collected and calm.

Reaney and Cooper sat tight on wingers Callaghan and Thompson, forcing the Reds to attack down the middle where they could be repelled by a compact white wall. Madeley offered a defensive screen to the back four while Charlton's aerial dominance, the assured tackling and covering of Hunter and a faultless performance by Sprake gave the United spine a resilient look.

The approach had worked hundreds of times before – the art of smothering, blanket defence had been perfected during their European forays.

Despite sustained Liverpool pressure, there were few early moments of real anxiety and it was 26 minutes before an attempt worthy of the name. Callaghan fired wide with an ambitious 25-yard effort, but the chance marked the start of a second wind for Liverpool. They pressed hard and came close to breaking the deadlock in the 35th minute.

Bobby Graham for once evaded United's defensive net to get in a cross for Evans, 14 yards out. In his eagerness the young striker snatched at the chance and fired high and wide.

There were few other chances in the half and Leeds' confidence was boosted by achieving their first milestone, goalless at the break. Shankly got into his men's ribs during the break and urged them to rouse themselves. Now they found some chinks in the white iron curtain.

After 61 minutes, Sprake pulled out all the stops to deny Callaghan and Liverpool then came close to a breakthrough. Ian St John fashioned an opening with a clever lob into the penalty area that found Evans unmarked. Again, the teenager failed to finish, shooting wide with the goal at his mercy.

That was as close as the Reds came while United created chances of their own over the last 15 minutes. For most of the game Jones was an isolated figure up front, but now he had some reinforcements. Giles nearly put O'Grady through, though the chance came to nothing.

There was the inevitable pounding of the United area over the frantic final minutes, but Liverpool simply did not have the inspiration to unlock such a wonderful rearguard – the game was up and United had survived in magnificent fashion.

They celebrated in style at the whistle and then received a most unexpected accolade. After acknowledging the travelling support, Revie instructed Bremner to lead the players up to the Kop. The Scot was apprehensive but took them slowly down to the other end.

There was hushed apprehension at what might be the reaction but one of the most sporting crowds in football provided the ultimate tribute, with warm chants of 'Champions, Champions'.

The moment sent shivers down the spines of the men in white and Revie described the reception as 'truly magnificent' before adding, 'and so, for that matter, was our defence tonight. It was superb in everything.'

Shankly came into the dressing room with a bottle of champagne for each of the Leeds players and asked Revie if he could speak. 'All I've got to say to ye, boys, is ye're a great side and ye deserved to win it. Ye didn't pinch it, ye didn't fluke it, ye're a wonderful team.'

'Coming from Shanks,' grinned Revie, 'that was praise indeed.' The two managers were fast friends and often telephoned each other on Saturday evenings after the match. Revie appreciated the gesture.

The championship secured, Revie turned his attention to the final match, two days later at Elland Road against Nottingham Forest, knowing that victory would bring a record 67 points.

For large parts of the game, it was very much a case of 'After the Lord Mayor's Show' as United struggled to impose any authority. With six minutes left and the match drifting towards a draw, Cooper moved forward. His shot was mishit but Giles was in the right place to coolly bring the ball down over his shoulder and fire it home from ten yards to send the crowd wild. It was only right that the master schemer should be the one to get the vital goal – he had enjoyed a tremendous campaign after putting early-season injuries behind him.

Five minutes after the final whistle, Len Shipman, president of the Football League, presented the championship trophy to Bremner in the centre circle. The players, who had run on to the field one by one, were then presented with their medals.

Victory brought a fitting end to a glorious season that United fans would never forget and one that set the record books spinning.

In addition to their record points total of 67, they achieved the most wins, most home wins and points and fewest defeats at a mere two. They conceded just 26 goals, only nine of which came at Elland Road.

Leeds were the worthiest of champions, a fact underlined by Revie's election as Manager of the Year. 'I accepted the title on behalf of Leeds United not on behalf of Don Revie,' he said.

On 1 May, a fleet of four coaches carried the players, staff and championship trophy in triumph from Elland Road to a civic reception and a tumultuous welcome by 10,000 cheering fans at the Town Hall.

The crowd began gathering two hours earlier; dozens of police were on duty and crush barriers were erected in front of Victoria Square steps. Shortly before 8pm a police escort led the procession down The Headrow, which had been closed to traffic. From the leading open-topped coach, Bremner showed the trophy to the crowd.

Cheering greeted the team as they were led on to the Town Hall steps by Lord Mayor John Rafferty, limping on crutches and with a cigarette drooping from his lips. Chants of 'Don Revie is our king' greeted the manager as he moved towards the microphones.

'I would like to thank the Leeds supporters for this wonderful turnout,' said Revie. 'But remember, it is not me but the lads. I hope you will support us next year and we will have a crack at the European Cup.'

Bremner thanked the gathered throng for 'the wonderful support you've given us this year, not only at Elland Road but also away from home, especially youse boys who've moved from the Scratching Shed up to the other end. We really appreciate it.'

Inside the Town Hall, Woodward told the guests he was the happiest man in the city. 'We have the greatest manager in the land,' he added.

There was more to come, much, much more, but for now Revie and his team were at the head of football's top table, the football press forced to acknowledge a great side.

Even Derek Wallis, a constant critic, offered praise. 'There has been no doubt in my mind for two seasons that Leeds are the best equipped of all the English teams for the traps, tensions and special demands of the competition they will now enter – the European Cup. Leeds United are the champions, the masters, the new kings of English football – at last.'

Woodward paid a tribute in the *Evening Post*. 'We have won the championship because Don Revie and his players have done every single thing humanly possible to win it. The board are intensely grateful to them, and so, I am sure, is our crowd. United have been very fortunate in having at the same time and working closely and harmoniously together two great natural leaders of men in Don Revie and our skipper, Billy Bremner. You do not find leaders of men every day, and still more rarely do you find two of them of the outstanding calibre of these two in their respective roles with us. Where the one leaves off the other takes over. Their devotion to duty and single-mindedness of purpose are inspiring.'

Revie had little interest in Woodward's words and when asked how United had won the title, he turned the discussion to the future. 'We still have achieved only about three-quarters of what I want the club to do. I want United to win the European

Cup, the World Club championship and, of course, the FA Cup. In the last two seasons we have won the League Cup, the Inter-Cities Fairs Cup and the championship, but we must go further still.'

Revie sloped off to enjoy a warming cup of tea with his beloved Elsie after the game before seeking out another loved one, his mentor Harry Reynolds, now club vice-president.

After the game Reynolds had told the press, 'This is something I dreamed about but something I knew could be done with the right approach. When we were in the Second Division I spoke to the crowd and said our aim and ambition was to win the Second Division championship, then go on to the First Division championship and then the European Cup!'

There was a huge beaming grin across his face and a warm handshake as Revie arrived at his house.

'We've done it, Don, well done.'

'Couldn't have done it without you, Harry. Just really disappointed we couldn't do it while you were in the chair. This should have been your achievement, not Woodward's.'

'Don't be saying that about Percy, Don, he means well.'

'I know he does, Harry, but he's not you.'

'Thanks very much, Don, but nothing stays the same for ever. You're Leeds United, Don, not Percy. Don't deny him his moment of glory, just enjoy your own. You've done a remarkable job and we've got everything we dreamed of. Now go and get us the European Cup.'

Reflections

'We all hate Leeds and Leeds and Leeds, Leeds and Leeds and Leeds, Leeds and Leeds and Leeds, we all f***ing hate Leeds!'

In November 2015, the *Daily Mirror* claimed that Leeds was the most sung-about football club by fans of opposing teams. They reckoned there were 117 anti-Leeds chants, a massive 67 more than those against second-placed Liverpool.

United had achieved little of genuine note since their Champions League odyssey in 2001 and have been without senior silverware since the championship in 1992. And yet, a bitter hatred of Dirty Leeds 'and all they stand for' percolates through supporters of other clubs.

Even future 'saviour' Ken Bates, chairman of Chelsea when United fans damaged a scoreboard at Stamford Bridge in 1984, had the bug, promising, 'I shall not rest until Leeds United are kicked out of the Football League. Their fans are the scum of the Earth, absolute animals and a disgrace. I will do everything in my power to make this happen.'

Those words were trotted out in later years by United's own fans, expressing their 'We're Leeds and we don't care' declarations of siege mentality. 'All Leeds aren't we?' and 'we've had our ups and downs' are regular rallying calls for the faithful.

So exactly why are Leeds United so universally reviled by rival football fans the length and breadth of the country?

It could be because Don Revie's Leeds United spearheaded the descent into gamesmanship, ultra-professionalism and defensive 'method football' during the 1960s.

One uncredited reporter wrote that 'The leaden football of the first 90 minutes has earned the 1965 Cup final a reputation as the worst final for years. This is the price the public must pay for the success it demands. Gates for years have shown that the fans will not settle for brave losers; they ought not now to complain of the way victories are won. Leeds and Liverpool did not play like this because they were at Wembley. Rather, they were at Wembley precisely because they play like this. Like it or loathe it, this was the football that got them there.'

Yet Liverpool were never accorded their share of the blame, painted as more elegant a club, one with more of a tradition.

The 1965 Cup semi-final against Man United brought this from *The Times*: 'The sooner Manchester United and Leeds United take a hard, appraising look at themselves and each other in the cracked mirror of Hillsborough, Sheffield, the better for all concerned ... This angry, shabby affair of naked intimidation and moments of physical violence should be held up as a permanent warning to all those who bow to Mammon at the expense of ethical standards. Those who live by the sword in the end may find it to be double-edged.'

Leeds had many wars of attrition against Chelsea and yet the Londoners were dubbed champagne-swilling playboys whose football was all swagger, poise and flair.

Tommy Smith, Peter Storey, Nobby Stiles and Ron 'Chopper' Harris represent the embodiment of the game at the time, dark-eyed destroyers who thought nothing of putting an opponent into the stands with one sly nudge at the right time or a blood-curdling sliding tackle, but Bobby Collins, Norman Hunter, Jack Charlton, Paul Reaney, Billy Bremner and Johnny Giles were the ones who were remembered. Perhaps it was just because Leeds were so much better at the art, had more of its exponents and were more evident in their strident attempts to influence officials.

And Don Revie, with his eternal, over-apparent chip on the shoulder, never earned the affection of those outside his club in the same way that Bill Shankly, Matt Busby Jock Stein and Bill Nicholson did; Revie, or 'Don Readies' as many would have it, was respected but reviled, forever branded as a scourge on football and sportsmanship. The greater the criticism, the more that Revie protested; the more that Revie protested, the greater the criticism. It was a vicious circle of epic proportions and one that would leave his club always referred to as Dirty Leeds, a term he detested.

There is no way of pinning down exactly when the myth of Dirty Leeds began: it could have been the day in early 1962 when Glasgow street fighter Bobby Collins answered Revie's call; it might have been over Christmas 1963, when United clashed twice with promotion rivals Sunderland and players on both sides indulged in onfield thuggery of the worst kind; or perhaps the month before, when United entertained Preston and the aggression was so intense that the referee halted the game after an hour to give the players a final chance to calm down and get themselves under control.

Whatever the truth, there was one specific day in the late autumn of 1964 that ranks prominently in the development of the legend – Leeds United's clash with Everton at Goodison Park has gone down in the annals of English football as one of its most notorious confrontations. It took both sides to generate the heat that ruined the day, but it certainly cemented the reputation of the Whites for provoking controversy and rancour.

It's a moot point as to whether Revie set out with the deliberate intention of his men kicking their way to success. He strenuously denied any such thing, choosing instead to lay the blame at the door of opponents, referees, commentators – anybody outside the confines of Elland Road would do. There are too many examples of the Yorkshiremen being involved in appalling scenes for such protestations of innocence to carry much credibility.

Jack Charlton provided a telling hint of the Elland Road approach, recalling the time he was lying in the treatment room alongside one of the young reserves, Jimmy Lumsden. The young Scot was talking about the previous evening's match and told Charlton that he had gone over the top of the ball to an opponent who had then been carried off.

'I gave him a beauty,' said Lumsden.

'You live by the sword, you die by the sword,' counselled Charlton. 'That guy might some day play against you again, he will remember you and he might just go over the top to you when you're not expecting it. You might finish up breaking your leg.'

Revie would point to the elegance of Gray, the fearsome shooting of Lorimer, the gorgeous passing of Giles and the spirit and heart of Bremner; his critics would see someone who would have been put down if he had been a racehorse, a diver, a dirty little bastard and a chain-smoking, beer-swilling thug. And, of course, there was the abominable Collins.

Giles earned himself a dark name after his arrival at Elland Road. He was unequivocal about the reality of the professional game: 'You had to establish a reputation that would make people think twice about messing with you ... It was a different game then, much more physical than it is today – vicious even – and people like Bobby Collins and myself were targets ... Now you either took it or you responded to it, and Bobby and I responded to it ... People might say, "Oh, that's not right – it's not sporting," but that's the way it was, a fact of life.'

The jutting-out chins, brash arrogance and shameless attitude brought out the worst in others, provoking them to outdo Leeds at their own game. As often as not, uptight opponents would forget to play football in their eagerness to fight fire with fire and that usually spelled their downfall: United had gained the upper hand, earned the right to dictate terms and usually finished off their opponents with equal measures of skill and brutality. It mattered not which weapon was required, Revie's men were equally at home with both bludgeon and rapier.

Hunter, Charlton, Reaney, Collins, Bremner, Giles ... Think of these icons of the Sixties and you cannot avoid recalling their fearful studs-up and elbows-out reputations, no matter how hard you try.

George Best used to recount the story of a team talk given by Matt Busby, a fiercely patriotic Scot, when Manchester United were playing Leeds: 'Gary Sprake, the goalkeeper, on his day a nasty piece of work. Right-back, Paul Reaney, dirty bastard. Left-back, Terry Cooper, even dirtier bastard. Johnny Giles, dirty little bastard. Centre-half, Jack Charlton, dirty big bastard. Right-half, wee Billy Bremner, good Scottish boy!'

For Best, Reaney came to be a feared spectre at the feast; he was usually detailed to man-mark the Irishman and did so successfully during one match in December 1964. Best had enjoyed even closer attention from another player. 'As the two teams walked down the tunnel, I felt a terrific pain in my right calf as someone kicked me with brute force. I turned. It was Bobby Collins. "And that's just for starters, Bestie," he said.'

Despite all the criticism and name-calling, Leeds and Revie were acknowledged as being the best team around when they were at their peak, an all-conquering juggernaut which swept aside the opposition with a fierce and passionate style of play that few could live with.

They were the most consistent of England's clubs in Europe in the Sixties with four attempts on the Inter-Cities Fairs Cup bringing one trophy, one final and one semi-final with five defeats from their first 39 games.

In the five years of domestic competition following 1964's promotion, Leeds were champions once, runners-up twice, fourth on two occasions, FA Cup finalists once, semi-finalists twice and raised the League Cup on one occasion. It is a glittering record but the period is more often characterised as the ultimate case of serial bottling it, with the club four times pulling up short at the final stage, crippled by nerves, self-doubt, an overly conservative approach and those damned dossiers.

The narrative does Leeds dreadful disservice. Theirs is the classic story of rags to riches, a mediocre club from a grimy northern city with no heritage tearing up from the depths of the Second Division to lord it over the best teams in world football.

Leeds United's title triumph of 1969 seemed light years from the days of Lambton and Taylor, and the knife's edge escape from the Third Division. The club was no longer either a one-man team or a music-hall joke – Leeds United had every right to lay claim to the title of Team of the Sixties.

The revered Geoffrey Green of *The Times* wrote in 1969, 'It has been a hard climb, a continuous and often discouraging assault. But now they have finally conquered the pinnacle, leaving the rest of the field behind.

'The image of defence dies hard. Yet this is no longer fair to Leeds. Certainly, there is little of the flashing rapier about their attack ... rather it is a slow, pounding process, a gradual crushing of the opposition, that is the Leeds method. If not a thing to excite the senses, it is effective, and the fact is that only Everton and Chelsea in the top drawer have scored more goals this season.'

The partnership of Don Revie and Harry Reynolds was one made in heaven and they fashioned a dynasty by building through the ranks. They recruited some of the finest young talent around when they had no right to do so, pitted against the glamorous giants from London, Liverpool and Manchester.

Revie shaped his young foot soldiers with outstanding insight. Bremner and Giles were right wingers whom he converted into central midfield playmakers; Reaney, Hunter and Cooper joined as centre-half, inside-forward and winger respectively, but Revie thought better and transformed them into the best defenders in Europe. His less successful attempt to rebrand Charlton as a striker was an isolated misjudgement. And it was the gelling of the players into a team with no stars that made Revie's name as one of the game's best coaches.

He bred a team spirit and sense of family togetherness and singlehandedly transformed Leeds United into one of the world's most successful clubs.

It's a moot point whether Revie could have succeeded at another club or without Reynolds, but the debt he owed to his mentor is incontrovertible. They established a mutual admiration society, two northern chaps who worked themselves up from their working-class roots with insight, intelligence, hard work and ambition. They took a drifting football club and transformed it into a slick and effective industrial giant, renouncing neither their homespun philosophies nor their commitment to looking after the little people, the cleaning ladies, the secretaries and the players' wives.

The story of Revie, Reynolds and Leeds United, the Team of the Sixties, is truly unique.

Bibliography

Armfield, Jimmy, *Right Back to the Beginning: The Autobiography* (Headline, 2005).

Bagchi, Rob and Rogerson, Paul, *The Unforgiven: The Story of Don Revie's Leeds United* (Aurum Press, 2009).

Ball, Alan, *Playing Extra-time* (Pan, 2005).

Butler, Bryon, *The Football League 1888-1988: The Official Illustrated History* (Queen Anne Press, 1987).

Chapman, Daniel, *100 Years of Leeds United: 1919-2019* (Icon Books Ltd, 2019).

Charlton, Jack, *Jack Charlton: The Autobiography* (Corgi, 1997).

Clavane, Anthony, *Promised Land: A Northern Love Story* (Yellow Jersey, 2011).

Coomber, Richard, *King John: True Story of John Charles* (Leeds United Publishing Ltd, 2000).

Edwards, Gary, *Fifty Shades of White: Half a Century of Pain and Glory with Leeds United* (Pitch Publishing Ltd, 2016).

Grainger, Colin, *The Singing Winger* (deCoubertin Books, 2019).

Gray, Eddie, *Marching on Together – My Life at Leeds United* (Hodder & Stoughton Ltd, 2001).

Greaves, Jimmy, *The Heart of The Game* (Sphere, 2006).

Hardaker, Alan and Butler, Bryon, *Hardaker of the League* (Pelham Books, 1977).

Hardy, Lance, *Stokoe, Sunderland and 73: The Story of the Greatest FA Cup Final Shock of All Time* (Orion, 2011).

Harrison, Paul, *The Black Flash: The Albert Johanneson Story* (Vertical Editions, 2012).

Howe, Jon, *The Only Place for Us: An A-Z History of Elland Road – Home of Leeds United* (Pitch Publishing Ltd, 2015).

Hutchinson, Roger, *'66: The Inside Story of England's 1966 World Cup Triumph* (Mainstream Sport, 2002).

Lorimer, Peter and Rostron, Phil, *Peter Lorimer: Leeds and Scotland Hero* (Mainstream Publishing Ltd, 2005).

McKinstry, Leo, *Jack and Bobby: A Story of Brothers in Conflict* (HarperCollins, 2009).

Mourant, Andrew, *Don Revie: Portrait of a Footballing Enigma* (Mainstream Publishing, 2003).

Peace, David, *The Damned Utd* (Faber and Faber, 2007).

Rees, Paul, *The Three Degrees* (Constable, 2014).

Risoli, Mario, *John Charles: Gentle Giant* (Mainstream Publishing, 2003).

Rowlands, Alan, *Trautmann: The Biography* (Breedon Books, 2005).

Saffer, David, *Bobby Collins: The Wee Barra* (Tempus, 2004).

Saffer, David, *Match of My Life: Leeds* (Know the Score Books, 2006).

Sprake, Stuart and Johnson, Tim, *Careless Hands: The Forgotten Truth of Gary Sprake* (The History Press, 2007).

Sutcliffe, Richard, *Revie Revered and Reviled* (Great Northern Books Ltd, 2010).

Thomas, Jason, *The Leeds United Story* (Littlehampton Book Services Ltd, 1971).

Thornton, Eric, *Leeds United and Don Revie* (Robert Hale Ltd, 1970).

Tyler, Martin, *Encyclopaedia of British Football* (Marshall Cavendish, 1979).

Tzu, Sun, *The Art of War* (Capstone Publishing, 2010).

Vasili, Phil, *Colouring Over the White Line: The History of Black Footballers in Britain* (Mainstream Publishing, 2000).

Wray, John, *Leeds United and a Life in the Press Box* (Vertical Editions, 2008).